Dangerous Offenders

In this era of unparalleled affluence the dangerous offender has become a figure of collective anxiety for the citizens of rationalised Western societies. Questions of why sexual and violent offences seem so ubiquitous and of how we should protect ourselves have produced a glut of political and media rhetoric in recent years.

Dangerous Offenders, however, takes a different view of the problem. The image of the dangerous offender and the idea that such individuals pose quantifiable 'risks' to the public are interrogated by scholars from the fields of criminology, sociology and law. The authors consider ideas of danger, social threat and legal responses to violent criminals in their historical contexts. They reflect upon the many systematic efforts made to predict truly dangerous individuals and on why these attempts have proven at best problematic. Furthermore, they interrogate the problematic nature of protecting women from the risks posed by dangerous offenders.

This collection invites us to rethink the received wisdom on dangerous offenders and will be of interest to students and scholars in the fields of criminology, sentencing and the sociology of risk.

Mark Brown is Lecturer in Criminology at the University of Melbourne.

John Pratt is Reader in Criminology at Victoria University of Wellington.

Dangerous Offenders

Punishment and Social Order

Edited by Mark Brown and John Pratt

London and New York

First published 2000
by Routledge
11 New Fetter Lane, London EC4P 4EE

Simultaneously published in the USA and Canada
by Routledge
29 West 35th Street, New York, NY 10001

Routledge is an imprint of the Taylor & Francis Group

Typeset in Garamond by Taylor & Francis Books Ltd.
Printed and bound in Great Britain by St Edmundsbury Press,
Bury St Edmunds, Suffolk

British Library Cataloguing in Publication Data
A catalogue record for this book is available from the British
Library

Library of Congress Cataloging in Publication Data
Dangerous offenders: punishment and social order/ [edited by]
Mark Brown and John Pratt.
p.cm.
    Includes bibliographical references and index.
    1. Recidivists. 2. Insane, criminal and dangerous. 3. Violent
crimes–Social aspects. 4. Danger perception. 5. Risk perception.
6. Criminal law–Social aspects. 7. Punishment–Social aspects. 8.
Criminal behavior, Prediction of. I. Brown, Mark II. Pratt, John.
HV6049 .D35 2000
364.6'01–dc21

                                                    99-057701

ISBN 0–415–20047–4 (hbk)
ISBN 0–415–20048–2 (pbk)

Contents

Contributors

Roderic Broadhurst is Associate Professor, Department of Sociology, University of Hong Kong, Honorary Research Fellow, Crime Research Centre, University of Western Australia, Fellow, Centre for Criminology, University of Hong Kong, and Associate Fellow of the Australian Institute of Criminology. Formerly, he served in the Western Australian Prison Department (1975–85) and Health Department (1986–8) and was Senior Research Fellow, Crime Research Centre (CRC 1990–4). He is a consultant criminologist for the Cambodian Criminal Justice Assistance Project and the newly established Centre for Criminology at the University of Hong Kong. His research interests include: recidivism and criminal careers; measurement of crime; sex and violent offenders; indigenous crime and justice; homicide and death investigation in Hong Kong; and comparative criminology.

Mark Brown is Lecturer in Criminology at the University of Melbourne, Australia. He is the author of a number of articles on serious offending, risk and penal policy. Despite recent forays into the worlds of crime prevention and drug law enforcement his interest remains principally in the ways violence and danger are constructed and the efficacy of political responses to such perceived threats. Currently he is interested in how the concepts of danger and social menace vary across cultural groups and how ideas of dangerousness are tied to colonialiam and to stages of national development.

Nils Christie is Professor of Criminology, Faculty of Law, University of Oslo, Norway. He is the author of numerous scientific articles and twelve books, some of them published in a great number of languages. Among them are *Limits to Pain* (Oslo: Oslo University Press, 1981) and *Crime Control as Industry: Towards Gulags, Western Style?* (London: Routledge, 1993, revised and enlarged edition 1994). Most of his writing has been in the field of crime and crime control, but he has also published books on education, on drugs, and on alternative communities. He has been the president of the Scandinavian Council for Criminology, and for many years was director of the Institute for Criminology and Penal law in Norway. He is a member of the Academy of Science in Norway (Oslo) and in Sweden (Lund). He has worked as a visiting professor in Berkeley, Jerusalem and Oxford.

Arie Freiberg was appointed to the Foundation Chair of Criminology at the University of Melbourne in January 1991 and has been Head of the Department of Criminology since January 1992. He has served as a consultant to the Victorian, South Australian, Western Australian and Federal governments on sentencing matters. Recent works include *Sentencing: State and Federal Law in Victoria* (Oxford: Oxford University Press, 2nd edn, 1999) (with R.G. Fox) and *Sentencing Policy and Penal Change: The Victorian Experience* (Sydney: Federation Press, 1999) (with S. Ross). He has published extensively in areas such as sentencing, confiscation of proceeds of crime, tax compliance, corporate crime, juries, juvenile justice, sanctions, victimology and superannuation fraud, trust in criminal justice and commercial confidentiality and the criminal justice system.

Eric Janus is Professor of Law at William Mitchell College of Law, St Paul, Minnesota. He has published extensively in the area of sex offender commitments and mental health law. He was Chair of the Section on Law and Mental Disability of the Association of American Law Schools (1998–9) and served on several commissions studying civil commitment in the State of Minnesota. He has served as co-counsel in lengthy litigation, challenging the constitutionality of Minnesota's Sexually Dangerous Persons Act. Eric Janus received his J.D. cum laude from Harvard Law School and his BA magna cum laude from Carleton College.

Pat O'Malley is Professor of Law and Legal Studies at La Trobe University, Melbourne. Recent research has focused on various topics in the area of risk, including crime prevention, harm minimisation strategies for drug users and insurance. Major publications include a number of works on risk and crime, most recently an edited book *Crime and The Risk Society* (Aldershot: Dartmouth, 1998). Currently he is working on a book length manuscript *Configuring Risk: Liberal Government and the Calculating Subject*.

John Pratt is Reader in Criminology at Victoria University of Wellington, Wellington, New Zealand. His main research interests are in the history and sociology of punishment. He has published extensively in this area, including *Punishment in a Perfect Society* (Wellington: Victoria University Press, 1993) and *Governing the Dangerous* (Sydney: Federation Press, 1997). He is currently working on a project that examines the development of penal culture in modern society.

Richard Sparks teaches criminology at Keele University, having previously worked in The Open University and the University of Cambridge. In addition to his interests in theoretical criminology, he has written on a number of aspects of prisons and penal policy including regimes in long-term prisons; prison disorders; international comparisons in prison populations; and the politics of prison privatisation. He is co-editor (with John Muncie) of *Imprisonment: European Perspectives* (Brighton: Harvester Wheatsheaf, 1991) and co-author (with Tony Bottoms and Will Hay) of *Prisons and the Problem of Order* (Oxford: Oxford University Press, 1996). He is also the author of *Television and the Drama of Crime* (Buckingham: Open University Press, 1992).

Elizabeth Stanko, Professor of Criminology, holds a Ph.D. in sociology from the City University of New York (1977). She taught for thirteen years at Clark University, USA, before taking a position in the Law Department of Brunel University in 1990. Her interest in criminology was sparked during her undergraduate sociology degree, awarded by Lehman College, CUNY in 1972. Serendipity fostered her interest in violence. She has been active in debates and dialogues about violence and gender since the late 1970s. Author of a number of books and articles, she is best known for *Intimate Intrusions: Women's Experiences of Male Violence* (London: Routledge, 1985) and *Everyday Violence: How Women and Men Experience Physical and Sexual Danger* (London: Pandora, 1990/95). She is now Professor of Criminology at Royal Holloway, University of London, and the Director of the Economic and Social Research Council's Programme on Violence.

Adam Sutton is a Senior Lecturer in the Department of Criminology at the University of Melbourne. He has an honours degree in Anthropology from the University of Sydney and a Ph.D. in Sociology from the University of New South Wales. His research and teaching interests are criminology and public policy, crime prevention and drug law enforcement. With Pat O'Malley he is co-editor of *Crime Prevention in Australia: Issues in Policy and Research* (Sydney: Federation Press, 1997).

Introduction

Mark Brown and John Pratt

At the present time, those of us who live in modern Western societies are living through an era of unparalleled affluence, an era of new found freedoms, an era of choice and self-fulfilling opportunities. But, simultaneously, as we ourselves are regularly made aware, we also seem to be living through an era when our fears of a particular kind of criminality – unprovoked, randomised, sexual and/or violent attack – seem to be constantly escalating. And thus, on the one hand, our everyday life brings with it the possibility of excitement, allurement and self-discovery. On the other, there is a growing sense of anxiety and insecurity as the starkest fears of those whom we consider to be society's most dangerous offenders intercede in such reveries and police our everyday pleasures. Indeed, in an era of neo-liberal polity, it is such fears that in recent years have fuelled a new and very illiberal set of dangerous offender laws targeted primarily at recidivist sex criminals. These new measures include sexual predator legislation, Megan's law, three-strikes measures and derivatives, and various other powers of quasi-permanent incapacitation, in either the mental health or penal arena: what is common to all of these new initiatives is that they allow for enhanced measures of surveillance and detention. If the United States has been foremost in their promulgation, then various traces and elements of them are now to be found across English-speaking societies as a whole.

But why should it be that the menace of such dangerous offenders should become so powerful an icon in modern Western societies? Is there any connection between these two contrasting paths of pleasure and excitement on the one hand, anxiety and danger on the other, as if the privileges of the former come at a price, or are these two possibilities of experience merely coincidental and nothing more than that? Even our awareness of dangerousness seems problematic: how do we know the kind of risks such offenders pose for us? Are our assessments based upon our own real-world experiences or are they conjured up for us by politicians able to draw on media fascinations with crime and images taken from the pages of popular fiction? If we are to move towards an understanding of what dangerousness is and its role and function in our society, then it would seem imperative to us that questions of this kind – which seek to establish its social, political, cultural and historical context in addition to the particular qualities that those offenders who fall within its rubric are thought to possess – be posed and addressed. Yet in the criminological literature on dangerousness there has been little sense of the need even to recognise the possibility of asking such questions, let alone of trying to find answers to them. In these respects, it is possible to discern three major shortcomings in the main body of criminological literature on this subject – shortcomings that this volume will attempt to address in the form of answers to the above and other attendant questions and which merit some introductory comment here.

Working from the general to more specific aspects of this critique, it is possible first to reproach criminology's approach to dangerousness for its disciplinary boundedness or insularity. Over the last two decades sophisticated analyses of the spectre of social danger and threat have been developed in such domains as sociology and social theory. Theorising about risk (see particularly Giddens 1990; Beck 1992), a term which paradoxically has become part of the common (if largely untheorised) parlance of modern criminology, has been at the heart of such analyses. In this new body of literature, risk is seen as a particular quality of modernity itself, one which not only provides us with a way of thinking – an attempt to calculate the future as it were – but which also acts as a kind of central organising dynamic of the social world itself. Risk, it seems, is something that modernity insists we tame and bring under control, and yet our very attempts to do so may only lead to the generation of new areas of unpredictability (see Beck *et al.* 1994). In these respects, far from being understood as a purely technical and mathematically calculable concept, the idea of risk and the structuring of possibilities that it represents has emerged as a central theme of social and academic thinking in the late twentieth century (see Beck 1992). The ubiquity of this way of thinking about and then ordering the social and technical world is illustrated in a recent popular history of risk and the probability theory that underlies it. Peter L. Bernstein's (1996) book *Against the Gods* is advertised as a 'worldwide bestseller'. At the heart of this 'remarkable story of risk' is the idea that risk management 'defines the boundary between modern times and the past' – thereby making possible 'the notion that the future is more than a whim of the gods and that men and women are not passive before nature' (p.1). And the rest of the book is concerned about what ultimately turns out to be the elusive and frustrating attempt to make risk serviceable and understandable. That it has remained such an elusive concept – in criminal justice as elsewhere – is one of the themes of this book: at least, the social context that makes the risk of dangerous offenders so central to modern penality but so elusive as well. That Bernstein's book has become so popular also tells us about how central the concept of risk has become to the dynamics of everyday life. Indeed, we would want to argue that it is this wider societal engagement with risk discourse that has acted as a kind of meta-context providing the ground upon which more narrowly conceived ideas of offender risk have gained credence. Thus, perhaps in something like the way that Foucault spoke of a carceral archipelago – a chain of disciplinary institutions spreading across the social frame – so too it might be possible to consider risk thinking as a cognitive habit that has penetrated all levels of Western thought. It has radiated out from scientific laboratories to enter the broadest level of popular consciousness and from there its influence has spread to the farthest corner of contemporary juridical procedure and penal administration. In these respects, the recent emergence of actuarialism in the penal world should be understood, as Feeley and Simon (1992) have argued, as a development that has a significance far beyond the technology it requires for its implementation. Instead, it becomes a key strategic device of 'the new penology' whereby, with risk as its organising dynamic, the legal rights of individuals begin to be over-ridden by the assumed qualities of sub-groups of the population to which individuals are thought to belong. By the same token, the need to both calculate and tame risk, not simply punish criminals, in the penal realm has the potential to bring into play new powers of surveillance and new forms of quasi-permanent incapacitation. In these respects, the foundations have been laid for very productive analyses of dangerousness and the modalities of calculation and punishment associated with it – and we wish to build on these foundations in this book.

However, it has been a measure of the disciplinary closure of criminological writing on dangerousness that such theorising is not widely known to criminologists nor these ideas widely debated or integrated in most of the contemporary dangerousness literature. That this is so might be explained by the structure of criminology as an academic discipline. Unlike sociology, for instance, it lacks the mechanisms that would provide for and drive an internal critique. Born as it was to meet the needs of governance, criminology reaffirms itself not by internal reflection but rather by reference to the material demands of penal administration. Recognising this administrative bias in criminology, together with its tendency to subscribe, perhaps too readily, to the methodologies of positivism, takes us some way toward understanding the second point in our critique. This is the rather elementary observation that criminological writing on dangerousness is inordinately fragmented for a discipline so tightly focused in its concerns. This fragmentation of approach is accompanied, however, by an almost perverse preoccupation with certain pieces of the overall picture. Perhaps not surprisingly, these tend to be those bits most amenable to scientific and administrative analysis. Thus, the vast bulk of criminological writing on dangerous offenders over the past three decades has concerned itself with either the quest for prospective identification of serious offenders (usually invoking the concept of reoffending risk) or with efforts to develop technical or principled responses to the dangerous individual in the realms of policy and sentencing practice. All the same, progress towards such ends has been uneven, notwithstanding the way in which three-strikes initiatives and the like would seem to ask for a reconsideration of the ethics of indeterminate detention and the efficacy of such measures. Indeed, little has been written to substantially revise the dangerousness guidelines that were proposed in the early part of this period (see e.g. *British Journal of Criminology* 1982; Floud and Young 1981; Moore *et al.* 1984; Walker 1980). This is not to say, of course, that a considerable amount has not been written on dangerous offenders over this time. In some areas of research, knowledge has become considerably more refined (for instance, in the work done on allocation of correctional resources on the grounds of risk – see e.g. Andrews and Bonta 1998) and some issues have been addressed in far greater detail (see e.g. Marshall 1996 on risk reduction through sex offender treatment). Yet this process often has tended to increase rather than reduce the distortions in attention to various areas we have noted here. Attendant with this dispersion and fragmentation has been a progressive decline within the field into detail and the technical minutiae of methods. Moreover, the literature has remained almost completely within the realm of journals and governmental reports, making it increasingly difficult to access and, as a discourse, increasingly difficult to maintain coherence within. These shortcomings, so characteristic of positivist correctionalism and managerialism, form the discursive background to dangerousness and stand generally as a kind of counterpoint to the form of reflexive criminology – that which, as David Nelken (1994) suggests, scrutinises disciplinary assumptions and emphasises the recursive interaction of systems and concepts – we have tried to develop here: correctionalism and managerialism in the field of dangerousness require analysis themselves rather than being allowed to serve as the organising principles of its discourse.

Third, as a consequence of this overriding concern with questions of how to identify dangerous offenders and then how to justify their semi-permanent incapacitation, any broader sociological significance that these offenders might have has been largely overlooked. However, if we turn to the field of cultural anthropology, Mary Douglas' work (see Douglas 1992; Douglas and Wildavsky 1982) on risk, shows us that what we assess to be a danger is not only telling us about the events or people so judged, it is also telling us about ourselves, and how we see and experience the world around us: in these respects, dangerousness, for example, is not only telling us about what types of offending we fear the most, it is also telling us what we value – and the lengths we are now prepared to go to in attempting to reduce any such risks to our wellbeing. As to why this should be so, within the criminological literature, Tony Bottoms' (1977) very prescient work stood alone for quite some time. Writing of the 'renaissance of dangerousness' in the mid 1970s, he recognised that this was a commentary on the times in which we were then living, in addition to anything that might be said in this renaissance about the particular qualities of dangerous offenders themselves. Using a Durkheimian framework, Bottoms argued that such a renaissance of interest might be attributable to the modern state being no longer able to maintain social cohesion, as the growing tide of social and political change began to fracture the conscience collective. To try to shore this up, the renaissance of dangerousness and its invocation of predatory monsters and demons helped to unite the public at large against a common enemy. It has only been in the more recent work of Jonathan Simon (1998) and in a some-what different context David Garland (1996) that such insights have been followed up. The criminological 'other' has been redrawn with colourings suited to our contemporary understandings of what we judge dangerousness to be, and the new anxieties and legislation they provoke is a reflection of the way in which the new penology allows for the identification and inca-pacitation of such intransigent evil (in the case of Simon); or it reflects the intellectual bankruptcy of the post-welfare state in providing solutions to such offending, other than through permanent incapacitation (Garland). In other words, and to go back to our opening paragraph, today's juxtaposition between pleasure in life and life in danger (Pratt 1997) is no mere coinci-dence: if we are to understand the socio-cultural significance of dangerousness today (and its escalating tendencies) then we must understand the social factors that have allowed for these interconnecting possibilities.

This volume has therefore been conceived as a corrective to the deficien-cies outlined above. It aims to place the issue of danger and threat in a broader social and disciplinary context than is commonly offered in crimi-nological treatments of this subject. New developments in social theory, and important overtures in the penological literature have helped to inform (although not uncritically) the way in which we have attempted to recon-textualise and readdress the issue of dangerousness in this book. To this end, we have attempted to produce a collection that not only situates social danger in a wider discourse but also highlights the way that ideas of danger assist and are constitutive elements of wider social debates. Furthermore, the critique of contemporary criminological writing on dangerousness that underpins this volume – that too much of this literature is excessively frag-mented, insulated and unreflective – is sustained in the efforts of each contributor to do more than simply summarise the 'state of play' in the particular area of their expertise. Instead, we have encouraged each writer to interrogate these niches of the criminological enterprise, to offer up crit-ical assessments of their theoretical or practical domain, to offer new ways of understanding seemingly incommensurable aspects of the literature they work with, or to integrate ideas across disciplinary boundaries and in doing so to broaden the field of analytical tools available for examining danger-ousness. The practical effect of this approach has been that the chapters in this volume do not function as contemporary literature reviews. They are not exhaustive surveys of the extant literature within the fields of criminology considered, but rather attempts to move thinking in those fields forward.

Neither has it been the purpose of this volume to provide a handbook-style overview of criminological writing on dangerousness. Indeed, given our critique of the current literature such a project would arguably be of limited value. Rather, we have been interested here first to identify and highlight the criminological frames or lenses through which it is possible to view the issue of social danger. The result is that chapters are grouped under the organising frames of history, law, penology and governance: four points at which criminological writing is forced into contact with wider academic and social discourses. Our second objective has been to offer a necessarily selective sampling from within those frames of reference. Within each there is much excellent and innovative work that, for mundane practical reasons like potential authors' workloads and the necessity to limit the size of this volume, could not be represented here. Though perhaps droll, this is an important point to recognise, for the subject matter dealt with in this volume and the attempts of the criminologists represented here to think beyond disciplinary orthodoxies do not describe the field in its whole. This volume does, however, provide a sampling of what we believe to be among the most important and progressive perspectives within each of the frames identified.

Following from these attempts to structure the various approaches to dangerousness there is a thread of logic to which we would draw readers' attention that joins the chapters in this volume. The observation was made above that contemporary understandings of danger are tied in important ways to the influence of risk thinking in the wider social sphere. The first section of chapters provides an historical account of these developments. In Chapter 1 Pat O'Malley interrogates current debates about the relationship between risk and modern society. He departs from what seems to be increasingly regarded as received wisdom that risk has only recently become an organisational dynamic of contemporary social arrangements by arguing that it can in fact be seen as a characteristic of all modern societies whose origins can be traced back to the late eighteenth century. In these respects, the key to understanding the concept of risk is not to see it as some monolithic, overarching characteristic of the last few decades, but instead as a concept that has moved in and out of the governmental strategies of the modern world, with corresponding consequences for our understanding of the governance of crime over the same period: risk-based strategies such as actuarialism have interacted with and emerged out of various other techniques – such as those based around discipline and surveillance.

John Pratt in Chapter 2 then provides an historical overview of the development of the concept of dangerousness. He tries to show how this emerged out of the social arrangements of modern society itself: the intermeshing of knowledges, of values, of class and gender relations, and of technologies, all helped to produce that figure which emerged towards the end of the nine-teenth century – the uncontrollable, unpredictable repeat offender. At a time when risk itself was steadily becoming calculable, the dangerous offender emerged as the antithesis of such developments – he (it was he and not she almost always in this context) became dangerous precisely because his conduct became so incalculable. He required special measures of control such as the indeterminate prison sentence, that were to be found at the margins of the cultural and legal boundaries of modern punishment – here lie the origins of the ethical dilemmas that have distilled from this posi-tioning ever since. From the creation of the dangerous offender, his colouring has periodically changed, his menace ebbed and flowed – as we would expect from a concept that is culturally relative. At the present time, however, that this figure has become so prominent – to the point where the measures of control necessary to constrain him are moving much closer to the centre of our penal arrangements – also reflects the much broader social, economic and political change that has taken place across most modern Western societies in the last two decades.

The most public and most symbolic encounter between the dangerous offender and the state occurs in the courtroom. In the second section of chapters two contributors examine contemporary responses of courts and legislatures to dangerous offenders and their behaviours. One of the most remarkable features of statutory provisions for the detention of dangerous offenders is in fact the reluctance of the criminal courts to use these powers. In Chapter 3 Arie Freiberg takes up the question of how judges are able to evade the obligation to detain serious offenders that the dangerousness statutes seem to imply and indeed why judges and the legal authorities in general should be so averse to invoking the special powers of detention these laws make available to them. Using the motif of guerrilla fighters chal-lenging central or established authority, Freiberg examines the techniques of judicial resistance to the superior authority of statute law. If such laws cannot be challenged as unreasonable on constitutional grounds, courts are required to work with them. Yet, as this chapter shows, there remain a number of ways in which judicial application or interpretation of statute law provides scope for the effect or meaning of the law to be turned. Although a large part of this chapter is concerned with the way such avenues of judicial resistance have been crafted by Australian courts, Freiberg also has been concerned to highlight the judicial rationale for such behaviour. In partic-ular, he argues that throughout the common law world, courts are increasingly engaged in a battle of principled wills, pitting their own princi-ples of legal justice against legislative efforts to express community sentiment and to force popular ideas of moral right into the juridical process.

The success of the criminal courts in guarding their domain has, in the United States at least, led to renewed interest in the possibilities for

detention available in civil law. In Chapter 4 Eric Janus considers the development since about 1989 of what have been termed civil commitment
statutes. These laws provide for the continued detention – under the jurisdiction of civil law – of an offender who has completed a criminal sentence
of imprisonment but who is thought to present a continuing threat to
public safety. It is the justice and logical coherence of these laws, straddling
as they do the jurisdictions of criminal and civil law, that forms the focus of
Janus' critique. These laws, he argues, are at heart contradictory and fundamentally flawed in the assumptions they make about causes of offenders'
behaviour. In particular, he highlights the incoherence of a system that on
the one hand holds an individual responsible for his or her behaviour and
thus able to answer criminal charges, yet which at a later date, and in a civil
court views the pattern of this individual's conduct as evidence of an inca-
pacity to control behaviour and thus finds them suitable for restraint under
civil detention. While this 'jurisprudence of difference' may satisfy short-
term instrumental needs of state legislators, Janus views it as a significant
breach of the social compact that legitimates and authorises state powers of
detention. The effects of this, he argues, are manifold but as is so often the
case it may in fact be fiscal rather than moral concerns that determine the
future of civil commitment.

Despite recent developments in the use of civil commitment in the
United States, most other common law jurisdictions continue to deal with
individuals convicted of serious crimes solely within the criminal justice
system. However, as the contributors in the third section of chapters show,
there have been a great variety of penal responses to, and uses made of, the
crimes committed by dangerous individuals. In penal responses to the
dangerous offender 'risk' is a central theme. In Chapter 5 Mark Brown
considers the way offender risk is conceptualised in current criminological
writing and questions why these theoretical prescriptions often bear so little
resemblance to the way risk is operationalised in practice. He is critical of
correctional risk research and theorising as a 'top down' enterprise, one that
attempts to deliver conceptualisations of risk to those working in penality
and that is dismissive of other ways of thinking about offenders. To address
this problem, Brown attempts to construct a taxonomy of risk grounded in
penal practice itself with the goal of accommodating within the taxonomic
scheme the full variety of practical penal responses to danger. This resulting
categorisation groups approaches to risk by the implicit models of
behavioural causation they reflect and thus by the causal logic they draw
upon in making calculations of offender risk. The majority of such calculations appear to draw upon just two underlying models of behaviour and thus
form two understandings of risk. Brown refers to the first of these as 'fluid
risk', the assumptions of which are that behaviour can be scientifically
understood and risk therefore predicted using the precepts and techniques of
science. The second he terms 'categorical risk', which he describes as

grounding risk in a broader social or philosophical understanding of behaviour and the categories of human virtue. Under this model of risk, notions of what an individual will do in the future are drawn not from mathematical equations but from social ideas such as remorse, and risk calculations are thus made upon what might be termed a metric of human virtue.

Despite the tendency of many decision-makers to adopt a categorical approach to estimating offender risk, there remains in criminology an enormous focus upon the scientific study of behaviour. However, as Roderic Broadhurst argues in Chapter 6, progress in this field has not been without difficulties of its own. To begin, recent years have seen a progressive move away from interest in recidivism (or the lack of it) as a central correctional goal and a shift instead toward risk assessment for the purposes of offender management. At the same time, however, there have been considerable advances in statistical modelling of offending behaviour made possible by the large and comprehensive databases that this managerialism has fostered. Survival analysis methodology pioneered in the life sciences has been applied to the problem of reoffending with more encouraging results than had been achieved with earlier cross sectional designs. Broadhurst illustrates the sort of results emerging from these projects using data from a Western Australian study with which he has been involved. He cautions, however, that neither penal administrators nor social theorists ought to make too much of these developments. In respect of the former, he emphasises that although improved, the risk and recidivism estimates currently available remain imprecise and should be used as adjuncts to careful decision making rather than replacements to it. With regard to the theoretical implications of these endeavours, he takes issue with writers such as Feeley and Simon (1992) whose predictions of an emerging era of actuarialism he finds overstated and lacking sufficient appreciation of the very real limits such methods have.

In Chapter 7 Richard Sparks, through his analysis of press coverage of the escapes of dangerous (i.e. maximum-security) prisoners in Britain, charts how such contingencies both help to define and are defined by broader political, technological and professional discourses/knowledges. In these respects, he shows how contemporary penal politics feeds on and digests such local events: one of the ignored features in teasing out the dynamics and direction of the new penology and its various motifs of 'three strikes' and so on has been 'the sociology of the scandal', wherein we can understand both the local and broader significance of a particular event, its contested possibilities of meaning and its subsequent emergence into popular/political discourse. The particular incident here – the escapes of dangerous prisoners – had reverberations both within the local prison system and in the development of the new penological discourse of danger, risk, tougher regimes and the like which set the agenda for punishment today and the place of dangerousness within it.

In the fourth section, two contributors challenge the conventional accounts and ground rules of research on dangerousness, each taking a different view of the relationship of danger to the tasks and priorities of governance. In Chapter 8, Elizabeth Stanko sheds new light on an enduring criminological issue: why is it that despite all empirical evidence to the contrary, 'stranger danger' continues to figure at the centre of debates on women's safety – and what can be done to rectify this matter? Both the problem and the solution, she suggests, lie in the difficulty women themselves, researchers of violence and writers of policy and crime prevention advice, have in finding a way through the contradictions of violence in our communities. Thus, women are most fearful in public spaces yet least likely to become victims of violence there; they are drawn to cohabitate with men by sexual desire and social pressures, yet these men they share intimacy with are the men most likely to hurt them; the criminal law treats violence against women as crimes born of individual responsibility, yet mens' violence is socially embedded and sanctioned in a wider community of males; the resources and individual agency of women successfully avoiding or escaping violence must be lauded, yet highlighting diversity among women's responses to danger reinforces images of 'deserving' and 'undeserving' victims. Running through these complex debates and analyses of women's risk of harm from men the image of the danger posed by strangers remains. Stanko argues that this is unlikely to change as long as frameworks for examining violence continue to see it as a phenomenon natural to the social relationships within which it occurs. Such accounts inevitably return to biological or psychological explanations of individual pathology or deviance. A better answer, she suggests, is likely to be found in a more complex social and relational analysis of gender and sexuality.

The need for more socially informed understandings of danger's context is a theme pursued in Chapter 9. Adam Sutton addresses two curiously neglected topics in writing on dangerousness, namely the drug-related offender (sexual and violent offences being the current staple) and disconfirming instances of governance wherein contemporary theories of risk and neo-liberal politics fail to account for current policies and strategies. Linking these two ideas Sutton asks what is special about drugs that shifts (or indeed forces) debates about their proper social role and modes of regulation outside the parameters of normal discourse. The answers he suggests are significant in at least two ways. To begin, he emphasises that tensions have historically existed between communities' symbolic and identity-based use or rejection of drugs and the wider efforts of governing elites to harness, shape or contest these uses and definitions. The importance of drug use is thus that it is tied to the very status, value and group formations that underpin the social fabric. That contemporary society has failed to modify attitudes and achieve a 're-framing' of the drug-use issue is therefore seen by him as evidence that in certain spheres of social life, 'archaic' modes of communication and social regulation continue to hold considerable force. Sutton is at pains to stress, however, that it is less formal, market based arrangements that neo-liberalism strives for – the self-sufficient clubs of private schools, gated housing estates and so on. The challenge facing theorists of the postmodern is, he argues, to account for the persistence of taboo and symbolism as tools of governance within neo-liberal societies.

The last chapter in this book, Chapter 10 by Nils Christie, presents a kind of epilogue to the preceding ruminations on the dangerous offender. He inverts the issue. He directs our attention to the problem of dangerous states rather than dangerous individuals and thus to the idea of govern-mental and bureaucratic deviance. The harms produced by state policies that criminalise wide sections of the community or that flow from over-burdened and neglected systems of penal administration are shown in this chapter to be equally as serious as any wrought by individual offenders. With particular reference to the current parlous state of the Russian prison system, Christie analyses how the failure of states to care about their population of prisoners as individuals leads inevitably to systematised brutality. In such cases the system of penal law can be seen not only to be deviant or deformed in its organisation and conduct, but also to amplify many of the dangers inherent in the structure of nation states themselves. These inherent dangers of state-hood must include factors like the state's power to make laws, to coerce its citizens and to punish in ways of its choosing. As Christie shows, the capacity of individuals to defend themselves in the face of such state power may be severely compromised if states fail to operate their penal machinery by common standards of civility and humanism. Our preoccupation with the problem of the dangerous offender therefore diverts our attention from problems of much greater magnitude – problems of dangerous states and how we might begin to control them.

These chapters, in addition to representing a diverse and vibrant discourse, also reflect upon a literature that shifts in its themes and preoccu-pations as it crosses national boundaries. Though it would be a mistake to overplay the discontinuities in writing on dangerousness and in the way it is viewed in the public eye – after all, each of the three principal areas repre-sented here, being the United States, Britain and Australia, experience broadly similar types of crime, operate broadly comparable legal frame-works, and seem able to understand each other's penal language – there are differences that require mention. The origin of these seems to lie in legal and penal cultures and consequently, perhaps following Garland's (1990) notion of punishment as a cultural agent, in public concern over particular types of crime and support for particular legal 'remedies'. Most notably, these differences are to be found in the contrasting approaches to dangerous-ness to be found, on the one hand, in the United States and, on the other, in Britain and its former colony of Australia. In the contributions to this volume, Janus' chapter on civil commitment reflects very clearly this sort of cultural opposition. In a contractualised and highly litigious society like the United States the recourse of communities and their legislatures to law in civil jurisdiction as a means of securing protection from dangerous offenders might be viewed as obvious, natural and reasonable. That such schemes have not emerged in Britain or Australia has less to do with their capacity to meet legal challenges there than with their fundamental inappropriateness in the cultural and legal climate of those nations. Beyond this particular legal response, there are broader differences also in the perception and management of risks that dangerous offenders pose. The pervasive risk culture described by O'Malley may have its origins in British capitalism and political theory, but it has found different expression in the legal and penal arrangements of these three countries. A crude characterisation of such differences would emphasise a preference in the United States for mechanistic and notionally 'scientific' responses, in Britain a greater prevalence of discretionary mechanisms and decision hierarchies that vest ultimate authority in a political figure, and in Australia a curious mixture of these two poles of response. Thus, in the chapters by Brown and by Broadhurst, both examining ideas about risk and its measurement, it is from the United States that the majority of quantitative, statistically grounded attempts to model offender behaviour, construct prediction tables and integrate such devices into structured decision-making systems emerge. Similarly, lying behind Australian responses to illicit drug use discussed in the chapter by Sutton is a rule-based 'say no' war on drugs policy originally developed in the United States and now exported to all those nations over which it retains economic leverage. The way drug users in Australia have become a central motif in its public discourse on dangerousness therefore reflects as much upon the relationship between these nations as it does something internal to Australian culture. Thus, the point to be recognised here is not one of simple continuities and discontinuities. Rather it is perhaps best captured in an image of an uneven mosaic, some threads of which are continuous, some more heavily weighted in one area than another, others isolated to a region wherein they blend more readily, but overall the whole object is connected and made possible by the common rules of construction. In the case of dangerousness these are the demands of governance and penality in the English-speaking societies of the West.

References

Andrews, D.A. and Bonta, J. (1998) *The Psychology of Criminal Conduct*, 2nd edn, Cincinnati, OH: Anderson Publishing.

Beck, U. (1992) *Risk Society*, New York: Sage.

Beck, U., Giddens, A. and Lash, S. (1994) *Reflexive Modernization*, Cambridge: Polity Press.

Bernstein, P.L. (1996) *Against the Gods: The Remarkable Story of Risk*, New York: John Wiley and Sons Inc.

Bottoms, A. (1977) 'Reflections on the Renaissance of Dangerousness', *Howard Journal of Penology and Crime Prevention* 16: 70–96.

British Journal of Criminology (1982) 'Special Issue: Dangerousness', 22, 3.

Douglas, M. (1992) *Risk and Blame: Essays in Cultural Theory*, London: Routledge.

Douglas, M. and Wildavsky, A. (1982) *Risk and Culture: An Essay on the Selection of Technological and Environmental Dangers*, Berkley, CA: California University Press.

Feeley, M. and Simon, J. (1992) 'The New Penology: Notes on the Emerging Strategy of Corrections and its Implications', *Criminology* 30: 449–70.

—— (1994) 'Actuarial Justice: The Emerging New Criminal Law', in D. Nelken (ed.), *The Futures of Criminology*, London: Sage.

Floud, J. and Young, W. (1981) *Dangerousness and Criminal Justice*, London: Heinemann.

Garland, D. (1990) *Punishment and Modern Society: A Study in Social Theory*, Oxford: Clarendon.

—— (1996) 'The Limits of the Sovereign State', *British Journal of Criminology* 36: 445–71.

Giddens, A. (1990) *The Consequences of Modernity*, Cambridge: Polity Press.

Marshall, W.L. (1996) 'Assessment, Treatment and Theorizing about Sex Offenders', *Criminal Justice and Behavior* 23: 162–99.

Moore, M., Estrich, S.R., McGillis, D. and Spelman, W. (1984) *Dangerous Offenders: The Elusive Target of Justice*, Cambridge, MA: Harvard University Press.

Nelken, D. (ed.) (1994) *The Futures of Criminology*, London: Sage.

Pratt, J. (1997) *Governing the Dangerous*, Sydney: Federation Press.

Simon, J. (1998) 'Managing the Monstrous: Sex Offenders and the New Penology', *Psychology, Public Policy and Law* 4: 162–78.

Walker, N. (1980) *Punishment, Danger and Stigma*, Oxford: Blackwell.

Part I

Dangerousness

A sociological history

Chapter 1

Risk societies and the government of crime

Pat O'Malley

In the past few decades, it is argued, the organisation of many fields of government and social life – and in particular the government of crime and 'social problems' – has been reshaped around techniques and models of risk management. The principal characteristics of risk in this sense are associated with the management of potential harms: risk identification; risk reduction; and risk spreading. Studies of criminal justice, psychiatry, health, industry, unemployment and the environment have all charted and attempted to explain this phenomenon of governmental planning around issues such as the dangerousness of criminals and of the mentally ill, environmental risks, traffic and industrial accidents, the centrality of insurance and so on (for example, Adams 1995; Green 1997; O'Malley 1998; Ericson and Haggerty 1997; Feeley and Simon 1992; Simon 1987; Beck 1992; Douglas 1992).[1] In this literature, the 'risk society' – a society substantially organised around risk management – is identified as a comparatively recent phenomenon, generally dating from the 1950s or 1960s.

While I have no doubt that we now live in societies in which risk occupies a prominent and distinctive place, I argue in this chapter that risk is a core characteristic of all modern liberal and capitalist societies, dating back to about the end of the eighteenth century. This suggestion arises out of a number of related difficulties with the risk society thesis.

All proponents of the risk society thesis assume that risk is identified with 'negative risk', that is, the risk of harm or danger. They depict contemporary societies as if they were not also, perhaps equally, characterised by governmental imageries of risk as positive. Thus for Ulrich Beck (1992), the most influential of risk society theorists, risk society is defined by the formation of a consciousness and form of government focused on the distribution of 'bads' (harms) rather than 'goods'. This seems strangely short-sighted in the present era of enterprise culture with its emphasis on the material rewards and personal fulfilments created by active participation in the competitive market. Yet as soon as this point is made, our attention is drawn not so much to the peculiar nature of the present, but to the crucial place that fostering and managing economic risk-taking has occupied in the government of capitalist economies for the better part of three hundred years. A little further reflection also draws to mind the prominence of social and moral discourses on risk throughout this period: prohibitions on gambling and some forms of market speculation; exhortations to be thrifty; furious debates over insurance and personal responsibility, and so on. What also becomes clear is that risk plays many different roles, and appears in many different guises and institutional forms, over this long period. Thus while the current era of 'enterprise culture' focuses on the autonomous management of risks by individuals and the benefits of rational risk taking, the welfare state was 'the insurance state' (Beck 1992) that governed to an unusual extent through collective or 'social' forms of risk minimisation and risk spreading, and in the nineteenth century, individuals were instructed to be prudent and risk averse. Of course these are simple and perhaps crude distinctions, but they indicate that we need a rather different approach to understanding the place of risk in contemporary societies than has been the case in the risk society literature. Such an approach will need to move beyond a monolithic notion of risk as the overarching characteristic of a society. It will need to account for variations in the relative prominence of risk-based governance over time, the kinds of political meaning and evaluation of risk, and the kinds of governmental roles to which risk is assigned. It will need to account for variations in the nature of forms taken by risk-based governance, and the diversity of techniques that are adopted. But in addition to recognising such variability in risk, it should recognise one of the major dangers inherent in the idea of risk society itself, namely, the tendency to interpret all major developments as if they are shaped by risk without recognising that risk is itself marginalised, fostered or shaped in different ways and degrees by multifarious other issues and developments. The welfare state, for example, was not simply shaped by risk, but by broader concerns with distributional justice and equality, fears of class unrest, issues of social and economic efficiency, and so on. Piecing all of these points together questions the utility of the unified and totalising image of 'the risk society' without negating or minimising the importance of risk as a feature of economically and politically liberal societies. In what follows, with special reference to the government of crime, I explore such an approach through a brief sketch of a genealogy of risk in three major epochs in modern government.

Punishment, discipline and risk in the nineteenth century

While it would be a parody to describe as backward looking the 'traditional' world and the 'moral' economy of the eighteenth century, nevertheless the development of capitalism and liberalism centred the future in new ways. By the beginning of the nineteenth century, the future was no longer understood to be shaped simply by sovereign commands, the will of God or the hand of fate. Rather, it was to be formed by the actions of free subjects. Free subjects were enjoined to think about the future in new ways, and to develop calculative techniques that enabled them to govern the future from the present. 'Freedom' and 'risk', this suggests, in many ways refer to the same mental set that envisages the future as governable primarily by calculation.

This was the imagined order of *laissez-faire* capitalism.[2] In the new economy, the market was to be governed by individual risk takers, whose calculations about the future were the foundation of capital growth. Neither tradition nor state should intervene in the freedom of the market. The law increasingly and rapidly took account of this, creating new institutions and new risk-based images of the citizen. In what is probably the central institutional shift, during the first half of the nineteenth century there was a revolution in contract as subjects were invested with new capacities, rights and obligations. The old order envisaged contract as the instantaneous transfer of rights in already existing things: it treated all exchanges as though they were exchanges of property. Access to legal redress for breach of contract required that someone already had acted on an agreement, the law sought to ensure that the parties performed exactly as they had agreed and redress involved the restoration of order through a requirement for the specific performance of the exchange. The emergence of executory contracts during the early 1800s, however, required only that a promise had been made, accepted, and protected a contracting party's *'expectation interest'* – including a right to profits that existed only as possibilities at the time of the agreement. In this way, contract law came to protect profits that always remain hypothetical – that never come to exist precisely because the breach of contract prevented their realisation. In the eighteenth century, all this most likely would have been regarded as socially dangerous speculation, and frowned upon rather than protected (Kercher 1990). But in the new order, the plaintiff was imagined to be someone who had correctly and rationally calculated the future, whose rational risk-taking was not only legitimate but vital to the economic wellbeing of the country, and who had full right to legal protection.[3]

Similar shifts occurred with respect to the setting of fair prices and exchanges. In the eighteenth century, these exchange rates were set largely by custom or fiat. However, in the 'will' theory of contract, the law began backing away from determining the fairness of prices or exchanges. Increasingly it imagined contract as an agreement in which all parties had examined the future, and – on the balance of probabilities – seen in the exchange some net advantage to themselves. It was not up to the court to protect those who 'miscalculated'. Even contract workers who suffered harms in their employment might not be protected by law if these were regarded as foreseeable risks of their trade. They were deemed to have built into their wage agreement the likelihood and the probable cost of these risks. Having thus voluntarily assumed the risk, they could, therefore, have no right to compensation in law for harms already compensated by the wage (Wrightman 1996).

More broadly, the liberal conception of 'freedom' assumed a subject possessed of this kind of rationality – one that was calculative about the future. The subject imagined by liberal political theory, was imbued with a form of risk consciousness. In Bentham's felicity calculus, for instance, this was understood to be a mental process of calculating two future states: the balance of pleasures and pains arising from a proposed course of action, and the probability of these various consequences being realised. In this sense, risk consciousness is built into the constitution of the liberal citizen. Liberalism's core principle of individual responsibility thus assumed an individual who had a moral duty to take account of foreseeable events, and indeed, to accumulate such available information as would assist such calculation. Consequently, while the poor of the eighteenth century were provided with relief when their means of support failed, nineteenth-century liberalism substantially stripped away this buffer. To a much greater extent it exposed individuals to the forces of the economy, and required them to be responsible for managing the consequences of such foreseeable calamities as the unemployment, sickness or death of a breadwinner. Some elements of this responsibility clearly applied old and familiar proscriptions against idleness. But increasingly the poor – indeed all subjects – were required to take on new attributes and learn new skills to govern the future. In particular, *thrift* became a core, preventative Victorian virtue, and the first half of the nineteenth century witnessed the formation of new institutions – such as savings banks and life insurance schemes – designed to render thrift a technology for governing the future even for the poorest of citizens (O'Malley 1999b).[4]

Needless to say, thrift was by no means alone in this role. Dean (1991: 219) argues that the morals of thrift, frugality, prudence and industry were drawn together in 'a continuous thread … provided by prevention' and that 'ultimately, the liberal government of morals would be concerned with the prevention of those modes of existence which elevate poverty to a "social danger" '. Liberal government's pivotal focus on prevention thus appears as a much more general and long-term characteristic of rule than might be assumed from a reading of the risk society literature. In the field of criminal justice this generated a:

> panoply of measures specifically designed for a systematic, effective and economical strategy for the prevention of crime. These measures include the establishment of a perpetually vigilant body concerned with the detection of crime, governed by a central board; an agency to collect such intelligence to ascertain the types and causes of crime; a ministry of police …
>
> (Dean 1991: 195)

These developments were linked to changes in the regime of criminal justice sanctions. Both the reduction in severity of punishment (to the point, in theory at least, where this exceeded only marginally the 'wages' of crime) and the regime of discipline, assumed a rational choice actor who weighed the probable costs and benefits of offending (Foucault 1977). In turn, through the work of Colquhoun, Peel, Chadwick and others, this was linked to the formation of a preventative police, for the emphasis in such Benthamite schemes was that the rational choice offender would be deterred as much by the probability of capture as by the calculus of probable costs and benefits.

Yet such preventative governance, while clearly implying that a conception of risk-management is central to government, is not to be associated with a notion of a society governed predominantly by actuarial techniques – such as social insurance or public risk analysis. Thus I would disagree with some risk society theorists who suggest that 'actuarialism' is risk society's core characteristic – that is, government through the manipulation of statistical distributions, rather than the disciplinary normalisation of individuals (e.g. Simon 1987).[5] It is worth recalling that for Foucault (1977), discipline is a technology of freedom: a technology for rendering free subjects predictable. 'Discipline' and 'risk' therefore are not hostile to each other, nor is actuarial governance the hallmark of risk society. Rather, within liberal frameworks of risk and freedom, disciplinary and actuarial techniques are set in variable relationships.

In the nineteenth century, this relationship was characterised by the overwhelming predominance of discipline and, as Simon suggests, the relegation of actuarial techniques to the margins of government. First, the liberal problematic of social danger linked the idea of dangerousness primarily to 'the dangerous classes' (Simon 1988; Pratt 1998). It was Foucault's (1977) view that no paradox existed in the resort to disciplines (which work on and through individuals) in order to govern the dangerous *classes*. Quite to the contrary, he argued that the disciplines' focus upon the individual had crucial political effects, for they disaggregated the dangerous classes in crucial ways. By focusing upon the pathological individual, the political reality of these classes was disrupted; by subjecting 'criminals' to scientific method, the apolitical reality of their pathology was neutrally confirmed; by locating such individuals in segregated buildings, their difference was graphically symbolised. Over and above this, as Simon (1988) has also stressed, the coercive substrate of the disciplines provided means to 'tame' the threat of mass disorder that confronted early liberal government.[6] The liberal imagery of 'responsible freedom' was enforced by disciplinary institutions such as the factory asylum, prison and school – coercive arrangements for transforming members of the dangerous classes into 'docile bodies'. In this sense, the creation of predictable, free individuals, governed the dangerous classes through individualised, disciplinary technologies of risk management.

Second, the sciences that were developed in large measure out of disciplinary institutional contexts – criminology from the prison, psychiatry from the asylum, medicine from the hospital – necessarily lagged behind the institutional developments themselves. In this era of the formation of disciplines, therefore, the governmental problematic of free will (and its particular take on risk) therefore had yet to be substantially conditioned by the deterministic causality of the disciplinary human sciences. The corollary was a particularly voluntarist conception of subjects' freedom and, accordingly, the primary forms of government were those that worked through and upon free will. Thrift and frugality, diligence, self denial, the voluntary subordination to 'superior' entities and values, the crystallisation of these into the notion of 'character', all reflect techniques for governing freedom and its risks, that were as yet hardly touched by the sciences of society and of the mind.

Third, given the problematic of the dangerous classes, and of social danger more generally, it is hardly surprising to find that the social allocation of risks and their government were structured by class. Positive evaluations of risk-taking, and the fostering of risk-taking, were associated almost exclusively with the entrepreneurial classes, and promoted in relation to business activity.[7] For all other classes and activities, and most especially for the mass of the working people, risk was identified with danger and harmful consequences. Through the lens of social danger, ungoverned exposure to negative risk, and 'unnecessary' risk-taking, thus already present 'risk' itself as a *problem* in the governance of the poor.

From this perspective, the scene was set for the rise of the welfare state, and its generally negative evaluation of risk. The ascendancy of the positive human sciences toward the end of the century, took this problematic of social danger and reframed it under scientific government. Viewed thus, the welfare state that many risk society theorists regard as the actuarial state or insurance state (Simon 1987; Beck 1992; O'Malley 1992) may have been founded and framed not solely in probability (which we almost inevitably associate with risk), but perhaps even more so through the deterministic disciplines that made up the positive human sciences.

The welfare state and the welfare sanction

The positive human sciences struggled (as they still do) with their poor predictive power. Yet they existed in an environment in which the advances of the natural sciences and technologies virtually assured the hegemony of positivism. The poor predictive capabilities of the human sciences, it was most generally assumed, was not a function of the intrinsically probabilistic nature of the social. Rather, it reflected the failure to discover the determining laws that governed society and the economy, and/or the difficulty of combining these in the sufficiently subtle ways required by the 'complexity' of social phenomena. This characteristic was not restricted to the social sciences, although it was far more visible there, for as Green (1997) shows, the divergence of outcome from prediction was almost universally understood in similar ways across the natural and medical sciences, thus insulating faith in determinism. The importance of such an observation is that however we choose to explain the rise of the welfare state – as a capitalist resolution of the legitimation crisis, as an effect of the scale of monopoly capitalism, as a victory of the working classes, or even as the first expression of the risk society – we should nevertheless recognise that one of its central characteristics was that actuarial elements were in key respects subordinated to the positive human sciences. This requires a little elaboration.

The human sciences played a key role in identifying problems as 'social problems'. Deploying actuarial data and statistical techniques, they had located the 'reality' of the social as a causal force shaping the distribution of health and mortality, education and employment (see generally Daston 1988). In so doing they helped undermine governmental faith in the risk-based *laissez-faire* arrangements of the previous century, by providing the promise of 'scientific' alternatives. In the quintessential example, 'freedom of contract' and the 'free market' were increasingly subordinated to the expertise of economists in order to correct deficiencies, inefficiencies and pathologies produced by market competition. In this sense, even economic risk-taking itself appears primarily as something to be governed scientifically (Reddy 1996; Bernstein 1992). The invention or discovery of the social or psychological 'determination' of health, mortality, education and a host of other sites for government, provided the basis for submitting these too to the regimes of the positive human sciences. Yet, while some of its critics (e.g. Aharoni 1981) were subsequently to deride the welfare state as 'the no-risk society' on the basis of such scientific intervention, this was incorrect. Generally speaking there was no sense in which capitalist risk-taking or individuals' responsibility for governing their futures, were to be squashed. Rather, in the light cast by the human sciences, economic risk taking and individual exposure to risk were to be assigned the roles and functions for which social engineers determined they were best suited. The 'welfare state' thus involved a quite specific relationship between risk and scientific determinism, in which the latter ideally was to be dominant, although this was articulated in different ways according to the nature of the 'problem' to be governed.

Generally, the causes of social problems were thought amenable – or at least ultimately amenable – to scientific elimination. Economic depressions could be prevented by state intervention; all manner of disorders could be resolved by scientific urban planning, identification of the causes of crime would mean that crime could be eradicated or greatly reduced, and so on. In the meantime, however, actuarial and disciplinary techniques were to be deployed in the management of risk and social danger. On the one hand, large-scale social actuarialism was deployed to manage the gross symptoms of market disorder and its inefficiencies: unemployment relief, national health schemes, free public education, a plethora of pensions for special categories of the (updated) deserving poor, and so on. In terms of their sheer scope of coverage and expenditures, these warrant viewing the welfare state as actuarial in important respects. However, at the level of the individual, welfare state interventions were characterised primarily by disciplinary work delivered by experts in the human sciences – particularly the 'psy' sciences – that had rather reshaped the voluntarist 'free will' based interventions of the previous century. Increasingly, these interventions were aimed at correcting pathologies and remedying deficiencies in the light of scientific knowledge that largely subordinated free will to a residual space defined by social or psychological determinants. In the process, as Pratt (1998) has pointed out, the rise of the disciplinary sciences was thereby instrumental in transforming the discourse of social danger – from the problematic of the dangerous classes, to that of the 'dangerous individual', even at a time when the actuarial management and distribution of risk had become institutionalised in social insurances.

Thus when we examine the characteristic expression of the 'actuarial' welfare state in the field of criminal justice, the 'welfare sanction' (Garland 1981), this 'takes as its object not a citizen but a client, activated not by guilt but by abnormality, establishing a relation that is not punitive but normalising' (p.40). This is not actuarial in the sense of government through statistical distributions and probabilities rather than the disciplinary government of individuals (cf. Simon 1988). Rather it is, precisely, disciplinary intervention guided by the human sciences, and primarily the 'psy' sciences, which are perhaps the least 'actuarial' of this constellation of knowledge.[8] In some respects, then, the welfare state represents the triumph of the deterministic human sciences, despite the massive actuarial institutions it established or embodied. What begins with the government of risk among the poor, extends to the attempt to subject entrepreneurial risk-taking to the problematic in which all risk appears as harmful unless itself governed by the positive sciences.

Actuarial sanctions and the 'post-social' state

In their analysis of recent trends in criminal justice, Feeley and Simon (1992, 1994) have alerted us to the emergence of 'actuarial justice' over the past quarter century. Actuarial justice involves the deployment of statistical probability in sentencing and parole decisions, in which the length of sentences is determined by the risk that offenders represent to others, rather than the moral wrong they have committed (punishment), or the nature of the correction needed to remedy their pathology (the welfare sanction). Increasingly, the nature of the sanction, too, is shaped by risk concerns, as punishment and correction give way to 'incapacitation' – in which institutional warehousing, home detention, curfews and electronic monitoring work to limit the opportunity of the 'risky' offender to offend. At first sight this is a conundrum, for an actuarial sanction emerges into the limelight just as the 'insurance state' is dismantled. The puzzle is all the more acute because as early as the 1920s it was widely recognised that actuarial methods provide a superior prediction of risk (particularly of post-parole offending) to that provided by the case-study methods of the positive human sciences (Glaser 1985).

Glaser suggests that the crucial reason for ignoring actuarial sentencing had been that judges and parole boards were concerned with pleasing the politicians and public upon whom their job security and advancement depended. The emergence of actuarial sentencing was put down to a political compromise in which 'researchers began to collaborate with judges and parole board members to develop new types of statistical tables' that gave greater autonomy to the judges (p.373). But why was a compromise not reached much earlier, and why was it reached during the late 1970s when punishment was well and truly back on the agenda? A more substantial answer would begin by observing that, apart from presenting problems for the judiciary, who might also object to seeing themselves as merely the dummies of statisticians, an actuarial approach flew in the face of the positive sciences that occupied a core place in the welfare state. It would have been resisted both by the army of 'case' practitioners within the criminal justice system, and by the political supporters of scientific correctionalism. It was not until the welfare state began to be dismantled, and the authority of the human sciences diminished, that actuarial techniques could be considered for a major role in criminal justice.[9]

The undermining of the positive human sciences may have some origins in the broader triumph of probability over determinism in science more generally during the past half century or more (Green 1997). But this more 'academic' issue is surely overshadowed by other, more political developments. While it has long been argued that the social sciences 'don't work', during the 1970s this critique was given considerable political muscle by its inclusion in the rising chorus of criticism – from the left and right – that was directed at the welfare state as a whole (Rose 1996a). Accusations of paternalism, the intrusive authoritarianism of experts, enormous costs coupled with low accountability, an inability to resolve a huge array of social problems, the creation of 'welfare-dependent' subjects, the 'over-regulation' of business, the stifling of initiative – these, and more, were part of a rising tide of opposition that gradually coalesced into the politics of neo-liberalism.

Crudely put, scientific government was regarded as an expensive and counterproductive failure. Competitive and quasi-contractual relations were built into state government procedures as they were recast in the image of the business enterprise. This reaction against scientific government did not involve reversion to the model of classical 'laissez-faire' liberalism, but went beyond that to make the state itself mimic the market. Markets, it was understood, are technologies, not natural phenomena, to be set up and engineered where and as required. In the process, of necessity, risk was re-evaluated and reformulated as a positive strategy for general application, and risk had to be tailored into new institutional forms. The private sector itself came under censure for being insufficiently innovative and too bound by submission to the 'anti-entrepreneurial' spirit of economic planners and bureaucrats (Clarke and Newman 1997; Peters 1987).

More generally, the governmental image of ordinary individuals was revised in the same way. Everyone now is to make an enterprise of their lives. This new credo goes beyond the belief of classical liberalism that people be exposed to risk in order to generate greater independence and responsibility. In many respects it overturns the equally venerable command to avoid 'unnecessary' risk, as was the stricture on the nineteenth-century masses. Rather, it requires individuals to embrace risk positively, to invest in the stock market, to create their own small businesses, to become entrepreneurs and petty capitalists in their own right (Rose 1990, 1996b). Certainly, individuals are expected as far as possible to avoid such negative risks as crime, ill-health or unemployment. But they must do so 'actively' and on their own behalf. They must become their own risk managers, and determine the ratio of risk-taking and risk-avoiding that suits their personal preferences and situations. Managing positive and negative risks is part of the enterprise of everyday life. Risk, now, is not *the problem*, as under the welfare state. Risk now is the *solution* to all manner of problems from 'welfare dependency' and bureaucratic unresponsiveness, to national economic inefficiency and the scale of state expenditure.

Unsurprisingly, the reassertion of government through competition over government through planning did not create a positive environment for the human sciences. As Rose (1996a) indicates, increasingly these have been displaced by, or subordinated to, calculative regimes of accounting and financial management. Audit, monetarisation, marketisation and other techniques have increasingly been deployed to bring scientific and other expertise to heel. Compared with the arcane, substantive, autonomous and sometimes conflicting sciences of the welfare professions, the 'know-hows of enumeration, calculation, monitoring, evaluation' (p.54) fit well with the enterprise culture, are more transparent to government inspection and provide universal criteria in terms of which all services can be simply measured. Accordingly positions formerly occupied by those trained in the human sciences increasingly are allocated to practitioners of managerial and entrepreneurial expertise (Clarke and Newman 1997). In criminal justice, the traditional claim that welfare sanctions were expensive and did not work, was given greater precision and authority. In the light of cost benefit analyses, expense ratios and the resilience of high crime rates, such criticisms broadened out into claims that 'scientific' criminology itself had failed, and that new approaches were required (Geason and Wilson 1989; National Crime Prevention Institute 1986). In this environment, cost effectiveness has even begun to displace recidivism as a key indicator of penal success, and accordingly, it is becoming a key element in shaping prison regimes and sentencing dispositions (Feeley and Simon 1994). Indeed, the definition and place of the 'social' shifts away from the locus of causes of crime, toward being the bearer of the harms produced by crime:

> (t)he criminal justice system ought to minimise the 'net social harm of crime' .... There is nothing mystical about these social costs. Home and business security systems, victim losses and prematurely abandoned buildings are as much expenditures on crime as prisons and police stations. These kinds of costs are involved: harm to victims, combating or preventing crime, and punishing offenders. Their sum represents the social cost of crime .... The trick is to find the balance among the elements that minimises the total crime bill.
>
> (Zedlewski 1985: 711)

In this regime, criminals, like the unemployed and the unhealthy, among many others (including potential victims of crime), are increasingly invested with personal responsibility for their status and actions (Greco 1993; Dean 1995; O'Malley 1992). Incapacitation or punishment (in the form of deprivation of liberty) displace correction, in part because scientific correctionalism – the welfare sanction – has 'failed', in part because the prioritisation of financial accountability strips expenditure from the treatment of prisoners. Deprivation of liberty remains as the residue of the penal sanction. Thus in the same moment that the imperatives of the new fiscal regime displace those of the human sciences, the prison and related sanctions (probation and parole especially), through the media of deprivation of liberty and incapacitation become aligned with imperatives to minimise social harm. In this sense, then, the 'triumph' of an individualised actuarialism emerges during the 1970s, at the cost of social actuarialism (social insurances) and the positive human sciences. Shaped by the individualism and new market focus of neo-liberalism, the mode of governing risk has changed yet again.

Neo-conservatism: monsters in the risk society?

As argued at the beginning of the paper, there is a danger inherent in any account that centres one or another dimension of life. The imagery of 'the risk society' almost inevitably blinds us to the role and impact of other developments that may do as much or more to shape government. Thus in the current context of criminal justice, while much attention has been paid to the ascendancy of actuarial justice, and to the erosion of criminology by more risk-centred knowledge, and while many have pointed to the role of neo-liberalism in shaping these developments (e.g. O'Malley 1992; Simon 1995; Pratt 1998), David Garland (1996: 445) has recently pointed to the emergence of a 'volatile and contradictory character in crime control policy' and criminology. Crime control policy is depicted as oscillating between two poles, alternately the punitive/authoritarian and inclusive/devolutionary.

> On the one hand there has been an attempt to face up to the problem (of crime) and develop pragmatic new strategies that are adapted to it. But alongside these difficult adaptations to the reality principle there has been a recurring tendency toward a kind of hysterical denial, and an emphatic reassertion of the old myth of the sovereign state.
>
> (Garland 1996: 449)

Likewise, we have witnessed the emergence not simply of an actuarial criminology, but of oscillating criminologies. On the one side is a neo-liberal criminology of the 'self', primarily envisaging a rational choice offender who, in a sense, could be anyone. This criminology links closely with currently ascendant risk-based strategies such as situational crime prevention, which are concerned more with 'criminogenic sites' than with criminal persons (see Geason and Wilson 1989). On the other, however, is a 'criminology of the other', associated with what Rose (1998: 35) refers to as 'the spectre of the monstrous': an image of evil that could not possibly be 'us' and that is beyond the rational.[10]

Linked to the volatility of penalty and criminology is the appearance of particular sanctions that owe little to risk models, and that are also contradictory – often appearing in the same jurisdiction. Some seek to create 'enterprising prisoners' capable of taking control of their lives and reinventing themselves in more 'positive ways'. Others have reinstated archaic sanctions such as chain gangs, or imported nostalgic programmes such as disciplinary boot camps, complete with military drill and uniforms – and for the monstrous there is permanent incarceration and death (O'Malley 1999a).

Such contradictory trends seem unintelligible solely in terms of the monolithic 'risk society'. Yet it requires only a slight lifting of the eyes from the risk focus to make sense of this. The oscillation noted by Garland, and the existence of contradictory punishments and criminologies that are involved, can be understood in terms of the fact that the assault on the welfare state, and the associated transformation of risk, almost nowhere has been carried through by neo-liberals alone. In most cases, they formed alliances with neo-conservatives under a loose banner of the 'New Right'. Neo-conservatives have much in common with neo-liberals. Support for the idea of individual responsibility, opposition to the welfare state, belief in the free market are the most evident examples. But there are also significant sources of difference and tension. For neo-conservatives, discipline is essential for the social good – and the concept of the 'social' in conservatism has very specific organic, traditional and authoritarian overtones that do not sit well with neo-liberals' radical individualism. Allegiance and loyalty to traditional collectivities such as the nation are paramount. Obligations, whether to the family, the community or the nation, are thought of as intrinsic to the nature of social beings, rather than contractually, rationally or voluntarily chosen. Consequently, the freedom and enhanced autonomy that is central to neo-liberalism 'cannot occupy a central place in conservative thinking …. Freedom is comprehensible as a social goal only when subordinate to something else, to an organisation or arrangement which defines the individual aim' (Scruton 1984: 24).

For neo-conservatives, the state, in particular in its role as the preserver of order and the governor of the nation is the privileged symbol of political rule, and allegiance to the state has little or nothing to do with neo-liberal 'charters' and 'partnerships' formed between states and their subjects. This strong assertion of state sovereignty in turn privileges law, morality and order as crucial, more so than the market and the individual. Thus for neo-conservatives, 'the law may not only control contract and crime, but may also regulate family relationships, personal morality and so on. And the state must possess severe and ultimate sanction and may utilise retributive punishment and social controls' (Hayes 1994: 137).

Much of the individualising of risk, and the erosion of social actuarialism that is visible in the present, may be quite compatible with neo-conservative agendas. But, the nostalgia for harsh disciplinary punishments as opposed to mere incapacitation; the assertion of the sovereign power of the state rather than delegating of control to all manner of community risk managers; the contrasting of the ideal community with the morally unintelligible, monstrous outsider – these resonate more with traditionally oriented, conservative rationalities than with the switched-on capitalism and technical risk management of the neo-liberals.

Thus, even with respect to a field as delimited as criminal justice, reduction of policy and practice to one dimension – such as risk technologies – provides insights that are paid for at the expense of considerable intelligibility. Risk societies are never simply societies dominated by risk.

Conclusions

Such an account, while inevitably partial, superficial and incomplete, begins to show how a genealogy of government through risk can be developed which can emphasise long-term continuities rather than the sudden emergence of 'risk society'. It can also, and more importantly, indicate that within this genealogy the meaning and place of risk has shifted rather than being a constant, and how the forms taken by risk techniques might vary accordingly. At the same time it alerts us to the ways in which the forces that influence the genealogy of risk may not only shape the nature of risk governance, but may also spin off quite distinct and in some ways conflicting or contradictory developments. One consequence, is that there is nothing very necessary about the course taken by the genealogy of risk. Its appearance has taken different forms, and its appearance in the form now recognised as 'the risk society' emerged as a result of pressures – such as neo-liberal politics – that themselves coalesced out of quite diverse origins.

Risk societies are thus contingent in their origins, and variable in their form, in part because their social foundation in political and economic liberalism is so broad. For this very reason, we should beware of regarding the present condition of risk as somehow the inevitable result of an historical logic of modernity or power (Beck 1992). Equally we should be circumspect about regarding the future as being simply the unfolding of a logic within the present – so that more and more institutions become increasingly dominated by the currently identified relationships of risk. Indeed, there are signs of quite different institutional arrangements that may transform the nexus between government and risk yet again. For example, it has been argued that in the economy, globalisation and technological shifts have rendered even medium-range probabilistic prediction redundant. The scene now is said to change so rapidly and dramatically, that plans and planners are inevitably doomed, and the figure of the entrepreneur is made still more central as the governor of the future. In this vision, chaos – with its own, non-probabilistic regularities – provides a more appealing model to many, not only in the sciences but also, and increasingly, in the business arena (e.g. Peters 1987). An argument could even be mounted that the 'volatile and contradictory punishments' noted above reflect the early onset of such a 'postmodern' environment of instability (cf. Simon 1995). There may equally be, via the 'third way', a partial return to the welfare state. Any of these three scenarios – continuation of the current regime of risk, its displacement by 'entrepreneurial chaos' or the 'third way' – would have its protagonists. The way we will govern risk, and govern through risk will be decided not by a logic of actuarialism, but by the outcome of struggles between those who imagine, design and deploy competing approaches to government. Nevertheless, as long as these are carried out within the encompassing frameworks of liberalism and capitalism, the societies they help to create will still be 'risk societies'.

Notes

1 'Government', in this paper, is not restricted to states, as in the sense of legislatures, judiciaries and state bureaucracies. Rather, it refers to all efforts to manage conduct, to direct it toward some ends rather than others, and to take some forms rather than others. It is thus possible to refer to the government of the self, as sensibly as to the government of the global economy.

2 'Imagined' here is not intended to imply an illusion. Rather, it refers to the imagery through which the problem to be governed is comprehended, and in terms of which the correct outcome of government is envisaged. One of the features of government, thought in this way, is that it attempts to intervene in the world in order to convert its philosophy into an actuality.

3 Consistent with this, the emerging law did not protect profits that could not have been foreseen by the contracting parties (Wrightman 1996).

4 Having its origins in parliamentary support for working men's fraternal life insurance schemes from about 1800, this grew into such pervasive institutions as industrial life insurance (characterised by the regular, door to door collection of 'penny premiums'). By the latter part of the century, it is estimated that three quarters of English working-class households were covered by such policies. Nevertheless, the issue was the site of major struggles over whether this provided an effective form of thrift for poor people (O'Malley 1999b).

5 Such techniques would include insurance, but also a wide variety of preventative strategies that do not discipline individuals – such as designing-out crime, providing sports facilities for schools in 'high risk' crime areas, or installing traffic obstacles to reduce speeding. It should be noted that Simon and others probably underestimate the extent to which actuarial techniques were deployed in this period: from massive public health measures aimed at disease reduction, to the rebuilding of large areas of metropolitan regions in order to break up criminal 'rookeries'. Arguably, preventative policing could be fitted into such schemata.

6 Simon (1988) goes on to argue that this fear of the dangerous classes rendered actuarial strategies – such as welfarism – impracticable, even had they appeared palatable on other grounds. In this view, the tolerance that actuarial strategies afford to individual deviance could not be risked until the dangerous classes had been tamed by the disciplines.

7 Other archetypical examples include the explorer and to a lesser extent the inventor. Both categories were linked with upper-class images of largely self-funded risk takers whose goals were nevertheless to foster the good of society. Naturally the consequences of failure were to be borne upon their own shoulders, or by the fiscal resources of voluntary societies.

8 For further discussion see Pratt (1998). It is important to recognise here that the welfare sanction involved a compromise in which the 'theoretical logic (of the human sciences) was continually interrupted by political calculation' in such a way that 'their positive aspects (interventionism, correction, individualism, the welfare sanction) were separated from their unacceptable ideological implications (determinism, the denial of responsibility and subjectivity, social reform etc)' (Garland 1981: 30–1).

9 Outside of the United States, actuarial sentencing has been little taken up. Pratt (1998), for example, suggests that the kinds of judicial obstacles noted by Glaser are unlikely to erode significantly, and that in consequence such actuarial techniques are likely to have only a marginal influence – and then mostly on parole decisions.

10   The call for justice is increasingly framed in terms of the rights of the innocent
victim and articulated in highly moral terms. And it singles out for its attention a new class of 'monsters'. Sex offenders, paedophiles, madmen or
quasi-madmen on the loose, drug dealers, violent children, serial killers and the
like.... Today the monstrous seem to have returned. The monstrous is the
anomaly, the exception, not merely a deviation from the norm but something
with a radically different nature, gross pathology, perhaps evil. Rather than
norm and deviation we have seductive fantasies of ideal communities of
harmony and civility threatened by terrifying fantasies of monsters.

(Rose 1998: 35)

References

Adams, J. (1995) *Risk*, London: UCL Press.

Aharoni, Y. (1981) *The No-Risk Society*, Chatham, NJ: Chatham House.

Beck, U. (1992) *Risk Society*, New York: Sage.

Bernstein, P. (1992) *Capital Ideas: The Impossible Origins of Modern Wall Street*, Princeton, NJ: Princeton University Press.

Clarke, J. and Newman, J. (1997) *The Managerial State*, London: Sage.

Daston, L. (1988) *Classical Probability in the Enlightenment*, Princeton, NJ: Princeton University Press.

Dean, M. (1991) *The Constitution of Poverty*, London: Routledge.

—— (1995) 'Governing the Unemployed Self in an Active Society', *Economy and Society* 24: 559–83.

Douglas, M. (1992) *Risk and Blame: Essays in Cultural Theory*, London: Routledge.

Ericson, R. and Haggerty, K. (1997) *Policing the Risk Society*, Toronto, Ont.: University of Toronto Press.

Feeley, M. and Simon, J. (1992) 'The New Penology: Notes on the Emerging Strategy of Corrections and its Implications', *Criminology* 30: 449–70.

—— (1994) 'Actuarial Justice: The Emerging New Criminal Law', in D. Nelken (ed.), *The Futures of Criminology*, London: Sage.

Foucault, M. (1977) *Discipline and Punish*, London: Peregrine Books.

Garland, D. (1981) 'The Birth of the Welfare Sanction', *British Journal of Law and Society* 8: 17–35.

—— (1985) *Punishment and Welfare*, Aldershot: Gower.

—— (1996) 'The Limits of the Sovereign State', *British Journal of Criminology* 36(4): 445–71.

Geason, P. and Wilson, P. (1989) *Designing Out Crime*, Canberra: Australian Institute of Criminology.

Glaser, D. (1985) 'Who Gets Probation and Parole: Case Study versus Actuarial Decision Making', *Crime and Delinquency* 31: 367–78.

Greco, M. (1993) 'Psychosomatic Subjects and the Duty to be Well', *Economy and Society* 22: 357–72.

Green, J. (1997) *Risk and Misfortune*, London: UCL Press.

Hayes, M. (1994) *The New Right in Britain*, London: Pluto Press.

Kercher, B. (1990) *Remedies*, Sydney: Butterworths.

National Crime Prevention Institute (1986) *Crime Prevention*, Louisville: National Crime Prevention Institute.

O'Malley, P. (1992) 'Risk, Power and Crime Prevention', *Economy and Society* 21: 252–75.

—— (1998) *Crime and the Risk Society*, Aldershot: Dartmouth.

—— (1999a) 'Volatile and Contradictory Punishment', *Theoretical Criminology* 3(2): 175–96.

—— (1999b) 'Imagining Insurance: Risk, Thrift and Industrial Life Insurance in Britain', *Connecticut Insurance Law Journal* 5(2): 675–705.

Peters, T. (1987) *Thriving on Chaos: Handbook for a Management Revolution*, New York: Knopf.

Pratt, J. (1998) *Governing the Dangerous*, Sydney: Federation Press.

Reddy, S. (1996) 'Claims to Expert Knowledge and the Subversion of Democracy: The Triumph of Risk over Uncertainty', *Economy and Society* 25(2): 222–54.

Rose, N. (1990) 'Governing the Enterprising Self', in P. Heelas and P. Morris (eds), *The Values of the Enterprise Culture*, London: Unwin Hyman.

—— (1996a) 'Governing "advanced" liberal democracies', in A. Barry, T. Osborne and N. Rose (eds), *Foucault and Political Reason*, London: UCL Press.

—— (1996b) 'The Death of the "social"? Refiguring the Territory of Government', *Economy and Society* 26(4): 327–46.

—— (1998) 'At Risk of Madness. Risk, Psychiatry and the Management of Mental Health', Unpublished paper, Goldsmiths College, London.

Scruton, R. (1984) *The Meaning of Conservatism*, London: Macmillan.

Simon, J. (1987) 'The Emergence of a Risk Society: Insurance, Law, and the State', *Socialist Review* 95: 61–89.

—— (1988) 'The Ideological Effects of Actuarial Practices', *Law and Society Review* 22: 772–800.

—— (1995) 'They Died with their Boots On: The Boot Camp and the Limits of Modern Penality', *Social Justice* 22: 25–48.

Wrightman, J. (1996) *Contract: A Critical Commentary*, London: Pluto Press.

Zelizer, V. (1994) *Markets and Morals*, New York: Basic Books.

Zedlewski, E. (1985) 'When Have We Punished Enough?', *Public Administration Review* 45(5): 771–9.

Chapter 2

Dangerousness and modern society

John Pratt

In most modern societies, dangerousness has come to have a specific penological meaning. It is usually taken to refer to that group of offenders whose propensity to repeatedly commit crimes of a non-capital but otherwise serious nature puts the wellbeing of the rest of the community at risk. How such offenders should then be punished has been a vexatious issue since the very conceptualisation of dangerousness across such societies around the end of the nineteenth century. The strategies that came to be adopted to punish and control those who were so judged went by a variety of names[1] but usually involved some form of indeterminate prison sentence. These powers have been periodically reviewed and reformulated but essentially they have remained on the statute books in most of these societies, sometimes drawing on mental health powers of compulsory detention as well.[2] This is because another problematic aspect of dangerousness is the way in which those offenders judged to possess this quality also tend to be regarded as 'neither sane nor insane' (Kozol *et al*. 1972). Again, this combination of repeated criminality in conjunction with a problematic but legally unclassifiable mental state has provoked the introduction of special measures of control. Much of the subsequent discussions on dangerousness have then centred around the ethical dilemmas associated with their use: to what extent is it legitimate to punish an offender for the kind of person they are judged to be, in addition to the crimes they have committed; and to what extent is it permissible in Western societies to detain an offender on the assumption that they might commit a crime in the future?

However, that there should be such ethical concerns associated with the use of these powers designed to remove such (apparently) high-risk offenders draws our attention to the broader (if implicit) political issues that underlie their introduction and subsequent presence. The first dangerousness laws in the early part of this century introduced strategies which remained on the statute books in one way or another – but for much of the time right at the boundaries of modern penality. Indeed, it was only in totalitarian societies (or other non-modern social formations) that such powers of indefinite detention became central penal features (see Morris 1951; Woolf 1993).

Certainly, in English-based societies, precisely because such powers effect-ively suspend taken-for-granted features of their penality (such as certain and proportionate punishments), they were always intended to be exceptional powers, to be used sparingly if at all. In the United States in particular, such powers have been, and still are, subject to regular legal challenge on the basis of their constitutionality.

In these respects, it is not the ethical dilemmas of dangerousness that I wish to address in this chapter but, instead, the problematic presence of these measures in modern society. Why were they introduced around a century ago; what utility were they meant to have; what has led to their reformulation and redirection at various times over the course of this century; and, finally, if, at the present time, there are indications that these powers are being repositioned to take a more central place in Western penality, why should this be so, and what is the particular significance of this?

From dangerous classes to dangerous individuals

For a good part of the nineteenth century, political and popular discourses were taken up with the supposed threat to social order posed by the dangerous classes. From the political manifesto of Karl Marx to the novels of Charles Dickens and Victor Hugo, it was as if the very structure on which modern society was being built was still, at this early stage of its develop-ment, a very fragile affair, with roots that still had to be firmly embedded in the social fabric. In these respects, and for good or bad, depending on the individual writer's point of view, the framework of modern society itself seemed to be regularly put at risk from disparate groups – trade unionists, urban masses, political agitators, dispossessed agricultural workers, crimi-nals, returning 'ticket-of-leave men' and the like who, in unity, constituted 'the dangerous classes' of this time; and who, in unity, seemed to possess this power of destruction. In these respects, their threats, their acts of insurrec-tion, the crimes that they committed in the course of such activities, came to be seen as having a wider purpose and significance than the damage or loss to the property and personal effects of the particular individuals who were their victims. It was as if their ultimate targets were the very founda-tion stones of modern society itself – hence the valorisation of their destructive potential in the writings of the time. If people or property were harmed as a result of these activities, this was likely to be in the course of the quasi-political struggle for existence between such proto-revolutionary forces and those classes which seemed to find favour in the arrangements of the modern social order.

However, during the second half of the nineteenth century, it is as if the threat from the dangerous classes comes to be dissipated. The combined effects of ameliorative social reforms and the embedding and settling down of the framework of modernity itself led to a number of the constituent elements of the dangerous classes being effectively siphoned off and them-selves enmeshed in the social alignments of modernity (see Davies 1980). For the most part, any subsequent questioning of it by oppositional groups came to be related to how it might be made to work more equitably for the interests they represented, rather than the need for its wholesale destruction. What we thus find is that, instead of dangerousness taking the form of a political quality associated with the insurrectional capacities of a particular class, it begins to be used in the second half of the nineteenth century more as a term to classify particular groups of criminals whose threat was of a very different order from that of the dangerous classes.

In one of the first depictions of this newly classified group of criminals, they were described as being:

> in the community, but neither of it, nor from it ... the large majority was so by descent, and stands completely isolated from the other classes in blood, in sympathies, in its domestic and social organisation – as it is hostile to them in the 'ways and means' of temporal existence.
>
> (Plint 1851: 153)

Those in whom such qualities were concentrated, such as repeat offenders, began to move to the forefront of penal policy concerns from the 1860s. The growing technology of modernity and its bureaucratic processes of record keeping both alerted the state and its penal commentators to the extent of this new formulation of dangerousness ('the number of men and youths that compose our criminal and dangerous classes now at large may be computed at about 40000 in England and Wales', Solly 1887: 763) – as well as raising the possibility of new systems of control and regulation over them. The English Habitual Criminals Act 1869 introduced a central register of recidivists which included their photographs. Later, a convict supervision office was opened at Scotland Yard, complete with photographs, a register of tattoos, initials, classification of distinctive marks and an index of the criminals' *modus operandi*, in a bid to make calculable and knowable such risks.

By the same token, those who demonstrated these propensities would no longer be celebratory, if infamous, figures living as it were beyond the boundaries of everyday life, as had been the case in the premodern world, with the highwaymen, for example, figures both of romance and fear (see Griffiths 1896); instead, by being located within the social body, such crim-inals came to be seen as insidious, cancerous threats to its wellbeing. The era of the criminal as a kind of folk hero preying on the powerful rather than the powerless was now coming to an end (although it was to live on for a while longer yet in some of the frontier societies of the new world). In its place, criminality came to be presented as a statistically verifiable omnipresent threat to all. By such means, the social enemy was transformed into a deviant, who brought with him the multiple danger of disorder, crime and madness. The carceral network linked, through innumerable relations, the two long, multiple series of the punitive and the abnormal.

(Foucault 1978: 300–1)

Furthermore, the state chose to act against such dangerous criminals not solely because it felt itself imperilled by them; in addition, during the second half of the nineteenth century, it became prepared to extend its powers of control over those who refused to conform to its laws and normative expectations on behalf of the citizens they endangered. It began to assume responsibility for their protection from the risks such offenders posed: and on such terms the penal arena itself can thus be developed as a form of social defence, reflecting the broader shifts in governance taking place at this time. In these respects, the moves to legislate against the dangerous belong to a pattern of measures designed to offer protection against risks of various kinds (unemployment, poor health, poverty in old age and so on). What it is possible to see by means of this various writing of protection from risk onto the political agenda of modern government, is the formulation of a new political relationship – which can also be seen as one of the hallmarks of modernity itself.

By being prepared to offer its citizens protection from risks, the modern state was thus granting them, in effect, 'a right to life' (Foucault 1979): a set of assurances were given, a set of expectations were created which thus marked out modernity from other social formations. Responsibility for risk management of varying kinds was being transferred from the individual to the state – and in return for the increased security and wellbeing this was intended to bring to its subjects, the state would assume greater powers of intervention and regulation over their lives.

Who were the dangerous?

Who, though, were these first 'dangerous offenders'? What kind of crimes had they committed and what other qualities might they possess? What is clear is that at this time those who tended to be regarded as dangerous (they would also be often referred to as 'habitual' or 'professional' criminals – the terms seem to have been interchangeable at this time, see Radzinowicz and Hood 1986) were likely to consist in the main of small-time recidivist property offenders who may often, as well, have displayed habits of vagrancy, itinerancy, have used aliases and have been well versed in the art of disguise. Horsley (1913: 35–6) thus referred to one such dangerous criminal as,

an old Southwark professional thief, though posing as a hawker. Has had two terms of penal servitude and six previous convictions ...

escaped identification lately, when in the burglary he planned his two companions got ten years each. One of his aliases was Sage and another Sausage.

What made them so dangerous at this time was not simply the issue of their repeated criminality – it was also the issue of their regularly changing or 'unknowable' identities.

Regarding their crimes, then it might be thought that the concerns to provide safeguards against the particular risks posed by recidivist property offenders were simply a reflection of the class and gender bias inherent in the criminal justice system at that time. In contrast to the gravity attached to property crime, those who committed violent/sexual crimes against women tended to receive far lighter sentences (see, for example, Peck 1878). This may well have been the case. But at the same time this coupling of property offending with dangerousness was also a reflection of a society where personal goods, for the most part, were both uninsurable and irreplaceable. Their loss would thus be a risk that was irreparable (Ewald 1991).

But the shifting identities of these criminals also made the risks they posed all the more incalculable. Their very rootlessness, their ability to shrug off one identity as it suited them and then assume another rendering them, as it were, 'unknowable' confirmed their status as dangerous. It was increasingly the case in the development of modern society that no one would be allowed to stand outside of the law or of its new administrative, regulatory mechanisms and, by so doing, remain unknowable to the state. In the development of modern society, one would not be allowed to remain anonymous, nor simply brush aside its persistent demands for information about oneself, that would be entered into registers concerning such matters as birth, health, education, criminality, marriage and so on. In this 'transcribing of real lives into history' (Foucault 1979) that became characteristic of modernity, the lives of ordinary people now became objects of knowledge and investigation. To try to remain unknowable in modern society was thus to threaten its very modality of governing. And it was precisely this quality of unknowability that made those who possessed it, particularly when coupled with criminal propensities, seem so dangerous at this time. In these ways, the initial concerns and anxieties about dangerous offenders were based on the way in which this concept was able to unify two registers of disobedience: continuous illegalities on the one hand, lives that remained unknowable and thereby unpredictable on the other. To prevent those who possessed such qualities from standing outside its power, it became necessary for the modern state to extend its penal apparatus to ensure that they too, along with all its other deviants and abnormals, could be brought within its carceral archipelago (Foucault 1978).

Punishing the dangerous

At this time it was as if those criminals who repeated their crimes were simply beyond the law, since they continually chose to break it. Indeed it was claimed that without special powers of detention being available specifically for them, the sanctions that such law breaking otherwise brought – short prison sentences – seemed to be regarded as nothing more than a professional risk by them: 'the sentence affects [them] much as an accident on the football field affects a player who has to retire from play for a while' (Anderson 1903: 496); but they were also beyond psychiatry since, notwithstanding the indications to the contrary of their repeated criminality, they were at one and the same time not insane as this term was understood in criminal law ('the law does not recognise any mental gradation between perfect sanity and absolute insanity', Haynes 1865: 548). Nineteenth-century penality had insisted on matching punishment to the crime one had committed rather than the person whom one was thought to be. As such, it was as if this group of offenders had placed themselves beyond the limits of modern penality and its classificatory framework.

In these respects, the subsequent introduction of indefinite sentences of imprisonment which did make it possible to match punishment to the kind of person one was thought to be reflected the influence of the new penology at this time, with its contributions from experts in the fields of eugenics, medico-psychiatry and criminal anthropology. This allowed some rewriting of the issue of criminal responsibility: it would now be placed on more of a sliding scale, with the categories of sanity/insanity representing the polarities of this continuum rather than the only modalities of classification: where one was placed on this continuum would be dependent on the way in which one's character was judged, assessed and ultimately constituted by the plurality of expert knowledges that would now begin to shape thinking about criminality. By such means, it would become possible to control the threat from those judged to be dangerous by indefinite imprisonment until they were no longer assessed as 'risky'. Even then, protection from them would continue – by making provision for the continuous surveillance of their habits when they were eventually released on license. This could be achieved by inserting a range of conditions in it designed to ensure their normalisation, not simply their desistance from criminality *per se*: addresses must not be changed without permission, punctual and regular attendance at work was a necessity, a 'sober and industrious' life had to be lived. Breach of normative stipulations such as these could lead to a recall to prison.

In line with this commitment from the state to provide risk insurance, the introduction of the indeterminate sentence provisions for those judged to be dangerous was accompanied, probably for the first time, by a commitment to 'public protection' being inserted into penal legislation. The

English Prevention of Crime Act 1908 seems to have been the first to specifically state this commitment, but there is no doubt that it was a crucial theme in the build up to the introduction of these measures in other jurisdictions, and from thereafter it began to be written into laws of this kind as a matter of course (see Pratt 1995). As part of the contractual arrangements between state and citizen in modern society, it had become an inescapable onus on the former to provide safeguards of this nature. Such measures have accordingly been reformulated and refurbished by whichever political parties have held power during the subsequent course of the twentieth century – both during the welfare era which lasted for the majority of this period and during the shift to neo-liberal polity during the last two decades or so. Changes in party political power might have an impact on the range and extent of this commitment, but not the commitment *per se*.

Notwithstanding the apparent ungovernability of these first dangerous offenders by the previously existing penal measures, the indeterminate prison sentence, precisely because it represented the farthest reaches of modern penality, was regarded as a sanction to be carefully scrutinised and sparingly used by the judges of this time (as has been the case since). It had to remain at the penal margins rather than be used as a general power because of its suspension of some of the established principles of modern penality. Hence the comments of the English Court of Appeal in *R* v. *Sullivan* (1913) Cr. App. R. 201:

> it was necessary in the interests of the prisoner that very watchful care should be exercised by this court and also by those who preside over trials in which a prisoner is charged with being a habitual criminal, to see that the prisoner's interests are jealously safeguarded, because he stands in a peculiar position, which is, to say the least of it, not a favourable one ... he is first of all convicted of the offence for which he is indicted, then he is put on trial as an habitual criminal, and consequently, it is enough to say that one must be scrupulously careful to protect him when this particular question whether he is a habitual criminal or not is put to the jury.

Initially, resistance to these new measures of control was not just confined to a judiciary schooled in *gesellschaft* law and classical jurisprudence; nor was it just confined to progressive liberal opinion (see Radzinowicz and Hood 1986). There had been significant opposition to these new penal measures from the general public, from the late nineteenth century when they were first suggested, through to the 1920s. The last formal note of public opposition towards the very principle of these special powers of detention is acknowledged in the English Report of the Committee on Sexual Offences against Young People (1925: 61):

we consider that special action is called for in cases of repeated sexual offences [against children] ... we are aware that the public mind is distrustful of any kind of indeterminate sentence, but we believe that a period of prolonged detention in a special institution might occasionally effect a cure. In any case it would protect the public more effectively than many short terms of imprisonment.

Why was it, though, that public opinion at this time could seem so hostile to measures which, today, have come to have an entrenched position in modern penal systems? The encroachments on the conduct of everyday life that such powers of punishment and surveillance allowed the state to make gave it a role that most of its citizens would take time to adjust to: it might well have been the case that by assuming such powers the state was prepared to act on behalf of its citizens to offer them a right to life; but at the same time the idea of a benevolent state still seemed novel to significant elements of the social body, as if such benevolence was a front to more sinister and coercive modes of control intimated by the dangerousness laws. Furthermore, while it was the case in the modern world that criminality would come to lose most of its romantic resonance with outlawry and so on, it was as if this period around the early twentieth century was a kind of transitional era: while criminality was beginning to be transformed from being an indicator of outlawry to one of cancerous depredation, until this transformation was complete, powers that led to what were thought to be excesses of punishment could still provoke public sympathy for the offender, as if the population at large were as yet unwilling to put its trust in the state's ability to manage risk on their behalf and the enlarged powers of regulation and intervention that this necessitated (see Pratt 1995, 1998). Instead, such powers were at that time seen by many as oppressive and unwelcome.

Dangerousness and the changing nature of risk

From around the 1930s onwards, though, there is something of a realignment in the dangerousness configuration. This touches on, first, the utility of the special powers of control. The state itself begins to question the need for the extra penal powers it had introduced in this area – particularly as regards their use against the initial group of dangerous offenders. The risks they had posed in terms of both their unknowability and their criminality came to be minimised by the very successes of the growing administrative framework, welfare infrastructure and economic programme of modern societies. By the 1950s, to remain unknowable had become an increasingly difficult, perhaps altogether impossible, task: in England, for example, the residual haunts and recesses of Sausage, Red Jim and their kind dramatically disappeared with the onset of postwar social reconstruction and the provision of more extensive social welfare assistance. Vagrancy as a social problem was being dramatically reduced at this time. Prosecutions for such conduct declined from over 1000 per year 1945–9 to 671 per year 1965–9 (Home Office 1974). In addition, new forms of social assistance that helped to reduce this problem were also accompanied by more extensive record-keeping, regulatory control, the investiture of further powers of intervention in state officials and so on. Overall, in the social development of this postwar period we find any last remaining vestiges of that micro-world which had provided cover for undesirables, into which they could enter in one identity then re-emerge in another, disappearing altogether.

By the same token, the growing availability of consumer goods and property insurance began to reduce the inherent risks associated until then with property crime. Now, such crime no longer meant irreparable damage. As a result, in most of these jurisdictions we find the state increasingly being prepared to refine and restrict the use of these laws against this category of offending (see, for example, Advisory Council on the Treatment of Offenders 1963; Department of Justice 1968). Such curtailments continued during the 1970s and 1980s but were also given a sharper economic and political focus: the relegation of prison to a last resort position, the bifurcation of the criminal population into 'the really serious' and 'the rest' with property offenders by this time firmly placed in the latter camp, not only led to the former dangerous offenders no longer having to face the possibility of indefinite imprisonment, but, in some jurisdictions, no longer facing imprisonment at all. Now we find more specific directions as to which offenders should be targeted by these powers by neo-liberal governments determined to ensure that respective elements of their programmes were not jeopardised or nullified by unsympathetic but powerful groups within the social body. The bid to relegate those with the characteristics of the initial dangerous offenders to a relatively insignificant position in the penal system perhaps reached its apogee with the British Home Office (1991) publication *Crime, Justice and Protecting the Public*. Not only were custodial sentences for property offenders frowned on, but in addition, past records were not to be taken into account when passing sentences – in effect, calling into question the very existence of dangerousness itself, as a particular form of risk that governments were prepared to manage. It had been precisely this element of past record that had been the critical feature of the status of those so judged. In large respects, it was almost as if the modern state had come to regard such laws – or at least as they had been directed at this group – as an unnecessary appendage to modern penality. Not only had the risks of at least this group of criminals diminished but, as in Britain, the growing political emphasis on the self-management of risk relieved the burden on the state to provide this.

In contrast, and in conjunction with a public that becomes increasingly anxious about various aspects of its personal security, we find a more focused and applied use of these laws in the area of sex crime. The immediate pre-war and postwar period sees a focus primarily on sex crimes against children, then in the post-1970s period, it brings into the frame such crimes against women. How do we explain the changing nature of risk and the reformulation of dangerousness in these ways?

By the 1930s, it was as if a special value had come to be attached to children (for example, the English Children and Young Persons Act 1933 emphasises the welfare of the child as being of paramount importance in all juvenile court proceedings). If we can see such sentiments gathering pace during the second half of the nineteenth century in law, literature and other discourses, perhaps it is at this point around the 1930s that they come to fruition. In an era of apparent population decline (see, for example, McCleary 1937) they begin to assume an irreplaceable commodity value, which largely remains today – hence the state comes to have a vested interest in ensuring the protection of its children, if purely for its own reproductive purposes. But there was more to the increasing emphasis on protecting children from this time than such instrumentalism. The normalisation of small families meant that children were more likely to be cherished in their own right than was the case a century or so earlier. Yet, simultaneously, it was as if the wellbeing and security of children only seemed more at risk because of the developmental nature of modern society itself and its attendant social changes. These took the form of mass urban development and an increasing emphasis on mobility of labour, which thereby led to the breakdown of informal systems of childcare, support and guidance. These features of modern society are likely to have increased the perceived immediate risks to children (such as the presence of 'strangers' in newly constituted communities and the absence of extended family support structures to offer guidance and protection). In such ways children had more value in themselves but, in addition, an increased vulnerability, owing to the uncertainties and incalculable nature of the dangers that now seemed to surround them. And again, harm to them would cause (literally it was thought, see, for example, Bowlby 1944; Friedlander 1947) irreparable damage.

Then, around the 1970s those who would commit sexual/violent attacks on women were added to the dangerousness framework. By this time, the homogeneous cultural framework of postwar welfare society was in the process of being broken down. The economic changes that made personal possessions more readily available and replaceable were accompanied by forms of social change that were beginning to completely revitalise and reorganise the conduct of everyday life. New opportunities for women in particular became available as normative social horizons for them were extended beyond domesticity and into a more pluralistic world of career opportunities and increased public visibility. These new-found freedoms and opportunities thereby bring with them additional risks and insecurities. As Karp *et al*. (1991: 147) write, the downside however to the urbane life in cities lies in this same phenomenon; that is, a world in which one frequently encounters strangers on public streets, in restaurants, and shops is a world that poses questions about possible dangers and personal harm. In this regard, women are particularly disadvantaged by both the larger cultural traditions of Western societies and the special structures within which such fears are shaped and nourished.

A growing sense of uncertainty and insecurity is brought home by the fragmentation of previously embedded cultural practices: if domesticity, for example, had been a form of entrapment for so many women in welfare society, at least the world then had a certainty and permanence to it. If very many more women were now given the opportunity to move beyond the domestic realm in post-1970s society, there was little by way of the traditional support structures to be found in the private, domestic world that had hitherto been their most expected location to structure and guide these new possibilities. Entry into the public domain came with a price – increased vulnerability and anxiety.

Second, alongside the changing nature of risk, there is the changing nature of risk assessment. It was as if the period from around 1930 marked a kind of crossover point in the way in which this task was accomplished: prior to this time, such assessments were likely to be based largely on discussions with neighbours or extended family. From this point in the twentieth century, however, it seems increasingly likely that risk is assessed on the basis of much more abstract sources of information; in such ways, risk becomes both more globalised and more localised (Giddens 1990). It now involved a reliance on the mass media rather than neighbours, for example, to find out 'what was going on'. Indeed, this trend had been gathering pace from the late nineteenth century onwards but perhaps during the 1930s became the predominant mode of risk assessment. The popularisation of the mass media round the end of the nineteenth century had begun this process; during the first half of the twentieth century, it accelerates and proliferates with the expansion and diversification of the media; then, with the technological revolution of the postwar period, our perceptions of risk become all the more intensified through this process.

At the same time, these sources of risk information are made increasingly authoritative by the harnessing of expert opinion to them, thus confirming the dangers so highlighted. One of the first examples of the way in which this concentrated power of definition is able to shape the concept of dangerousness is seen in the immediate pre-war and postwar period. Psychological experts of one kind or another were provided media space to proclaim the presence of the dreaded 'sexual psychopath' and colour in his alleged propensities (Sutherland 1950). Even so, there is of course no necessary unity to such expertise. If the mythical qualities of this creature had been exposed by the 1960s in a further realignment of the knowledge which had hitherto constituted it (see, for example, Tappan 1957), nonetheless, the value of children in modern society continued to mean that those who were thought to pose a threat to them represented an irreparable risk; hence such offenders, although no longer known as sexual psychopaths, remained in the dangerousness focus.

The anxieties that were generated through these forms of risk assessment serve to revitalise the perceived necessity for the presence of the dangerousness laws. The risks that children face have been rearticulated and are now thought to be embodied in the figure of today's 'sexual predator', as if such monsters may surreptitiously move into our neighbourhoods, and against such eventuality the entire community must be mobilised.[3] Equally, women not only become the new targets of dangerous offenders but also, in line with their enhanced social status and visibility begin to claim the right to protection from such attacks. The incalculable and irreparable nature of the risks that they now seem to face and the very marginality of such powers of protection that the laws have always represented leads to members of the public – but particularly women – being exhorted to assume increasing responsibility for self-management of such risks: 'police want people to create strongrooms in their houses to barricade themselves away from intruders ... "for women living alone or people not in close proximity to their neighbours, it is often safer to barricade yourself in a room than venture outside where they may be other offenders" ' (*The Dominion*, 4 May 1998). In these respects, 'taking care of oneself' – one of the most significant political catch phrases of the 1990s – is both empowering and threatening. It addresses on the one hand all those forms of conduct and etiquette aimed at perfecting personal appearance and wellbeing that are now available to us; but on the other hand, it represents the way individuals (rather than the state) have been given responsibility for an increasing array of risk management.

Beyond modernity?

From the birth of dangerousness until the early 1990s, notwithstanding its own kaleidoscopic nature during this time, it remained a kind of boundary marker of modern penality: it was a reserve not a general power of punishment. But in the last few years it has been clear that modern penality has been subjected to a considerable refiguring (Garland 1996): crime, and real and perceived risks from crime, no longer seem manageable within the established arrangements of modern penality. By the same token, the increasing exhortation from the state to its citizens that they should 'take care of themselves' creates, paradoxically, a demand for more protection from the state, as the more alarming and risky the world seems to become. One aspect of the refiguring of penal arrangements has seen the dangerousness laws and their kind being shifted from the far reaches of the penal system to a much more central place, particularly, but not exclusively, in the United States. That this should be so is, at one level, a reflection of the extent to which the anxieties and uncertainties which impinge upon everyday life, and which themselves have been let loose by the shift towards neo-liberal governance in the last two decades, make risk seem unmanageable within the existing arrangements of policing and punishment. The risks posed by dangerous offenders not only seem to grow but seem to be beyond the capabilities of the modern state to manage.

In these respects, the increasing reliance on dangerousness laws of the United States' three-strikes nature both illustrate the way in which it has become a much more general form of penal power and of the way in which the erstwhile boundaries of modern penality are now being breached in these latest bids to govern the dangerous. From being largely confined to those who would put at risk the wellbeing of women and children the concept now comes to have the potential to remove an increasingly broad range of the socially undesirable. To achieve this, it seems that democratic states increasingly have to have recourse to penal powers of totalitarian and other non-modern social formations. If we are now prepared to ignore the political and cultural stigma that these powers bear as a result of their ancestry in Nazi Germany and Soviet Russia, then we are also able to live with the consequences of so doing: massive increases in the prison populations of these societies (cf. Christie 1993). What lies behind them, surely, is the emergence of a new culture of intolerance, a cheapness and expendability of human life. Ironically, these measures, with their totalitarian parallels are justified on the grounds that they are designed to protect personal freedom and individual rights, even if these new dangerousness laws themselves seem to be at odds with such values.

Notes

1 For example, in England, the sentence of preventive detention was introduced in the prevention of Crime Act 1908; in New Zealand, the Habitual Criminals Act 1906 allowed such criminals to be detained indefinitely by means of an Habitual Criminal Declaration.
2 See particularly the United States sexual psychopath laws from the late 1930s to the early 1950s.
3 As in current sexual predator legislation in the United States; for a more general discussion of these laws against sex criminals, see Pratt (2000).

References

Advisory Council on the Treatment of Offenders (1963) *Preventive Detention*, London: HMSO.

Anderson, R. (1903) 'The Crusade against Professional Criminals', *The Nineteenth Century* March: 496–508.

Bowlby, J. (1944) *Forty Four Juvenile Thieves*, London: Penguin Books.

Christie, N. (1993) *Crime Control as Industry*, London: Martin Robertson.

Committee on Sexual Offences Against Young People (1925) *Report*, London: HMSO (cmnd 2561).

Davies, J. (1980) 'The London Garrotting Panic of 1862', in V. Gatrell, B. Lenman and G. Parker (eds), *Crime And The Law: The Social History Of Crime In Western Europe Since 1500*, London: European Publications.

Department of Justice (1968) *Annual Report to Parliament*, Wellington: Appendices to the Journal of the House of Representatives.

Ewald, F. (1991) 'Insurance and Risk', in D. Burchell, C. Gordon and P. Miller (eds), *The Foucault Effect*, Brighton: Harvester.

Foucault, M. (1978) *Discipline and Punish*, London: Allen Lane.

—— (1979) *The History of Sexuality*, vol. I, London: Allen Lane.

Friedlander, K. (1947) *The Psychoanalytic Approach to Juvenile Delinquency*, London: Kegan Paul.

Garland, D. (1996) 'The Limits of the Sovereign State', *British Journal of Criminology*, 36: 445–71.

Giddens, A. (1990) *The Consequences of Modernity*, Cambridge: Polity Press.

Griffiths, A. (1896) *The Chronicles of Newgate*, London: Chapman and Hall.

Haynes, S. (1865) 'Clinical Cases Illustrative of Moral Imbecility', *Journal of Mental Science* 10: 533–49.

Home Office (1974) *Working Party on Vagrancy and Street Offences*, London: HMSO.

—— (1991) *Crime, Justice and Protecting the Public*, London: HMSO.

Horsley, J. (1913) *How Criminals are Made and Prevented*, London: Unwin.

Karp, D., Stone, G. and Yoeb, W. (1991) *Being Urban: A Sociology of City Life*, New York: Praeger.

Kozol, H., Boucher, J. and Garofalo, R. (1972) 'The Diagnosis and Treatment of Dangerousness', *Crime and Delinquency* 18: 371–92.

McCleary, G. (1937) *The Menace of British Depopulation*, London: Faber.

Morris, N. (1951) *The Habitual Criminal*, London: Longman.

Peck, F. (1878) 'The Miscarriage of Justice', *Contemporary Review*, p.100ff.

Plint, T. (1851) *Crime in England*, London: Charles Gilpin.

Pratt, J. (1995) 'Dangerousness, Risk and Technologies of Power', *Australian and New Zealand Journal of Criminology* 28: 1–31.

—— (1998) *Governing the Dangerous*, Sydney: Federation Press.

—— (2000) 'Sex Crime and the New Punitiveness', *Behavioural Sciences and Law* (in press).

Radzinowicz, L. and Hood, R. (1986) *A History of English Criminal Law*, vol. 5, London: Butterworths.

Solly, H. (1887) 'Our Vagrant and Leisure Classes', *The Leisure Hour* 36: 763–7.

Sutherland, E. (1950) 'The Sexual Psychopath Laws', *Journal of Criminal Law and Criminology* 40: 543–54.

Tappan, P. (1957) 'Sexual Offences: The American Context', in L. Radzinowicz (ed.), *Sexual Offences*, London: Stevens and Sons Ltd.

Woolf, J, (1993) 'Crime Policy against Juveniles and Crime Control during the Nazi period in Germany', paper presented at the 11th International congress on Criminology, Budapest.

Part II

Legal responses and responsibilities

Chapter 3

Guerrillas in our midst?

Judicial responses to governing the dangerous

Arie Freiberg

The persistence of dangerousness

Like the poor, the dangerous have always been with us. The dangerous, those who persist in their crimes because of their psychological, biological, economic, alcoholic, drug dependent or political condition or simply by their rational choice, have long posed difficult problems for Anglo-Australian jurisprudence. On the one hand, their persistence, resistance or sheer unamenability to traditional criminal justice interventions stands as a stark reminder of the system's failure to deal with a small, but highly visible group of offenders. Courts and penal authorities, past and present, need no sophisticated criminological analysis to identify the core of offenders who are multiple recidivists. Judges, in sentencing, have before them the offender's prior record which so often is a depressing litany of defeat, disappointment or defiance. Prison authorities know that fifty to seventy per cent of their intake are repeat customers.

While logic, common sense, medical and social science, the public and politicians, urge that the persistent and dangerous should be the subject of special measures designed to deter, divert, incapacitate, habilitate or quarantine them, a juridical tradition built up over the last century remains firmly resistant to such legal and social innovations. To a community subject to repeated victimisation, this resistance on the part of the courts appears incomprehensible, obstructive and unresponsive. These opposed responses to dangerousness raise important questions about the distribution of political power and the accountability of the courts to parliament and the people.

This chapter examines judicial responses to legislative mechanisms introduced to deal with recidivist or violent offenders over the past century in Australia. In his book, *Governing the Dangerous* (1997), John Pratt explores a range of measures introduced over the last century designed to deal with two classes of offender, the minor but persistent property offender and the violent offender. He identifies these as the 'dangerous' classes. In noting the 'remarkable commonality between jurisdictions to the way dangerousness has been thought about and responded to' (Pratt 1997: 5) and the various attempts to 'govern'[1] the dangerous, he makes two important observations. The first is that despite the widespread existence of an array of legislative measures, they were remarkably little used at any one time in any jurisdiction. Though highly symbolic of the state's power to act, and of considerable sociological significance, they were, in practice irrelevant, offering little effective protection to the public (Pratt 1997: 192). The second, is that throughout their histories, they were often strongly and continuously opposed by those charged with their implementation – the judiciary. As Pratt notes: 'one of the most striking features of the history of these laws has been the continuous opposition to and suspicion of them that the judiciary has demonstrated' (Pratt 1997: 159).

This chapter briefly examines the techniques of governance, but focuses particularly upon the techniques of judicial resistance and their legal justifications. The revival and reshaping of statutory provisions directed against the dangerousness over the last two decades has provoked a predictable set of judicial responses. Just as there are continuities and discontinuities in societal responses to dangerousness, there are patterns in courts' reactions. Moral panics and symbolic crusades come and go and with them, the modes of judicial accommodation (Feeley and Kamin 1996: 135). Understanding the dynamics of these responses may assist in predicting whether this wave of legislation will meet the same fate as those which preceded it.

Techniques of governance

Recidivism, or persistence in crime has long been a component of the concept of dangerousness, and at common law the offender's prior criminality has a powerful influence in sentencing. Historically, and still today, the most common statutory or judicial response to recidivism is an increase in penalty for a second or subsequent offence of the same type. Prior convictions may defeat any claim or inference that the defendant is a first offender or is of prior good character or they may satisfy the statutory requirement of a relevant previous conviction for the purpose of subjecting the offender to increased penalties allocated for second and subsequent offences (Fox and Freiberg 1999: paras 3.702–3). However, the perceived failure of these techniques against certain groups of recidivists produced a new range of measures to deal with them across England-based jurisdictions in the early part of the twentieth century (see Pratt 1997).

Under these schemes, courts retained a discretion whether or not to invoke their new powers of detention against those declared to be 'habitual criminals'. In practice, these laws tended to be applied to the petty offenders whose dangerousness was founded in the repetition of their offences: the drunks, the vagrants, petty property offenders and the mentally ill.

The second wave of laws, as identified by Pratt (1997: 70), were those which related to specific classes of offenders who were perceived as particularly dangerous. The laws became more narrowly drawn and focused more upon the offender who inflicted physical violence than upon the frequent, but minor recidivist (Pratt 1997: 170). In 1940, South Australia introduced amendments to its Criminal Law Consolidation Act (SA) (now Criminal Law (Sentencing) Act 1988 (SA) ss.23, 24) which permitted a person to be detained at the Governor's pleasure if there were medical evidence which showed that the person was incapable of controlling their sexual instincts. The Criminal Law Amendment Act 1945 (Qld), s.18, was in a similar vein, being introduced after a 1944 parliamentary inquiry into sex offences (Finnane 1997: 104). The Northern Territory's provisions were found in the Criminal Code 1983 (NT), s.401.

The third wave of measures emerged in Australia and elsewhere in the early 1990s. In some ways, they combined elements of the earlier measures, but extended the range of techniques available to the courts. Their focus tended to be upon future physical danger rather than past conduct (Pratt 1997: 171), though the repeat property offender remained of concern. The relevant knowledge was psychological or actuarial, rather than legal/historical. Some laws were aimed at extending the length of sentence that could or should be imposed by a court, in some cases to indefinite terms, some attempted to increase not the sentence but the length of time the offender was held in custody while others removed judicial discretion altogether. In two states, *ad hominem* laws were introduced to deal with named offenders deemed too dangerous to release from custody.[2] These most recent Australian measures are briefly outlined.

Indefinite sentences

In 1992, Queensland introduced legislation permitting a court, instead of imposing a fixed term of imprisonment, to impose an indefinite sentence on an offender convicted of a violent offence and who is considered by the court to pose a serious danger to the community (Penalties and Sentences Act 1992 (Qld), s.163). Under these provisions, the court must state a 'nominal sentence', that is, the sentence it would have imposed had it not imposed an indefinite sentence. The court is required periodically to review the sentence and cannot discharge the offender from the sentence unless it is satisfied that the offender is no longer a serious danger to the community. In 1993, Victoria followed suit (Sentencing Act 1991 (Vic.), s.6A and s.18A) in relation to serious and violent offenders, extending the reach of the legislation in 1997 to serious drug and serious violent offenders. Similar provisions have been enacted (or, in some cases, updated and re-enacted) in Western Australia (Sentencing Act 1995 (WA), Part 14), the Northern Territory (Sentencing Act 1995 (NT), ss.65–78) and Tasmania (Sentencing Act 1997 (Tas.), ss.19–23).

Mandatory sentences

Mandatory sentences are not unknown in Australian legislation, but, other than mandatory life imprisonment for murder, no longer in vogue, have generally been confined to minor offences, especially traffic offences. Some drug offences carry mandatory sentences, but these are rare, as are mandatory minimum sentences. Since the early 1990s a spate of measures have been introduced to restrict judicial discretion in relation to sentencing offenders to prison. These provisions are directed both at the manifestly dangerous, in modern terms, as well as to those regarded as dangerous because of the repetition of their criminality. In 1992, the Crimes (Serious and Repeat Offenders) Sentencing Act 1992 (WA) required a court to impose a mandatory twelve month prison sentence upon a person classified as a repeat burglar. This legislation, which was designed to deal with a spate of aggravated burglaries, or, as they became more popularly known, 'home invasions', is directed at offenders with at least one prior conviction for burglary (Morgan 1995). It was repealed and replaced by Criminal Code Amendment Act (No 2) 1996 (WA).

In the Northern Territory, amendments to the Sentencing Act 1995 (NT) and the Juvenile Justice Act 1983 (NT) introduced what effectively amounted to 'one-strike' legislation in relation to both first time and persistent offenders (Flynn 1997). The legislation requires a court to impose a mandatory minimum term for persons convicted of a range of property offences: fourteen days for adult first offenders; ninety days for an adult with one prior property conviction and twelve months for an adult with two or more prior property convictions. A juvenile (fifteen to seventeen years old) with one or more prior property convictions must be sentenced to twenty-eight days in a detention centre.

Increasing sentence lengths

Aiming to increase sentence lengths for the purposes of deterrence, incapacitation and retribution, legislators have encouraged or urged sentencers to alter their sentencing practices. This they have done in a variety of ways. One is to require sentencers to redefine the purposes of sentencing in relation to specified groups of offenders, such as the violent or dangerous, to emphasise the protection of the community. Thus, the Sentencing Act 1991 (Vic.), s.6D, states that in sentencing such offenders, the court must regard the protection of the community from the offender as the principal purpose (as opposed to merely one of a number of purposes) for which the sentence is imposed; and, in order to achieve that purpose, may impose a sentence longer than that which is proportionate to the gravity of the offence considered in the light of its objective circumstances. Provisions such as s.6D are specifically designed to defeat the principle of proportionality which has acted as a common law restraint on excessive punishment (*Veen (No. 1)* (1979) 143 CLR 458; *Veen (No. 2)* (1988) 164 CLR 465; Fox and Freiberg 1999: para 3.501; Fox 1988).

Another method of increasing sentence lengths is to require or encourage the court to sentence multiple or recidivist offenders cumulatively, rather than concurrently. Another is to deny dangerous offenders access to remissions (where they still exist), thus increasing effective sentence lengths. In Queensland, the Penalties and Sentences Act 1992 (Qld) requires that a person convicted of a serious violent offence serve at least 80 per cent of their sentence before being eligible for parole or remission which is an increase from the 50 per cent offenders are generally liable to serve (Mason 1998). Queensland legislation, introduced in 1997, excludes the operation of the principle that imprisonment be sentence of last resort where the person is being sentenced as serious offender. These last three methods are intended to increase sentence lengths without any alteration in statutory maximum penalties for the predicate offences.

Ad hominem *legislation*

An *ad hominem* Act is one which is directed at a named individual and this technique was used frequently in the seventeenth and eighteenth centuries in the form of Acts of Attainder. Though expressly prohibited in the United States by Article 1, s.9 of the Constitution, no similar constitutional bar exists in Australian law. In 1990, Victoria introduced preventive detention legislation of an extraordinary nature directed against a single individual, Gary David, permitting the Supreme Court to order his continued detention beyond the expiry of any existing sentence of imprisonment (Community Protection Act 1990 (Vic.); see Williams 1990; Victoria 1992; Fairall 1993). Following David's death in 1993 while still in custody under the Community Protection Act 1990 (Vic.), the legislation lapsed and was replaced by provisions of more general application. They retained the form of the 1990 legislation which authorised the Supreme Court to make an order of a civil nature for the post-sentence detention of persons thought to represent a continuing danger to others, despite the expiry of their sentence. In 1993, by the Sentencing (Amendment) Act 1993 (Vic.), this approach was abandoned in favour of the reintroduction of the concept of the 'indefinite' sentence described above.

In New South Wales, in 1994, Parliament passed the Community Protection Act 1994 (NSW) intended to allow the imprisonment of a single allegedly dangerous offender following civil proceedings, without the need for charges to be laid. The legislation was enacted just prior to the offender's release from a long term of imprisonment after fears had been raised over his potential for future violence based on a series of threats made by him while in prison (Zdenkowski 1997). Following his release after some six months of preventive detention, the Act was struck down by a majority of the High Court (*Kable* (1996) 138 ALR 577; see p.63).

Symbolic security

> the history of English measures aimed specifically at persistent offenders is a history of failure.
>
> (Ashworth 1995: 150)

Whether the dangerous are defined as the persistent or the violent or both, Ashworth's observation of English practice is as true for Australia as it is for England. Over the century of their existence, what has distinguished the techniques of governance outlined above is their lack of use relative to their intended population and to the sentenced population as a whole. If the dangerous were being governed at all, it was not through these measures. Time and again, in England, Australia, New Zealand and the United States, committees of inquiry and commentators have noted the remarkable lack of application of whatever forms of special laws were available to deal with the persistent and/or dangerous. In the same way that judges over the centuries have found ways to subvert the operation of mandatory penalties (Morgan 1995; Tonry 1996: Chapter 5; Feeley and Kamin 1996), they have resisted governmental attempts to remove or shape their discretion in relation to the dangerous.

In England, between 1908 and 1930 the Prevention of Crime Act 1908 was rarely invoked and by 1932 it was effectively moribund (Daunton-Fear 1972: 573; Radzinowicz and Hood 1980: 1377). Fewer than one offender in a thousand received punishment under the Act (Radzinowicz 1969 cited in Pratt 1997: 72) despite the ready supply of qualified offenders. Morris notes that although nearly 3,000 offenders each year were received in prison with six or more prior sentences, an annual average of only thirteen men were declared habitual criminals (Morris 1951: 2–27). Few were sentenced for offences of personal violence.

In Australia, commonwealth habitual criminal legislation (Crimes Act 1914, s.17) was never invoked in the six or seven decades of its existence (Fox and Freiberg 1985: para. 9.206). In Victoria, between 1908 and 1947 an average of approximately eight criminals per year were declared habitual (Morris 1951: 105). In comparison, the average number of prison receptions each year was between 6,000 and 10,000 of which many were well qualified to be declared under the legislation. In the last five years of the scheme, only ninety-five prisoners were so dealt with, or a mere 3 per cent of all sentences imposed (Murphy 1996).

Queensland courts were similarly reluctant to apply their habitual criminal legislation introduced in 1914. According to Morris, writing in 1951, there were about three to five habitual criminals in custody at any one time, and no separate facilities were ever developed for them (Morris 1951: 113). Between 1963 and 1972 only two persons were declared habitual criminals and only four were in custody in 1970 (Daunton-Fear 1972: 584). In South Australia, thirty-six men were relevantly declared in the thirty years between 1909 and 1939 (Morris 1951: 122) and six between 1965 and 1969 (Daunton-Fear 1972: 590).

New South Wales was slightly more enthusiastic in its use, with approximately twenty-three offenders sentenced each year between 1934 and 1944 (Morris 1951: 98), though such offenders rarely made up more than about 5 per cent of the prison population. Though still on the statute book in 1997, the Habitual Criminals Act 1957 (NSW) was last used in 1973. Campbell (1991: 91) reports that fifteen prisoners were held under Criminal Code (WA), s.662, as at 30 June 1991, which represented less than 1 per cent of the State's daily muster. Between 1982 and 1987, there was a total of thirty-six receptions under the indefinite sentence provisions, representing 0.001 per cent of all sentenced prisoner receptions in that period. Following the High Court's decision in *Chester* (1988) 165 CLR 611, which, following *Veen*, re-affirmed the rare and exceptional nature of non-proportional sentences, receptions fell to zero by 1991.

The reluctance to use these laws is not just historical. Although Queensland introduced provisions for indefinite sentences for serious violent or sex offenders in 1992, to date only one such sentence has been imposed. The Western Australian Court of Criminal Appeal recently upheld two indefinite sentences under s.98 of the Sentencing Act 1995 (*Lowndes* (1997) 95 A Crim. R 516; *Jones* 8/5/98) while in Victoria only two sentences have been imposed, in each case in relation to offences and offenders who would, in any case, have received extremely long sentences (*Carr* [1996] 1 V.R. 585; *Moffatt* (1997) 91 A Crim. R 557). Provisions requiring courts to cumulate have had minimal impact. Although there is some evidence that prison sentence lengths as a whole have increased marginally in Victoria (Freiberg and Ross 1999), these increases more probably reflect an overall hardening of popular attitudes than the specific effect of statutory directions. Prison sentences for the relevant offences are still well within the boundaries of proportionality and totality principles.

The sex offender provisions are even less used. In South Australia the Mitchell Committee (1973: 91) noted that the provisions were 'very little used'. While there were many preliminary reports, only offenders with serious mental illness were considered suitable for intervention, in which case they were dealt with under other provisions. One of the few declarees has bitterly litigated his confinement, though his frequent relapses seem only to reinforce the need for such legislation (*O'Shea* (1982) 31 SASR 129; *South Australia* v. *O'Shea* (1987) 163 CLR 378; *O'Shea* (1997) 94 A Crim. R 560). In Tasmania, dangerous offender declarations are rare. Warner (1990: 174) noted that between 1921 and 1990, only two declarations had been made, one in 1981 and the other in 1985. Since then two more have been reported (*McCrossen* [1991] Tas R 1; *McCrossen* (1997) 91 A Crim. R 254; *Read* (1994) 3 Tas SR 387; *Read* (1997) 94 A Crim. R 539).

These data make it plain that the special provisions, whatever their form, were applied to a tiny minority of all offenders coming before the courts or even of eligible offenders. Accepting Pratt's argument that these laws in particular, or mandatory penalty in general, have always been symbolically important (see also Craze and Moynihan 1994; Tonry 1996: 160), in practice, they were almost completely irrelevant to the control of criminal individuals or populations. No matter how patent the failures of those laws, no matter how often offenders returned to courts and prisons, and no matter how frustrated judges may have been with the inadequacies of the criminal justice system, they were not prepared to countenance legislative alternatives which were regarded by them as being more dangerous than the dangerous they sought to govern. Why was this so, and how did the judiciary respond to the special measures which were made available with so much enthusiasm?

Techniques of resistance

> Today it can sometimes seem that it is only the judges and the jurists who stand in the way of the successful implementation of these initiatives.
>
> (Pratt 1997: 193)

Consciously or unconsciously, Anglo-Australian judges have been steeped in the principles of classical jurisprudence. Sceptical of the ends of power, suspicious of 'experts' and jealous of their independence and autonomy, the judiciary have often adopted what appear to be conservative positions in the face of sometimes considerable social and political pressure. In hindsight, these positions now seem prescient, cautious rather than reactionary, reflective rather than resistant. 'Resistance' in this context is too strong a term, for it implies a conscious, concerted and co-ordinated effort. 'Questioning' is probably a more apt description. For example, where the executive has promised to provide special facilities or programmes in support of the special legislation, but failed to deliver, the courts have declined to use the powers vested in them. In many jurisdictions, recidivist offenders were not separately confined, were not provided with treatment or were not held in special 'reformatory' prisons (Pratt 1997: 62, 73; cf. *Jackson* [1923] St R Qd 276). Containment without care, restraint without rehabilitation or reform were considered unacceptable to judges already reluctant to invoke unusual or unwelcome powers.

Where mandatory sentencing laws have been introduced, they have provoked an opposite, and often unequal reaction. For every symbolic or political reason for their introduction there is usually a good instrumental and normative reason for not applying them (Tonry 1996: 16). Such laws increase public expense, are generally inflexible, result in unjust punishments and encourage prosecutorial and judicial hypocrisy (Tonry 1996: 160).

The judicial actions described below have not been planned or plotted. They have occurred over decades and across many jurisdictions. They have been neither consistent nor cohesive. Not all judges have subscribed to these ideas nor adopted these techniques. Some have enthusiastically embraced social and legislative change designed to control the dangerous. The judgements and attitudes of both the appeals courts and courts of first instance also affected the attitudes of prosecutors who had the responsibility of bringing cases before the court. Prosecutors are not only lawyers, but lawyers with an administrative responsibility to be efficient, effective and economical with state resources. Prosecutors who may themselves be antipathetic to special laws, may refuse to bring cases before the courts if the chances of obtaining a successful outcome are slim.

Most, if not all, of the initiatives intended to govern the dangerous challenge the paradigms within which the courts have operated. Though sometimes disparagingly described as 'nineteenth-century liberalism', many of these paradigms are considerably older and have continued throughout the twentieth century. Many lie at the heart of the judicial function. Although the courts must ultimately be respectful of the will of parliament, they are not subservient to it. The common law provides a range of techniques that can be employed to limit the scope of legislation. While some can be described as 'guerrilla tactics' (though certainly not by the judges), others amount to open confrontation.

Proportionality

The bedrock of resistance to special laws is the principle of proportionality, whose origins have been traced back to the Magna Carta 1215 and the Bill of Rights 1688 (both cited by Mildren, J. in *Trenerry* v. *Bradley* (1997) 93 A Crim. R 433, 444).[3] The principle holds that a judge or magistrate is prohibited from awarding a sentence which exceeds that which is commensurate to the gravity of the crime then being punished. It is therefore impermissible for any punishment to be extended above this limit in an effort to isolate potentially dangerous persons, or to punish offenders with criminal histories more severely than the offence itself warrants.

Though courts have recognised that the principle can be overridden by competent legislation such as those described above, they have attempted strictly to circumscribe the operation of such provisions. Even under the first wave of habitual criminal legislation, the finite component of a dual track sentence was subject to proportionality principles (*Roberts* [1961] SR (NSW)

681). Courts were reluctant to impose long sentences of penal servitude for 'trifling' subsequent offences where they formed the trigger for the invocation of the special provisions (Radzinowicz and Hood 1980: 1358). Under second wave laws, they have consistently held that special provisions 'should be confined to very exceptional cases where the exercise of the power is demonstrably necessary to protect society from physical harm' (*Chester* (1988) 165 CLR 611, 618, High Court of Australia; see also *McCrossen* [1991] Tas R 1, 7; *Tunaj* [1984] WAR 48, 51; *Cooper* (1987) 30 A Crim. R 19, 21; *Connell* [1996] 1 VR 436). The Court in *Chester* went on to observe:

> The stark and extraordinary nature of the punishment by way of indeterminate detention, the term of which is terminable by the executive, not by judicial, decision, requires that the sentencing judge be clearly satisfied by cogent evidence that the convicted person is a constant danger to the community ...

Courts have frequently observed that the criminal law as a whole, not merely special legislation, is designed to protect the community. Before they will invoke the special provisions they must first be satisfied that it is necessary for the protection of the community that a disproportionately long sentence be imposed. If that objective can equally be achieved by a proportionate sentence, particularly since such a sentence may be quite lengthy if the accused has been found guilty of multiple serious crimes, then it will be unnecessary to impose a longer sentence (*Robertson* (1995) 82 A Crim. R 292, 298; *Connell* [1996] 1 VR 436, 443; *Cowburn* (1994) 74 A Crim. R 385). These principles will also apply when courts are considering the totality of sentences in the cases of multiple offending when directed to cumulate sentences. In other words, the courts indicate to the legislature that they have adequate powers to deal with habitual criminals or dangerous offenders without the need to invoke any special provisions (Daunton-Fear 1972: 581 and 594; Pratt 1997: 91).

Where special legislation lays down mandatory minimum sentences which courts consider unjust, they have attempted to reconcile the competing imperatives of the legislation and the common law by holding that although the legislation overrides judicial discretion to the extent of the minimum term specified, the fundamental principle of proportionality in sentencing continues to apply to a sentence in excess of that mandatory minimum (*Fergusson* v. *Setter and Gokel* (1997) 7 NTLR 118).

Strict construction

The principle of strict construction underpins, or provides the ideological framework for, the range of other techniques, mechanisms or approaches adopted by the courts in applying or construing special legislation. It reflects the long-held judicial view that although parliaments are sovereign, albeit subject to constitutional limitations and protections, law and justice are transcendent concepts which embody and protect fundamental historical national and international 'rights, freedoms and immunities' the curtailment of which will not be readily conceded by the judiciary (*Coco* (1994) 179 CLR 427, 436–7 per Mason, C.J., Brennan, Gaudron and McHugh, JJ).

Where the judiciary suspects or believes that legislation represents an attack on fundamental human rights, it will 'strictly construe the language of the statute in order to give it the narrowest interpretation consistent with the intention of the statute and the preservation of those human rights' (Sebba 1971: 233). Courts presume that parliament does not intend to abrogate fundamental human rights (*Coco* (1994) 179 CLR 427, 436–7 per Mason, C.J., Brennan, Gaudron and McHugh, JJ) and will require clear and explicit language to be used before they give effect to a statute.

The tension between the courts and parliaments again erupted in the Northern Territory in the context of legislation requiring the mandatory imprisonment of first and recidivist property offenders. Martin, C.J. observed that there was (*Trenerry* v. *Bradley* (1997) 93 A Crim. R 433, 435–6, see also Mildren, J. at 447):

> open conflict between the established order of sentencing considerations, developed upon the basis of judicial discretion within a particular statutory framework, and discriminatory legislation boldly entitled 'Compulsory Imprisonment'. Parliament expects that any Act which apparently intrudes upon the established rights of people before courts exercising criminal jurisdiction will be closely scrutinised to determine the extent to which, if any, those rights have been adversely affected by the will of the people expressed in the words enacted by the Parliament .... Approaching the matter in this way is not to raise the false image of a contest between Parliament and the courts. It is to do no more than reiterate and apply principles long established and well understood by both institutions which together provide the essential foundation for a well ordered democratic society.

Due process: the requirement for notice

'Natural', or 'procedural' justice, holds that the way a decision is reached is as important as the decision itself. Justice is found in process as well as outcome. Whether they be constitutionally enshrined or available at common law, due process requirements such as the right to know the case made against the alleged offender, the requirement of notice, specificity of charges, the right to participate and be heard, appropriate burdens and standards of proof and others are carefully respected. Special legislation intended to govern the dangerous often fell foul of these rules. The Prevention of

Crime Act 1908 (UK), for example, failed, partly because it was too widely drawn, without clear and precise guidelines as to the offenders to be included (Ashworth 1995: 151). Morris (1951: 42) notes that the courts laid down strict requirements, such as sufficient notice of the charge of being an habitual criminal, of the previous convictions upon which that charge was founded, of the evidence to be led and of any 'other grounds' upon which the charge was to be laid. The defendant had to be provided with sufficient opportunity to provide an answer to the allegations, which had to be made with sufficient specificity to enable a response to be made.

Meaning of 'prior conviction'

When courts have been given the power to increase or enhance a sentence on account of an offender's prior conviction they have been careful to construct a meaning of prior and subsequent conviction which appears to conform to the intent of the legislation. At common law, a person is not regarded as a second offender for the purposes of statutory escalations in penalty unless the conviction or finding of guilt for the first offence was recorded prior to the acts which constitute the second offence. Such provisions are intended to be deterrent, and the courts have generally taken the view that for deterrence to operate, the offender must have had the opportunity to become aware of the certainty and severity of punishment for the crime (*Schluter* (1997) 6 NTLR 194).

Attacking the meaning of 'prior convictions' is one of the most common means of restricting the operation of special legislation. In some cases, a finding or admission of guilt has been held not to amount to a prior conviction (*G (A Child)* (1997) 94 A Crim R 586; see also Morgan 1995: 43). In others cases the argument that the requirement of conviction and sentencing on separate previous occasions requires separate court hearings has met with mixed success, often depending upon the precise wording of the legislation (*Schluter* (1997) 6 NTLR 194; *Cowburn* (1994) 74 A Crim. R 385; *Braham* (1994) 73 A Crim. R 353; *White* (1968) 42 ALJR 10; *Ciemcioch* [1963] SASR 64; *Nesbitt* (1946) NZLR 505).

Retention of judicial discretion

Judicial discretion, with its concomitant principle of judicial independence, is central to the self-concept of the judiciary. The distribution of sentencing authority between the legislature, the courts and the executive varies over time and between jurisdictions. Though it is not denied that parliament may constitutionally remove or limit a court's discretion in sentencing (*Palling* v. *Corfield* (1970) 123 CLR 52; Ashworth 1995: 42) Anglo-Australian parliaments have traditionally left the courts with a wide discretion, though in the United States this is currently becoming less and less true.

Anglo-Australian courts, and courts established in that tradition, have generally been distrustful of unaccountable administrative authority with the result that attempts to restrict the amount of judicial discretion have been strongly resisted (Sebba 1971: 234; Tonry 1996: 143). The recent revival of mandatory penalties in the Northern Territories has re-kindled these tensions between the desire of the legislatures to control crime and criminals and that of the courts to do the same, but with the discretion remaining with the courts to individualise justice. In *Trenerry* v. *Bradley* (1997) (93 A Crim. R 433, 445) Mildren, J. stated:

> Prescribed minimum mandatory sentencing provisions are the very antithesis of just sentences. If a court thinks that a proper just sentence is the prescribed minimum or more, the minimum prescribed is unnecessary. It therefore follows that the sole purpose of a prescribed minimum mandatory sentencing regime is to require sentencers to impose heavier sentences than would be proper according to the justice of the case.

Angel, J., in a similar vein, struck out against these provisions, but ultimately conceded to the ultimate authority of parliament (*Trenerry* v. *Bradley* (1997) 93 A Crim. R 433, 442):

> mandatory sentences by their very nature are unjust in that they require courts to sentence on a basis regardless of the nature of the crime and the particular circumstances of the offender, cf. *Palling* v. *Corfield* (1970) 123 CLR 52.
>
> It appears that Parliament intended that the courts impose the blunt instrument of imprisonment in lieu of other sentencing dispositions which might more truly reflect the circumstances of the offence and offender in the hope or expectation of lessening property offences and perhaps of making victims feel better – about something.
>
> But a judicial tribunal must apply the Act, even if it thinks the policy of the Act unwise and even dangerous.

Constitutional and international law principles[4]

Linked to the question of the distribution of powers is that of the separation of powers. Lacking the firmer bases that the United States' constitution provides, Australian lawyers have been more restricted than their American counterparts. Direct constitutional challenges are therefore few. In the case of *Kable* (1996) (189 CLR 51) the New South Wales legislature had attempted to authorise the Supreme Court to make a preventive detention order which directed that Kable be imprisoned for six months following the expiration of his sentence (Community Protection Act 1994,

NSW). The order was not imposed by way of sentence for a specific criminal offence but was a special means of seeking to control what the executive and legislative arms of government feared he might do in the future. Like the legislation in Victoria from which it was copied, the law was not of general application, but one which authorised a sanction only to be applied to Kable.

The High Court held that the separation of judicial from executive and legislative powers under Chapter III of the Constitution also applied to state courts invested with federal jurisdiction. Because the Act imposed upon the Supreme Court such an extraordinary function and invested it with powers of such an exceptional nature as to make it appear that the court was acting at the behest of the executive, thus impairing public confidence in the impartial administration of judicial functions, it was incompatible with the standing of the court as one upon which federal jurisdiction could be conferred under the Constitution. The New South Wales legislation was therefore invalid (Fairall 1993).

In *Moffatt* (1997) (91 A Crim. R 557) Kable's case was relied upon to mount an attack upon the indefinite sentence provisions of the Sentencing Act 1991 (Vic.). It was argued that the legislation was invalid because an indefinite custodial sentence was so alien to the traditional sentencing role of the courts as to bring them into disrepute when they administered it, thus rendering them unfit for the investment of federal judicial power. It was contended that the scheme of the legislation required the court to impose such an extreme form of punishment as would, or would likely, breach the fundamental judicial principle of proportionality in sentencing. Furthermore it required the court to perform a non-judicial function in administering the sentence through a process of periodic review. The Victorian Court of Appeal rejected all these arguments and upheld the validity of the legislation. The Victorian situation was distinguished from that in New South Wales in that the sanction complained of was an actual criminal sentence based on a proven or admitted allegation of crime in the normal exercise of the courts' jurisdiction.

Arguments to the effect that a grossly disproportionate sentence can amount to a 'cruel and unusual punishment' for the purpose of the Bill of Rights have been mounted in Australia with little success (see *Boyd* (1995) 81 A Crim. R 260) as have attempts to invoke international covenants such as the International Convention on Civil and Political Rights and the Convention of the Rights of the Child. In relation to the latter, it was argued in *Fergusson* v. *Setter and Gokel* (1997) (7 NTLR 118) that mandatory minimum sentences were contrary to the principle that imprisonment should be a sanction of last resort. The court accepted the existence of the principle, but ruled that the Northern Territory's legislation took precedence.

Scientific evidence: risk and probability

Unlike the United States, there have been few cases in Australia where the question of the prediction of danger has been the focus of an attack on legislation (cf. Janus and Meehl 1997). Australian courts have been reluctant to make too much use of probabilistic data. This attitude is well summarised by the Supreme Court in Victoria when it was asked to take into account the release policies of the Parole Board in setting a non-parole period. In *Morgan and Morgan* (1980) (7 A Crim. R 146, 155–6), Jenkinson, J. noted the unpredictability of both the life course of the offender and the behaviour of the Board. But he went even further to state:

> The liberty of the subject under the common law is not to be set at hazard upon a statistical probability, nor curtailed in the expectation, no matter how well grounded, that an agent of the Executive Government or a Parole Board will choose to set him free before the law's sentence has run its course.

However, the courts still prefer human diagnosis and judgement to clinical diagnosis or statistics although they will not ignore the latter completely (*Pollentine* v. *Attorney-General* (1998) (1 Qd R 82). In *Attorney-General* v. *David* ([1992] VR 46), Hedigan, J., noted the vast body of scientific literature on the difficulty of predicting dangerousness but declined to enter their 'serpentine depths', preferring to base his judgements on estimating the risk to public safety on his own assessment of David's past record of violence, aided by the psychiatric evidence in relation to this individual case.

As Pratt concedes in relation to the use of scientific predictions of risk (1997: 178):

> The emphasis on 'rights' and due process of law, at the expense of utilitarianism and broader social defence philosophies, during the development of neo-liberalism, seems likely to ensure that there is very little space for it to be developed as a significant tactic of control in this space for the foreseeable future.

Overcoming resistance

The dialogue between legislatures and courts is an ongoing one. Each responds to the other with a wary diffidence and deference, each conscious of its own powers and responsibilities, its electorate or constituency, its history and its historical relation to the other. This discourse, or interaction, is implicit rather than explicit and may span periods of years or even decades. Its dynamics may not be obvious to the uninvolved observer.

In their recent analysis of the effect of 'three-strikes' laws on the courts in the United States, Feeley and Kamin (1996: 136) identify a standard pattern of responses to laws created in the midst of moral panics: first, vigorous opposition with exaggerated claims of the effects of the laws on courts and prisons; second, a period of hyper-concern and confusion which produces an amount of injustice. Third, once the hysteria subsides, the employment of a host of discretionary devices to adapt the law. Finally, the laws are repealed or amended to reinstitutionalise traditional procedures.

The thesis tentatively proposed in this chapter is that the Anglo-Australian courts have generally resisted measures introduced to 'govern' the dangerous which conflict with fundamental principles and approaches of the common law outlined above, in particular proportionality, discretion and natural justice. As Pratt has observed, the 'measures of social protection traversed existing boundaries of penality' (Pratt 1997: 53). They were perceived as inhumane and transferring too much power to administrative authorities (Pratt 1997: 54; Radzinowicz and Hood 1986: 235). History has shown that both lawyers and judges will seek to avoid the application of laws which are considered to be unduly harsh (Tonry 1996: 147). Where possible, the judiciary have opposed the reduction or removal of their discretion in individual cases, they have narrowed the operation of the special laws. In one sense, their actions are 'anti-democratic' in that they nullify the will of parliament (Ashworth 1998: 24).

To the current crop of interventions, the courts have responded as they have historically. In reply, the legislatures seem to be redoubling their efforts. However, the conflict is not simply between principle and expediency, between the public and professionals. Historically and presently, the conflict seems to lie more deeply in the psyche of the body politic. In their recent study of public support for punitive policies such as the 'three-strikes' laws in California, Tyler and Boeckmann (1997), developing Durkheim's thesis concerning the expressive values and functions of punishment, have argued that public punitiveness is linked more to judgements about social conditions and underlying values than to concern about the level of crime and the work of the courts. Support for three-strikes laws, in the United States, they suggest, is not related to judgements about the future dangerousness of offenders as much as to moral cohesion. In other words, the instrumental effects of sentencing policy, that is, reducing the rate of crime or the chances of being victimised, are less important than judgements about social conditions: concern over the decline of social institutions such as the family, the lack of a moral and social consensus, the decline of social ties and a discomfort with growing social and ethnic diversity. They suggest that declining moral cohesion leads to more punitive attitudes because people who are sceptical of the courts, of politics and of society in general are also sceptical of the ability of social, welfare and penal agencies to rehabilitate offenders; to integrate or remoralise them.

Many of the initiatives outlined earlier in this chapter, including the more recent three strikes and similar legislation, are part of a wider move to remove discretionary authority from the courts, signalling a repudiation of legal authority more generally. General confidence in legal and political authority seems to be waning leading to greater support for non-legal means of dealing with crime or for reducing the role and scope of courts' discretion. The fluctuations in the use of measures to govern the dangerous are possibly symptoms of changes in public confidence in the legal system and their feelings of security and cohesion.

Judges and penal authorities are now less trusted. Sentencing is regarded as fraudulent, untruthful and ineffective. The first legislative riposte has therefore been to further remove judicial discretion: mandatory sentences proliferate, leaving the judiciary with less scope to manoeuvre. The second response is to place pressure upon the judiciary to be more attentive or responsive to public opinion and to legitimise its role in judicial decision making. Thus judges may be asked to take into account possible community reaction to the release of dangerous offenders (see discussion in *Pollentine* v. *Attorney-General* (1998) 1 Qd R 82; and also *Mott* v. *Community Corrections Board* [1995] 2 Qd R 261; *In re Findlay* [1985] AC 318; *South Australia* v. *O'Shea* (1987) 163 CLR 378) and the legislature may institutionalise public opinion by placing representatives of the public or victim groups upon parole or release boards. Finally, attempts may be made to change the judiciary itself: to appoint judicial officers more sympathetic to the agenda of the government of the day.

As Pratt notes in the conclusion to his book, it is ironic that it is only in totalitarian societies that the laws against the dangerous have been used to any significant extent (Pratt 1997: 192). Following the public will is not necessarily a recipe for safety and freedom and, as he observes, it sometimes seems that only judges and jurists stand in the way of a 'new kind of totalitarianism' (Pratt 1997: 193).

But, in my view, the danger comes not from new technologies of prediction of risk, or of the processes of actuarialism, but from an emerging philosophy of despair. As communal fear, anger and frustration over the perceived failure of the criminal justice system to curb crime grows and more mandatory exclusionary sanctions are invoked, they are no longer justified on the basis of the gravity of the precipitating offence or even on the basis of the offender's predicted future conduct, but simply on the basis that the offender has forfeited his or her right to participate in society. Nigel Walker has recently well encapsulated this new justification (Walker 1996: 7):

Someone who has harmed, or tried to harm another person, can hardly claim a right to the presumption of harmlessness: he has forfeited that right, and given society the right to interfere in this life .... The justification [of the right to interfere] is not a duty based on retribution but the offender's forfeiture of an immunity.

In an increasingly contractualised society, the social contract between the state and its errant citizens is brought to an end. However, the guerrilla warfare continues, and it may be that the dangerous, now defined to include the judiciary as well as the offenders, are no longer governed, but subdued.

Notes

1 In his terms, governance 'means not just actions of political executive, nor state arrangements, but whole ensemble of institutions, procedures and tactics of power over given population. It is a force, an array of knowledges, expertise and technologies' (Pratt 1997: 3).
2 Other than some special laws dealing with named dangerous offenders, I will not be examining civil commitment or general mental health laws which could be applied to mentally ill and dangerous offenders.
3 Magna Carta 1215 (UK): 'A free man shall not be amerced for a small offence, but only according to the degree of the offence'; Bill of Rights 1688 (UK): 'Excessive baile ought not to be required nor excessive fines imposed nor cruell and unusual punishments inflicted'.
4 This material is drawn from Fox and Freiberg 1999: paras 1.228–1.229.

References

Ashworth, A. (1995) *Sentencing and Criminal Justice*, 2nd edn, London: Butterworths.
—— (1998) 'The Decline of English Sentencing, and Other Stories', Unpublished conference paper, Sentencing Policy in Comparative International Perspective, Minneapolis.
Campbell, I. (1991) 'Indeterminate Sentences and Dangerousness', in Victoria, Social Development Committee, Inquiry into Mental Disturbance and Public Safety, *Second Report*, Melbourne: Government Printer.
Craze, L. and Moynihan, P. (1994) 'Violence, Meaning and the Law: Responses to Garry David', *Australian and New Zealand Journal of Criminology* 37: 30–45.
Daunton-Fear, M. (1972) 'Sentencing Habitual Criminals', in D. Chappell and P.R. Wilson (eds), *The Australian Criminal Justice System*, Sydney: Butterworths.
Fairall, P. (1993) 'Violent Offenders and Community Protection in Victoria – The Garry David Experience', *Criminal Law Journal* 17: 40–54.
Feeley, M.M. and Kamin, S. (1996) 'The Effect of "Three Strikes and You're Out" on the Courts: Looking Back to see the Future', in D. Shichor and D.K. Sechrest (eds), *Three Strikes and You're Out: Vengeance as Public Policy*, Thousand Oaks, CA: Sage.
Finnane, M. (1997) *Punishment in Australian Society*, Melbourne: Oxford University Press.
Flynn, M. (1997) 'One Strike and You're Out', *Alternative Law Journal* 22: 72–6.
Fox, R.G. (1988) 'The Killings of Bobby Veen: The High Court on Proportion in Sentencing', *Criminal Law Journal* 12: 339–66.
Fox, R.G. and Freiberg, A. (1985) *Sentencing: State and Federal Law in Victoria*, Melbourne: Oxford University Press.

—— (1999) *Sentencing: State and Federal Law in Victoria*, 2nd edn, Melbourne: Oxford University Press.

Freiberg, A. and Ross, S. (1999) *Sentencing Reform and Penal Change: the Victorian Experience*, Sydney: Federation Press.

Janus, E.S. and Meehl, P.E. (1997) 'Assessing the Legal Standard for Predictions of Dangerousness in Sex Offender Commitment Proceedings', *Psychology, Public Policy, and Law* 3: 33–64.

Mason, B. (1998) 'Queensland gets Tough with "Serious Violent Offenders": A Critique of the *Penalties and Sentences (Serious Violent Offences) Amendment Act 1997*', Unpublished paper.

Mitchell Committee (1973) *First Report: Sentencing and Corrections*, South Australia, Criminal Law and Penal Methods Reform Committee, Adelaide: South Australian Government.

Morgan, N. (1995) 'The Sentencing Act 1992: Subverting Criminal Justice', in R. Harding (ed.), *Repeat Juvenile Offenders: The Failure of Selective Incapacitation in Western Australia*, 2nd edn, Nedlands: University of Western Australia, Crime Research Centre.

Morris, N. (1951) *The Habitual Criminal*, London: London School of Economics and Political Science.

Murphy, P. (1996) 'Indeterminate Sentences: The Victorian Experience', Unpublished Master of Criminology Thesis, The University of Melbourne.

Pratt, J. (1997) *Governing the Dangerous*, Sydney: Federation Press.

Radzinowicz, L. and Hood, R. (1980) 'Incapacitating the Habitual Criminal: the English Experience', *Michigan Law Review* 78: 1305–89.

—— (1986) *A History of English Criminal Law*, vol. 5, London: Butterworths.

Sebba, L. (1971) 'Minimum Sentences: Courts v. Knesset', *Israel Law Review* 6: 227–39.

Tyler, T.R. and Boeckmann, R.J. (1997) 'Three Strikes and You are Out, But Why? The Psychology of Public Support for Punishing Rule Breakers', *Law and Society Review* 31: 237–65.

Tonry, M. (1996) *Sentencing Matters*, New York: Oxford University Press.

Victoria, Social Development Committee (1992) *Inquiry into Mental Disturbance and Community Safety*, Melbourne: Government Printer.

Walker, N. (1996) *Dangerous People*, London: Blackstone Press.

Warner, K. (1990) *Sentencing in Tasmania*, Sydney: Federation Press.

Williams, C.R. (1990) 'Psychopathy, Mental Illness and Preventive Detention: Issues Arising from the David Case', *Monash University Law Review* 16: 161–83.

Zdenkowski, G. (1997) 'Community Protection Through Imprisonment Without Conviction', *Australian Journal of Human Rights* 3: 8–54.

Chapter 4

Civil commitment as social control

Managing the risk of sexual violence

Eric Janus

Introduction

The use of civil commitment to control sexual violence has had episodic currency in the United States. This chapter traces the history and present manifestation of this practice, describes its legal and social policy context, and offers critiques of both theory and practice.

Sex offender commitment laws incarcerate 'mentally disordered' individuals who are judged to pose a danger of future sexual violence. Like standard mental illness commitment laws, the sex offender laws use civil, rather than criminal, procedures. Confinement is not in prisons, but in secure treatment facilities. Commitments are for an indeterminate period, ending only when the individual is no longer dangerous. In practice, committed individuals are rarely discharged.

The first wave of sex offender commitment laws began in the late 1930s and fell into disuse in the decades that followed. Beginning in the late 1980s, a second generation of sex offender commitment laws developed. While the first generation laws were designed as an alternative to prison for offenders deemed too sick for punishment, the second aimed to extend the incarceration of convicted sex offenders deemed too dangerous to release from custody.

The central controversy underlying contemporary sex offender commitment laws concerns the appropriateness of using the civil system of social control to address behaviour that is clearly within the purview of the criminal system. The contests generated by these laws illuminate the legal, moral and public policy issues underlying the control of dangerous individuals, and map the borderland between civil and criminal approaches to the problem.

Sex offender commitment laws

Using a 'civil commitment' model, contemporary sex offender commitment schemes incarcerate sexually dangerous persons, diagnosed with mental disorders, in secure treatment facilities. The majority of those committed have just completed criminal sentences for sexual crimes (Program Evaluation Division, Office of the Legislative Auditor, State of Minnesota 1994: 8). The primary, articulated purpose for these laws is incapacitation, the prevention of future sexual violence by means of direct physical constraint. The laws claim treatment as an additional purpose (*Kansas* v. *Hendricks* 1997: 2085).

Sex offender commitment laws are 'civil' as opposed to 'criminal' in at least three senses. First, the laws make an explicit claim to be civil. Second, they claim a purpose and effect that are not 'punitive' and are therefore consistent with civil proceedings. Third, they claim exemption from key constitutional protections constraining the state's exercise of its criminal jurisdiction. Normal application of the constitutional prohibitions on *ex post facto* laws and double jeopardy prevents the state from lengthening previously imposed criminal sentences. Further, the Constitution prohibits criminal punishment based on a 'status' or on predicted future crimes (Janus 1997a: 71). Civil commitment provides a method of social control that is unconstrained by these constitutional limits.

Contemporary sex offender commitments occupy the borderland between civil and criminal confinement. They use civil commitment to accomplish a core criminal justice task, protecting the public from the sexual crimes of mentally competent criminals. Standard civil commitment laws traditionally have addressed people whose behaviour is 'crazy' (Morse 1985), the 'furiously mad' (*Kansas* v. *Hendricks* 1997), people whose ability to perceive and reason is seriously impaired by psychotic illnesses (Winick 1995; Janus 1996). In sharp contrast, the targets of contemporary sex offender commitment laws are most often people whose ability to reason and perceive is not psychotically impaired, who can care for themselves and are properly held responsible for their behaviour. These individuals have 'mental disorders' that are characterised by strong 'deviant' sexual desires (paraphilias), or maladaptive, persistent personality patterns (personality disorders). Almost all of the commitments are individuals who have been held criminally responsible for their conduct.

The history and evolution of sex offender commitment schemes

The first wave of sex offender commitment laws: their rise and fall

The first civil commitment laws aimed specifically at sexually dangerous individuals were enacted in the late 1930s. Despite a variety of forms, their espoused purpose was to create an alternative to punishment for a certain subclass of sex offenders, those 'too sick to deserve punishment' (*Millard* v.

Harris 1968: 966). If these individuals did not fit the traditional notions of 'insanity', the laws were understood as creating new legal categories to reflect a new 'scientific' understanding of the links between sexual deviance and mental disorder (Brief of the Minnesota Attorney General, *State ex rel. Pearson* v. *Probate Court of Ramsey County* 1940: 22). Writing in 1955, Hacker and Frym state that the California sexual psychopath act 'recognised and adopted [the principle] that "our collective conscience does not allow punishment where it cannot impose blame"', and that 'the commission of a sex crime was usually, if not always, evidence of a mental disorder which should be treated rather than punished' (Hacker and Frym 1955: 767). Some twenty-seven states and the District of Columbia enacted some form of mentally disordered sex offender commitment law (Erickson 1995: 3).

Litigation challenging the early Minnesota commitment law asserted that its reach was unconstitutionally broad. Defending the law, the state relied on two lines of authority. First, consistent with the 'too sick to deserve punishment' theory, the state invoked its *parens patriae* power (Brief of Respondent, State of Minnesota, *State ex rel. Pearson* v. *Probate Court of Ramsey County* 1940: 13). The second argument invoked a much broader notion of state power to regulate the dangerous. Citing the Supreme Court's public health cases, *Jacobson* v. *Massachusetts* (1905) (immunisation) and *Buck* v. *Bell* (1927) (sterilisation), the state claimed broad authority under its police power to protect itself against manifest danger, even when that means curtailing the rights of 'innocent' citizens.

Both the Minnesota and United States Supreme Courts upheld the commitment act, but neither court relied on the police power arguments advanced by the state. Instead, the courts limited the reach of the act to dangerous sex offenders who are dangerous by reason of an 'utter lack of power to control their sexual impulses', suggesting that a broader reach for this commitment statute 'might render it of doubtful validity' (*State ex rel. Pearson* v. *Probate Court of Ramsey County* 1940: 273). The implication is that civil schemes to incapacitate the dangerous will be received restrictively rather than expansively.

The frequency and nature of the use of these early laws were quite varied. Erickson reports that in the 1940s and 1950s these laws were characterised by 'commitment of relatively harmless individuals for relatively trivial crimes' (Erickson undated: 10). During the period 1939–69, approximately 15 per cent of those convicted of sex offences were diverted to civil commitment in Minnesota (Hausman 1972: A–3, 4), whereas, during the 1950s, the proportion was 35 per cent in California (Freedman 1987: 97).

Over time, the use of civil commitment declined and its focus shifted from non-violent to violent offenders (Erickson undated: 10–12). In 1977, the Group for the Advancement of Psychiatry issued an influential report entitled 'Psychiatry and Sex Psychopath Legislation: The 30s to the 80s' (hereinafter the 'GAP Report'). This report, along with the President's

Commission on Mental Health, and the American Bar Association's Committee on Criminal Justice Mental Health Standards, recommended the repeal of the sex offender commitment legislation (Brakel *et al.* 1985). The GAP Report characterised sex offender commitment statutes as an 'experiment [that] has failed', providing neither effective treatment nor incarcerating truly dangerous individuals (Group for the Advancement of Psychiatry 1977: 942, 935). By the 1980s, most of the states with sex offender commitment laws had either repealed them or had ceased actively using them (Bodine 1990: 109–10).

The second wave of sex offender commitment laws: rebirth and constitutional litigation

The second wave of sex offender commitment laws resulted from the confluence of three forces in the late 1980s and early 1990s. The first was the tenet of contemporary Western society that it is a duty of the state to prevent violence to its members (Pratt 1997). The second was the transformation of the penal sentencing systems in many states during the 1970s and 1980s from indeterminate to determinate systems based on standardised guidelines (Tonry and Hatlestad 1997: 6). The third was associated with the feminist agenda to change societal attitudes and behaviour about sexual violence against women (D'Emilio and Freedman 1997: 314). By the late 1980s, feminist-inspired views of sexual violence had transformed social judgements about punishing sex offenders. Existing penal sentences for violent, recidivist sex offenders were judged to be too short. Sex offender commitment laws aimed to fill the 'incapacitation gap' created by this change of viewpoint.

The beginnings of the second generation of sex offender commitment laws took root in about 1989. Task forces in the states of Washington and Minnesota proposed a renewed use of civil commitment as a tool for containing sexually violent individuals. Both states were addressing public outrage at heinous crimes committed by sex offenders recently released from prison. Both states faced the same dual-faceted problem: first, in the early 1980s both states had replaced 'indeterminate' sentencing schemes with 'determinate' schemes under which incarceration terms were set at sentencing (Tonry and Hatlestad 1997: 6; Lieb 1997: 20; Dailey 1997: 35). This change deprived the states of their power to exercise long-term, flexible control over offenders deemed 'too dangerous' to release from prison (Boerner 1992: 548; Office of the Attorney General, State of Minnesota 1989: 19). Second, both states replaced indeterminate sentences with a system of 'presumptive sentencing guidelines' (Tonry and Hatlestad 1997: 7–8). By the late 1980s, 'society's increased attention to sexual assault' had produced a 'change in its perceived seriousness' (Governor's Task Force on Community Protection, State of Washington 1989: II–5). The sentencing guidelines were seen as 'inadequate punishment', 'too short to permit mean-ingful treatment of sex offenders in prison', and potentially inconsistent with 'supervised release after the prison doors are opened' (Office of the Attorney General, State of Minnesota 1989: 10, 19). By the late 1980s and early 1990s, individuals imprisoned under the new sentencing guidelines became eligible for release. This exposed a gap in the states' ability to protect against recidivist sexual violence.

Contemporary Western thought endorses a strong obligation on the state to protect its citizens from violence (Pratt 1997). As the 1980s saw a public mood that was 'fearful and punitive', tolerating 'zero risk to public safety', this protection imperative manifested itself as the principle of incapacitation – the notion that public protection against violence is best accomplished by locking up criminals (Zimring and Hawkins 1995: 10–16). Zimring and Hawkins point out that the principle of incapacitation has no internal point of balance. By its internal logic, it tends to be expansive rather than limited (Zimring and Hawkins 1995: 12). Thus, the emergence of a sexual-violence protection-gap produced a strong push to extend the systems for the inca-pacitation of sex offenders.

Key constitutional constraints prevented the states from addressing this incapacitation imperative simply by increasing criminal punishments for sexual violence. Retroactive increases would have run afoul of prohibitions on *ex post facto* laws and double jeopardy prosecutions (Janus 1997a: 71). Prospectively, the states could – and did – increase sentence lengths for sex offenders (Lieb 1997: 27; Dailey 1997: 38). But both Washington and Minnesota rejected a return to 'long indeterminate sentences for sex offenders' (Boerner 1992: 572; Kirwin 1995: 25) at least in part because such a scheme would be inconsistent with the 'principle of desert' (Boerner 1992: 548). Finally, the Constitution prohibited the state from imposing criminal punishment simply for the 'status' of being mentally disordered and dangerous, or for the punishment of future predicted crimes.

Searching for an escape from these constraints on the criminal law, both states turned to civil commitment to close the 'gap' in social control. Soon, Wisconsin, Kansas and California followed suit. Though the statutory language differed from law to law, the structure of all was similar. All required a demonstration of a past course of harmful sexual behaviour, a current mental disorder or abnormality, and the resultant prediction of future harmful sexual behaviour (Janus 1997a).

Litigation challenging the constitutionality of these provisions was launched in each of these states and eventually reached the United States Supreme Court. The litigation centred on the location of the constitutional border between civil and criminal incarceration. As the Minnesota Court put it: 'Arguably, then, the question is not whether the sexual predator can be confined, but where. Should it be in prison or in a security hospital?' (*In re Blodgett* 1994: 917).

The courts hearing these challenges were badly split. Trial courts in Wisconsin and California held that the statutes were unconstitutional, as did a federal court in Washington State and the Kansas Supreme Court. On the other hand, the supreme courts of Wisconsin, Minnesota and Washington upheld the constitutionality of these types of commitments (Janus 1997a: 72). In *Kansas* v. *Hendricks*, the US Supreme Court reversed the Kansas Supreme Court in a 5–4 decision and upheld the civil commitment of a recidivist paedophile.

Hendricks *and the limits of the state's power to control the dangerous*

Hendricks, and the litigation leading up to it, teaches important lessons about the state's power to control the dangerous. First, states may supplement the criminal justice system with a civil system of control, but the civil system must be extremely limited, and it may not impinge on the primacy of the criminal system. Second, the 'principle of desert' (Boerner 1992) marks an important boundary between the two systems. Blame is a central feature of the criminal law, but is banished from the discourse of civil confinement. Third, civil commitment is limited to the 'disordered' mental conditions that have traditionally supported civil confinement.

Civil control of the dangerous is allowed, but it is a restricted practice that must not impinge on the primacy of criminal law.

Civil commitment has long been understood to furnish a tool for the management of the dangerous. But the sex offender litigation highlighted the fact that the courts had rarely dealt with the substantive limits on the state's power to use civil process for this purpose (Boerner 1992: 554). Nonetheless, all of these cases made the same fundamental assumption: mental disorder is a constitutionally required predicate for civil commitment.

The significance of this foundation lies in its rejection of a 'jurisprudence of prevention' (Richards 1989). The rejected theory posits a broad state right to 'regulate' the dangerous using civil processes: to confine dangerous persons preventively, the state must simply establish that its interest in preventing a future danger overbalances the individual's interest in liberty (Richards 1989). Civil preventive detention is not limited to the mentally ill dangerous, for the foundation of the state's power is the magnitude of the danger, not its aetiology. This is an exceedingly broad theory that would allow civil control schemes to threaten the primacy of the criminal law.

The sex offender commitment courts clearly rejected this expansive view of state power. At the base of the rejection is the recognition that the 'moral credibility' (*In re Blodgett* 1994: 918) of the criminal justice system is strongly tied to the integrity of the stringent constraints which contain it. The legitimacy of the civil commitment system, in turn, depends centrally on whether it provides too broad an escape from these criminal constraints and thereby compromises their integrity.

Hendricks teaches that civil commitment is 'limited ... to a small segment of particularly dangerous individuals' (*Kansas* v. *Hendricks* 1997: 2085) and reinforces the court's clear statement in *Foucha* v. *Louisiana* (1992) that the 'ordinary criminal processes ... are the normal means of dealing with persistent criminal conduct' (*Foucha* v. *Louisiana* 1992: 82). The Minnesota Supreme Court expressed the same idea: the Constitution 'forecloses the substitution of preventive detention schemes for the criminal justice system' (*In re Linehan* 1996: 183).

Civil commitment may occupy only a small – and principled – portion of the social control function of the state. The mental disorder element must perform the limiting function, and also must explain why the state is justified in circumventing the constraints of the criminal law. 'Mental disorder' provides the basis to *discriminate* between those dangerous individuals who are appropriate in the criminal system, and those for whom civil commitment is justified (Schopp and Sturgis 1995; Janus 1997b).

The boundary of criminal and civil control is informed by the principle of desert.

Pratt traces the re-emergence of a 'just deserts' understanding of the criminal justice system during the 1980s (Pratt 1997: 166). As stated above, it was in part such a concern for maintaining the 'principle of desert' (Boerner 1992: 548) that led to the enactment of Washington's sex offender commitment law. Following the same understanding, the sex offender commitment cases suggest that the principle of desert is a central feature of the boundary between criminal and civil systems of control. Blame is a necessary condition for criminal punishment. Thus, in the criminal system, incapacitation must be but a happy by-product of punishment. If the state wishes to exercise control beyond deserved punishment, it ought to do so outside of the criminal system:

> The concern with enhanced criminal punishment on the basis of dangerousness is that the punishment may tend to become divorced from moral blameworthiness, thus adversely affecting the criminal justice system's credibility, which largely rests on a sense of blameworthiness.
>
> (*In re Blodgett* 1994: footnote 16)

Blame and desert are not only necessary conditions for the criminal law, but sufficient, as well. If civil management of the dangerous is to preserve the primacy of the criminal law, then it must banish the discourse of blame. As the Supreme Court put it: 'Its [civil commitment's] purpose is not retributive: It does not affix culpability for prior criminal conduct, but uses such conduct solely for evidentiary purposes ... ' (*Kansas* v. *Hendricks* 1997: 2075).

Civil commitment is limited to traditional mental impairments.

In rejecting the 'jurisprudence of prevention', the sex offender commit-ment courts established that 'mental disorder' is a constitutionally required predicate for civil commitment. A diagnosis of 'mental disorder' provides the platform for psychological *explanations* of violence that replace the blame-based *judgements* of the criminal law. Civil commitment depends on psychological explanation for violence – this is the essence of diagnosis and prediction – and such explanation is inconsistent with the judging that leads to blame and desert (Wilson 1997: 7).

Hendricks appears to reject the notion, however, that *any* disordered mental condition could form the basis for commitment. Instead, the Court repeatedly focused on a particular kind of mental impairment, Mr Hendricks' inability to control his behaviour. It is the 'lack of volitional control' that 'adequately distinguishes Hendricks from other dangerous persons who are perhaps more properly dealt with exclusively through crim-inal proceedings' (*Kansas* v. *Hendricks* 1997: 2079, 2081).

Historically, the courts have limited commitments to a small subgroup of mental impairments, such as inability to care for oneself, inability to control one's own behaviour, and criminal non-responsibility (*State ex rel. Pearson* v. *Probate Court of Ramsey County* 1940; *Addington* v. *Texas* 1979; *Jones* v. *United States* 1983). By invoking the 'inability to control' standard for sex offender commitments, *Hendricks* characterises sex offender commitments as within the mainstream of traditional civil commitment law. Such a characterisation avoids violation of the principle of criminal-primacy. A high percentage of criminals are diagnosable with some form of mental disorder (Cunningham and Reidy 1998: 340). Limiting commitments to a narrow band of tradi-tional impairments serves to insure that mental commitments do not swallow the criminal law.

Second wave sex offender commitment law: in practice

As of October, 1998, fourteen states and the District of Columbia have sex offender commitment laws on their books. About half of these laws were passed after the Supreme Court's *Hendricks* decision. Thirteen states have legislation under consideration (Fitch 1998).

Contemporary sex offender commitment statutes are designed to extend incapacitation for sex offenders deemed too dangerous for release at the end of their sentences. An essential feature of these laws is a system by which sex offenders in prison are screened and selected for referral to the commitment process (see, e.g., Minnesota Statutes §244.05). In Minnesota, screening is undertaken by the Department of Corrections, which uses a combination of an actuarially developed screening tool and clinical judgement based on file review and interviews. During the years 1993 through 1996, the

Department referred between 8 per cent and 9 per cent of about-to-be-released sex offenders for commitment. Approximately half were eventually committed (Minnesota Department of Corrections 1999: 2). On average, about 5 per cent of sex offenders released from prison are committed each year (Janus and Walbek 2000: 25). Commitments in Wisconsin follow a similar pattern (Harris 1998), while Washington, California and Illinois commit only about 1 per cent of sex offender releasees (Washington State Institute for Public Policy 1998: 24; Leyva 1998; California Department of Mental Health 1998; Gross 1998).

Though many commitment schemes are rather new, evidence indicates that incarceration will be extremely long term. Once committed as a dangerous sex offender, individuals have rarely been discharged. In Minnesota, no individual admitted as a sex offender since 1983 has been granted a full discharge from commitment. No individual committed after 1988 was on provisional discharge as of November, 1998 (Janus and Walbek 2000: 26).

Because discharges are rare, the population of committed sex offenders continues to grow, both in absolute terms, and as a percentage of the total body of incarcerated sex offenders. In 1989, sex offenders under civil commitment accounted for about 3 per cent of the incarcerated sex offenders in Minnesota. By the end of 1997, committed sex offenders numbered 128, and accounted for 11 per cent of all incarcerated sex offenders. Officials predict that approximately eighteen additional offenders will be civilly committed each year through the year 2010 (Minnesota Department of Corrections 1999: 2). Sex offender commitments are exceedingly expensive (see p.80–1). Thus, as the committed population grows, so will its allocation of treatment and prevention resources.

The critiques

The goal of sex offender commitment statutes – the prevention of sexual violence – is a compelling goal. But the laws are built on a foundation made precarious by its placement directly on the fault-line separating civil and criminal. This section summarises the critiques that have exposed the contradictions, questionable morality, self-defeating symbolism and poor policy choices that arise from this border location.

The civil liberties critique

The civil liberties critique argues that sex offender commitment laws are really punishment, are based on inaccurate predications of future violence, and extend beyond the proper scope for civil commitment.

Critics argue that statements of commitment proponents (e.g., 'these "animals" should be kept in prison beyond their scheduled sentences and never allowed out'), show a punitive intent (Campbell 1998: 125–6). But courts point out that incapacitation is a proper purpose for civil commitment laws. As further evidence of improper intent, critics argue that states have failed to provide treatment for committed sex offenders, or that there is no effective treatment for sexual violence or the mental disorders underlying it (Janus 1998: 306–9). In response, the courts hold that even 'meagre' treatment, 'ancillary' to the states' primary purpose of incapacitation, will not invalidate a commitment statute (*Kansas* v. *Hendricks* 1997: 2085). Further, there is no constitutional bar to civilly committing individuals for whom there is no effective treatment (*Kansas* v. *Hendricks* 1997: 2084).

Some critics claim that the prediction of future dangerousness is too uncertain to support the indefinite deprivation of liberty (Blacher 1995: 912–13). Pointing out that such prediction is ubiquitous in the law, courts have uniformly rejected this argument (Janus and Meehl 1997).

The core of the civil liberties critique is that sex offender commitment schemes extend beyond the constitutional scope of the states' police power. This is an argument under 'substantive due process', the constitutional doctrine that 'bars certain arbitrary, wrongful government actions regardless of the fairness of the proceedings used to implement them' (*Zinermon* v. *Burch* 1990: 125).

As pointed out above, the criminal law must be the primary means of addressing antisocial behaviour. Therefore, 'dangerousness alone' is insufficient to support a civil commitment. Rather, civil confinement is proper only for those dangerous individuals who are 'mentally disordered' and therefore lack the ability to control their sexual behaviour. But courts routinely apply the 'inability to control' standard to sex offenders who have been held fully responsible for their behaviour. This apparent contradiction renders the 'inability to control' standard a meaningless legal fiction (Janus 1997a: 81–4). In practice, commitment requires nothing more than a history of sexual violence and a diagnosed 'mental disorder'. Such a definition, rather than distinguishing civil commitment from criminal confinement, allows commitment to virtually swallow the criminal law. More than 70 per cent of all prisoners are diagnosable with 'antisocial personality disorder' (Cunningham and Reidy 1998: 340). Up to 69 per cent of all convicted sex offenders are diagnosable with a 'personality disorder' (Romero and Williams 1985: 58). Thus, the sex offender commitment schemes sweep within their reach most of the criminal population, undercutting the argument that commitment schemes are limited and principled exceptions to the primacy of the criminal justice system.

The utilitarian critique

The utilitarian critique argues that sex offender commitment schemes are an unwise approach to an important social goal, the prevention of sexual violence.

The *resource allocation* critique cites the hugely disproportionate expenditure of resources on civil commitment, and questions whether it is the wisest expenditure of sexual-violence prevention funds. For example, in the State of Minnesota, the annual cost to civilly commit and confine a sex offender is about 100 times the per capita amount spent on sex offender treatment in prisons (Minnesota Department of Corrections 1999: 23; Huot 1998b, 1998a). The disproportion will grow as more sex offenders are committed but few, if any, are released. A recent Minnesota Study Group report estimates that the annual cost of 'current practice' will increase by 450 per cent (from $17 million to $76.9 million) in the twelve years from 1998 to 2010 (Minnesota Department of Corrections 1999: 23).

This critique suggests that the resources spent on commitments would be better expended on expanding and intensifying correctional treatment, including follow-up supervision for sex offenders released into the community. Despite the growth in the committed population, most imprisoned recidivist sex offenders are not committed when their prison terms expire, but are released into the community (Doren 1998). It is for this reason, as pointed out by Harris, that 'prisons provide the point of greatest opportunity for the treatment of persons convicted of serious sex offences' (Harris 1995: 569). Yet the evidence shows that correctional treatment efforts are underfunded and overwhelmed (Washington State Institute for Public Policy 1998: 21). The National Center for Missing and Exploited Children warns that 'While community supervision and oversight is widely recognised as essential, the system for providing such supervision is overwhelmed', and 'State-sponsored [sex offender] treatment programs are under attack and are disappearing around the country' (National Center for Missing and Exploited Children 1998). Resource-allocation critics argue that the vast sums of money spent on commitment would more effectively be spent on correctional and community treatment and supervision.

The *therapeutic jurisprudence* critique seeks to determine whether sex offender commitment laws create conditions that either encourage or discourage therapeutic outcomes (Winick 1998: 507). Sex offender commitment schemes may discourage full participation in correctional sex offender treatment (Klotz 1996: 139). Sex offender treatment requires full disclosure, which, for many sex offenders, includes sex crimes that are unknown to the authorities. Disclosures in correctional treatment sometimes form the core evidence for subsequent commitment proceedings. Since commitment is a deprivation of liberty akin to a life sentence, even a small risk of commitment may serve to dissuade some sex offenders from full participation in prison-based treatment.

A second potential anti-therapeutic effect arises from the symbolic social meaning of sex offender commitments (see below). Sex offender commitment schemes 'psychologise' the discourse of sexual violence, and push it in a deterministic direction. To squeeze into the civil commitment paradigm, sexual violence must be described as 'caused by' mental disorder, and sex offenders as without the 'power to control' their sexual impulses. But both of these images run directly counter to central premises of contemporary treatment approaches, in which '[o]ffenders are informed that urges do not control behaviour. Rather, giving in to an urge is an active decision, an intentional choice for which he is responsible' (Pithers 1990: 355).

The moral critique

Civil commitment entails a massive deprivation of liberty (*Humphrey* v. *Cady* 1972: 509–10), and therefore needs moral justification. A partial justification is provided by the *goal* of commitment laws: self-defence against sexual violence. The important remaining question concerns *means*: when is non-blame-based preventive detention a morally justified means to social control? The quest to justify civil commitment as a means to violence-control produces the contradictory holding that a criminal can be at the same time held responsible and yet unable to control their behaviour. As I suggest in this section, this contradiction leads down a dangerous moral path.

The courts have made clear that preventive incarceration is not justified by reference to 'dangerousness' alone. Rather, the justification for non-blame-based incapacitation turns on the 'mental disorder' of the individual. There are two ways in which a person's mental condition might justify such different treatment at the hands of the government. First, the condition might invoke an extraordinary interest of the state, an interest over and above the state's normal interest in combating serious interpersonal violence (Janus 1998). Second, the mental condition might mark a degraded moral status, in which the individual is not entitled to the full benefits of civic personhood (Unsworth 1987: 36, 41).

A central example of the first type of justification is the traditional use of civil commitment to incapacitate the criminally insane. 'Insanity' is a mental condition that excuses the person's crime, placing him or her beyond the reach of the criminal law. The state is unable to protect itself by the criminal law, and thus is justified in turning to the alternative civil commitment system for self-protection.

But the central feature of contemporary sex offender commitments negates this traditional justification. These laws target individuals who are fully accountable for their criminal acts, past and future. Thus, if sex offender commitments are justified, it must be on the second basis. Here, the mental condition marks a degraded moral status. It is this degraded status that permits the state to incarcerate the individual to prevent future predicted crimes, a remedy unavailable against all other members of the community, including those who are 'dangerous'.

I suggest that the justification for sex offender commitments is founded on the construction of its subjects as different *in kind* from 'normal' human beings, and, by reason of the difference, entitled to diminished rights. This 'jurisprudence of difference' taps into a shameful tradition in American law, and ought to call into question the morality of sex offender commitments.

Underlying this jurisprudence of difference is the portrayal of sex offenders as individuals whose bad behaviour flows inexorably from a being who is essentially different from the norm. It is this essential difference that justifies the degraded status that permits the abrogation of constitutional rights.

Sex offender commitment schemes construct an essentialist view of sex offenders in three ways. First, a central tenet of sex offender commitment courts is that sex predators constitute an 'identifiable' group suffering from a particular 'condition' (*In re Blodgett* 1994; *In re Young* 1993). Second, sex offender commitment schemes rely centrally on diagnosis, a process of explicit categorisation and classification. Diagnosis seeks the essence, discarding or ignoring the individual. Third, commitment requires prediction. Prediction is possible only to the extent that individuals 'belong' to groups whose statistical probability of exhibiting the target behaviour can be measured or estimated (Janus and Meehl 1997: 42). An individual 'belongs' to the group only to the extent that he or she is 'essentially' – rather than 'accidentally' – associated with the group.

At bottom, I suggest, lies the fundamental divide between criminal and civil approaches to danger-management. Constrained by strict protections, criminal law judges that the individual deserves punishment. The judgement is based on a past act. Civil commitment judges that the individual is not entitled to the procedural protections of the criminal law. But the lack of entitlement cannot arise from a desert-based reasoning. It cannot be the result of the individual's past wrongs. Rather, it must be the individual's condition or status that diminishes their entitlement to the protections of the criminal law. The blame-based foundation of the criminal law requires a human act as a predicate, whereas the regulatory, future-oriented civil commitment is predicated on human condition or status.

Thus, at the centre of the regulatory model of danger-management is the notion that it is appropriate only for those persons who are 'essentially' dangerous, whose 'true nature' is dangerousness (Pratt 1997: 42; Zimring and Hawkins 1995: 23). This is what the courts must mean by their invocation of 'inability to control' rhetoric. To say that a person lacks the power to control their dangerous behaviour is to say that dangerousness is their true nature – rather than a contingent choice of behaviours, dependent on a variety of environmental and developmental factors.

Thus, it is not dangerousness 'alone' that justifies regulatory detention – but dangerousness as a condition, as an essence, that is the predicate. It is through this process of essentialisation that these laws are able to isolate a small group for specially disadvantaged treatment under the law. If the discourse of sex offender commitment schemes establishes its subjects as different in kind from the norm, then it is only a short step to the conclusion that this difference in 'personhood' justifies a difference in legal rights. A 'different' essence is tantamount to a degraded essence. After all, in

American jurisprudence, there is a long and ignominious history of according diminished rights to those who are perceived as essentially different (see, e.g., *Dred Scott* v. *Sandford* 1856). Whether intended or not, sex offender commitments partake of this history.

The social meaning critique

Law reflects and helps create social meaning, especially in areas of high contention (Wilson 1997: 46). As a society, our efforts to curb sexual violence depend heavily on how we define and explain it. Sex offender commitment schemes create a set of social meanings that, paradoxically, may undercut the very advances in understanding and combating sexual violence that led to their creation.

In *Intimate Matters: A History of Sexuality in America*, D'Emilio and Freedman analyse the history of sexuality into three realms: sexual meaning, sexual regulation and sexual politics. Sex offender commitment laws are clearly in the realm of sexual regulation. But, as the authors argue, these areas often are interrelated, with regulation both reflecting and influencing sexual meaning and politics. Sex offender commitment schemes can be seen as a counter-move in the politics of sexuality, a move that adopts the sexual violence agenda of the feminist movement into the mainstream of politics, and then contains it by establishing a set of sexual meanings that place sexual violence safely in the medical and psychological realm of discourse.

Beginning in the 1970s, a variety of movements, most prominently the feminist movements, have pushed for broader definitions of sexual crime, more vigorous enforcement of sex crime laws, and the removal of traditional procedural impediments to enforcement (D'Emilio and Freedman 1997: 314). As I argue above, it was in part these changes that led to the enactment of sex offender commitment laws.

A key aspect of the feminist-led changes entails challenges to traditional gender roles and the sexual politics of the society. Arguments over the definition of rape reflect a 'desire to change the power relationship between men and women, or to reflect a change that is taking place' (Seminar Summary, Sexuality and American Social Policy 1995: xvii). Sexual violence is a reflection of broadly dispersed societal values and attitudes (Ellis 1993: 17–18, 20). Changing broadly held values and attitudes about sex and gender is fundamental to the reduction of sexual violence (Office of the Attorney General, State of Minnesota 1989: 4). Society, as well as the individual perpetrator, bears responsibility for sexual violence.

Contemporary sex offender commitment schemes were born in 1989, the same year as one of the major measures of crime in the United States – the Crime Victimization Survey – was being redesigned to improve the reporting of sexual assaults and domestic violence. The redesign 'substantially increased the number of rapes and aggravated and simple assaults reported' (US Department of Justice 1997). These changes in survey methodology, and their results, both reflect and validate the emerging view that sexual violence is a reflection of broadly held societal attitudes and values.

The coincident birth of sex offender schemes reflects a congruent new awareness of the seriousness of sexual violence. But sex offender commitment schemes construct a paradigm of sexual violence that is at odds with the emerging feminist view of sexual violence. These laws seek to explain sexual violence through its connection to mental disorder. To the extent that this imagine prevails, it is incongruent with a broad-based effort to change prevailing social values. The mental disorder explanation suggests an aberrational, rather than systemic or societal, source for sexual violence. It is a model that emphasises the absence of both personal and societal responsibility for sexual violence (Dinovitzer 1997: 149–50). It suggests a source that is within the individual – and thus not in the society – but beyond the individual's control. This is a model for non-responsibility, both of the society and the individual.

By constructing the sex offender as the mentally disordered 'other', offender commitment schemes absolve the mainstream of society of responsibility for sexual violence, and thus support a *status quo* sexual politics. Sex offender commitment schemes harness the symbolic power of 'madness'. This concept has long enabled European culture to 'establish its range by its own derangement'; to establish through 'ritual exiles' and 'rigorous divisions' that which it is, by showing that which it is not (Foucault 1988: xi, 10). The 'ritual exile' of 'mentally disordered' sex offenders confines sexual violence to a small, aberrational group of 'others'.

Sex offender commitment discourse both exemplifies, and limits, the feminist agenda to broadly redefine, and eventually control, sexual violence. If feminists saw sexual violence as the 'product of a society which devalues women' (Dinovitzer 1997: 149), and as a 'key element maintaining the subordination of women' (D'Emilio and Freedman 1997: 314), then sex offender commitment laws provided a means to remedy the failure of criminal justice practices to fully reflect this understanding. But by banishing the discourse of blame, and embracing the psychologised explanation of sexual violence, the rhetoric of sex offender commitment laws represents a paradigm of sexual violence that undercuts the need for broad changes in social values. Sexual violence is not us, it is the other.

Conclusion

The criminal justice system is based on a simple social compact: the deprivation of liberty is limited by strict procedural constraints and may be imposed only on those who deserve their punishment. The moral legitimacy of the criminal system depends on the integrity and primacy of this compact. The *blameless* dangerous fall outside of this compact, and thus the state is justified in developing an alternative system of control – civil commitment – to vindicate its need for self-defence. Civil commitment of the blameless dangerous does not threaten the criminal justice compact because the social aversion to excusing violent acts serves to contain the civil system to a narrow and secondary territory.

Sex offender commitments fit neither of these paradigms. Born of the feminist-led heightening of attention to sexual violence and an expansionist incapacitation-imperative, sex offender commitments impose social control outside of the criminal law social compact. This social control is outside of the compact not because its targets are incapable of blame, but rather because blame-derived incapacitation has been exhausted. Thus, sex offender commitment laws create a third category of social control. This category aims at individuals whose mental state is 'sane' enough to deserve punishment, but who nonetheless are not entitled to the constraints normally flowing from the social compact.

To create this third category, sex offender commitment laws must turn to a 'jurisprudence of difference', creating a degraded civil status for individuals whom the law labels as different in kind from the norm. This rhetorical move maintains the primacy and legitimacy of the blame-based criminal law, but at a price.

First, there is a moral price: Justice Alan Page of the Minnesota Supreme Court expressed the danger inherent in the legal construction of degraded status: 'Today the target is people who are sexually dangerous. Which class of people, who are different from us and who we do not like, will it be tomorrow?' (*In re Linehan* 1996: 202). Second, there is a public policy price: the construction of sex offenders as aberrational and the emphasis on psychological and 'causal' explanations for sexual violence undercuts the feminist-led advances in the understanding of sexual violence. Finally, there is a cost in allocation of scarce public resources. Huge, and growing, sums are being spent with no empirical assurance that these schemes are the most effective use of limited treatment, confinement and supervisory funds.

In the end, second generation sex offender commitment schemes likely will follow their predecessors into failure. Worried about the growing cost, the 1998 Minnesota legislature ordered a study to examine the sex offender commitment system and recommend 'alternative methods of addressing sexually dangerous persons ... while balancing the need for public safety ... and financial prudence' (Minnesota Laws 1998, Chapter 367, Article 3, Section 15). The study projected a growth in cost of 450 per cent over the next eleven years. The view of one 'alarmed' member of the legislative oversight committee that such costs are 'unsustainable' (Minnesota Senate Hearing 1999) will likely be widely shared. It will be this unacceptable demand for resources that will, in the end, shed a clear light on the moral and public policy contradictions of these laws. As these laws fail, the question will be how badly these contradictions will have damaged the critical fight against sexual violence.

References

Addington v. *Texas* (1979) 441 U.S. 418.

Blacher, R. (1995) 'Historical Perspective of the "Sex Psychopath" Statute: From the Revolutionary Era to the Present Federal Crime Bill', *Mercer Law Review* 46(2): 889–920.

Bodine, B.G. (1990) 'Washington's New Violent Sexual Predator Commitment System: An Unconstitutional Law and an Unwise Policy Choice', *University of Puget Sound Law Review* 14(1): 104–41.

Boerner, D. (1992) 'Confronting Violence: In the Act and In the Word', *University of Puget Sound Law Review* 15(3): 525–77.

Brakel, S.J., Parry J. and Weiner, B.A. (1985) *The Mentally Disabled and the Law*, 3rd edn, Chicago, IL: American Bar Foundation.

Brief of the Minnesota Attorney General, *State ex rel. Pearson* v. *Probate Court of Ramsey County* (1940) 309 U.S. 270.

Brief of Respondent, State of Minnesota, *State ex rel. Pearson* v. *Probate Court of Ramsey County* (1940) 309 U.S. 270.

Buck v. *Bell* (1927) 274 U.S. 200.

California Department of Mental Health (1998) 'Sex Offender Commitment Program (SOCP): All Cases as of 9/28/98', in W.L. Fitch, *NASHMPD Update: Civil Commitment of Sex Offenders in the U.S. (A Quick and Dirty Survey)*, National Association of State Mental Health Program Directors, Forensic Division, 19th Annual Conference, 1 October 1998.

Campbell, A.D. (1998) 'Note, Kansas v. Hendricks: Absent a Clear Meaning of Punishment, States are Permitted to Violate Double Jeopardy Clause', *Loyola University of Chicago Law Journal* 30(1): 87–131.

Cunningham, M.D. and Reidy, T.J. (1998) 'Antisocial Personality Disorder and Psychopathy: Diagnostic Dilemmas in Classifying Patterns of Antisocial Behavior in Sentencing Evaluations', *Behavioral Sciences and the Law* 16(3): 333–51.

D'Emilio, J. and Freedman, E.B. (1997) *Intimate Matters: A History of Sexuality in America*, 2nd edn, Chicago, IL and London: University of Chicago Press.

Dailey, D. (1997) 'Minnesota's Sentencing Guidelines – Past and Future', in M. Tonry and K. Hatlestad (eds), *Sentencing Reform in Overcrowded Times: A Comparative Perspective*, New York: Oxford University Press.

Dinovitzer, R. (1997) 'The Myth of Rapists and Other Normal Men: The Impact of Psychiatric Considerations on the Sentencing of Sexual Assault Offenders', *Canadian Journal of Legal Studies* 12(1): 147–69.

Doren, D.M. (1998) 'Recidivism Base Rates, Predictions of Sex Offender Recidivism, and the "Sexual Predator" Commitment Laws', *Behavioral Sciences and the Law* 16(1): 97–114.

Dred Scott v. *Sandford* (1856) 60 U.S. 393.

Ellis, L. (1993) 'Rape as a Biosocial Phenomenon', in G.C. Nagayama Hall, R. Hirschman, J.R. Graham and M.S. Zaragoza (eds), *Sexual Aggression: Issues in Etiology, Assessment and Treatment*, Washington, DC: Taylor & Francis.

Erickson, W.D. (undated) 'Critical Analysis of the Psychopathic Personality Statute', unpublished manuscript, on file with author.

—— (1995) ' "Northern Lights": Minnesota's Experience with Sex Offender Legislation', *American Academy of Psychiatry and Law Newsletter* 20(1): 3–6.

Fitch, W.L. (1998) 'NASHMPD Update: Civil Commitment of Sex Offenders in the U.S. (A Quick and Dirty Survey)', National Association of State Mental Health Program Directors, Forensic Division, 19th Annual Conference, 1 October 1998.

Foucault, M. (1988) *Madness and Civilization*, Vintage Books edn, New York: Vintage Books.

Foucha v. *Louisiana* (1992) 504 U.S. 71.

Freedman, E.B. (1987) ' "Uncontrolled Desires": The Response to the Sexual Psychopath', *Journal of American History* 74(1): 83–106.

Governor's Task Force on Community Protection, State of Washington (1989) *Final Report to Booth Gardner, Governor, State of Washington*, Olympia, WA: Governor's Task Force on Community Protection.

Gross, T., Kansas Attorney General's Office (1998) Personal communication with author, 28 October 1998.

Group for the Advancement of Psychiatry (1977) *Psychiatry and Sex Psychopath Legislation: The 30s to the 80s*, New York: Mental Health Materials Center, Inc.

Hacker, F.J. and Frym, M. (1955) 'The Sexual Psychopath Act in Practice: A Critical Discussion', *California Law Review* 43(5): 766–80.

Harris, L., Wisconsin Department of Corrections (1998) Personal Communication with the author, 12 June 1998.

Harris, P.M. (1995) 'Prison-based Sex Offender Treatment Programs in the Post-sexual Psychopath Era', *Journal of Psychiatry and Law* 23(4): 555–81.

Hausman, W. (1972) 'Report on Sex Offenders: A Sociological, Psychiatric and Psychological Study', unpublished manuscript, on file with author.

Humphrey v. *Cady* (1972) 405 U.S. 504.

Huot, S.J., Minnesota Department of Corrections (1998a) 'Development and Use of the Minnesota Sex Offender Screening Tool', Presentation to the Minnesota Sex Offender Civil Commitment Study Group, on file with author.

—— (1998b) Personal communication with the author, 10 June 1998.

In re Blodgett (1994) 510 N.W. 2d. 910 (Minn.).

In re Hendricks (1996) 912 P. 2d 129 (Kans.).

In re Linehan (1996) 557 N.W. 2d 171 (Minn.), certiorari granted, judgment vacated, 118 S. Ct. 596, 1997.

In re Young (1993) 857 P.2d 989 (Wash.).

Jacobson v. *Massachusetts* (1905) 197 U.S. 11.

Janus, E.S. (1996) 'Preventing Sexual Violence: Setting Principled Constitutional Boundaries on Sex Offender Commitments', *Indiana Law Journal* 72(1): 157–213.

—— (1997a) 'Sex Offender Commitments: Debunking the Official Narrative and Revealing the Rules-in-use', *Stanford Law and Policy Review* 8(2): 71–102.

—— (1997b) 'Toward a Conceptual Framework for Assessing a Police Power Commitment Legislation: A Critique of Schopp's and Winick's Explications of Legal Mental Illness', *Nebraska Law Review* 76(1): 1–50.

—— (1998) '*Hendricks* and the Moral Terrain of Police Power Civil Commitment', *Psychology, Public Policy and Law* 4(1/2): 297–322.

Janus, E.S. and Meehl, P.E. (1997) 'Assessing the Legal Standard for Predictions of Dangerousness in Sex Offender Commitment Proceedings', *Psychology, Public Policy and Law* 3(1): 33–64.

Janus, E.S. and Walbek, N.H. (2000) 'Sex Offender Commitments in Minnesota: A Descriptive Study of Second Generation Commitments', *Behavioral Sciences and the Law* 18.

Jones v. *United States* (1983) 463 U.S. 354.

Kansas v. *Hendricks* (1997) 117 S.Ct. 2072.

Kirwin, J.L. (1995) 'Civil Commitment of Sexual Predators: Statutory and Case Law Developments', *The Hennepin Lawyer* 66(7): 22–6.

Klotz, J.A. (1996) 'Sex Offenders and the Law: New Directions', in D.B. Wexler and B.J. Winick (eds), *Law in a Therapeutic Key*, Durham, NC: Carolina Academic Press.

Leyva, M., California Department of Mental Health (1998) Personal communication with the author, 2 November 1998.

Lieb, R. (1997) 'Washington State: A Decade of Sentencing Reform', in M. Tonry and K. Hatlestad (eds), *Sentencing Reform in Overcrowded Times: A Comparative Perspective*, New York: Oxford University Press.

Millard v. *Harris* (1968) 406 F. 2d 964 (D.C.).

Minnesota Department of Corrections (1999) *Civil Commitment Study Group: 1998 Report to the Legislature*, St Paul: Minnesota Department of Corrections.

Minnesota Laws (1998) Chapter 367, Article 3, Section 15.

Minnesota Senate Hearing (1999) Senate Crime Prevention Committee, Presentation by Civil Commitment Study Group, 20 January.

Minnesota Statute (1996) 244.05.

Morse, S.J. (1985) 'Excusing the Crazy: The Insanity Defense Reconsidered', *Southern California Law Review* 58(3): 777–836.

National Center for Missing and Exploited Children (1998) *A Model State Sex-Offender Policy*, Arlington, VA: National Center for Missing and Exploited Children.

Office of the Attorney General, State of Minnesota (1989) *Attorney General's Task Force on the Prevention of Sexual Violence Against Women*, St Paul, MN: Office of the Attorney General.

Pithers, W.D. (1990) 'Relapse Prevention with Sexual Aggressors: A Method for Maintaining Therapeutic Gain and Enhancing External Supervision', in W.L. Marshall, D.R. Laws and H.R. Barbaree (eds), *Handbook of Sexual Assault: Issues, Theories and Treatment*, New York and London: Plenum Press.

Pratt, J. (1997) *Governing the Dangerous: Dangerousness, Law and Social Change*, Sydney: Federation Press.

Program Evaluation Division, Office of the Legislative Auditor, State of Minnesota (1994) *Psychopathic Personality Commitment Law*, St Paul, MN: Office of the Legislative Auditor.

Rice, M.E. (1997) 'The Treatment of Mentally Disordered Offenders', *Psychology, Public Policy and Law* 3(1): 126–83.

Richards, E.P. (1989) 'The Jurisprudence of Prevention: The Right of Societal Self-Defense Against Dangerous Individuals', *Hastings Constitutional Law Quarterly* 16(3): 329–92.

Romero, J. and Williams, L. (1985) 'Recidivism Among Convicted Sex Offenders: A 10 Year Follow Up Study', *Federal Probation* 49(1): 58–64.

Schopp, R.F. and Sturgis, B.J. (1995) 'Sexual Predators and Legal Mental Illness for Civil Commitment', *Behavior Science and Law* 13(4): 437–58.

Seminar Summary, Sexuality and American Social Policy (1995) in M.D. Smith, J. Besharov and K.N. Gardiner (eds), *Was it Rape? An Examination of Sexual Assault Statistics*, Menlo Park, CA: Henry J. Kaiser Family Foundation.

State ex rel. Pearson v. *Probate Court of Ramsey County* (1940) 309 U.S. 270.

Tonry, M. and Hatlestad, K. (1997) 'Sentencing Reform in the United States', in M. Tonry and K. Hatlestad (eds), *Sentencing Reform in Overcrowded Times: A Comparative Perspective*, New York: Oxford University Press.

Unsworth, C. (1987) *The Politics of Mental Health Legislation*, New York: Oxford University Press.

US Department of Justice, Bureau of Justice Statistics (1997) *Redesign of the National Crime Victimization Survey*, Washington, DC: US Department of Justice.

Washington Revised Code (1998) Annotated section 71.09 (WestGroup).

Washington State Institute for Public Policy (1998) *Sex Offenses in Washington State: 1998 Update*, Olympia, WA: Washington State Institute for Public Policy.

Wilson, J.Q. (1997) *Moral Judgment: Does the Abuse Excuse Threaten Our Legal System?*, New York: Basic Books.

Winick, B.J. (1995) 'Ambiguities in the Legal Meaning and Significance of Mental Illness', *Psychology, Public Policy and Law* 1(3): 534–611.

—— (1998) 'Sex Offender Law in the 1990s: A Therapeutic Jurisprudence Analysis', *Psychology, Public Policy and Law* 4: 505–70.

Young v. *Weston* (1995) 898 F. Supp. 744 (W.D. Wash.).

Zimring, F.E. and Hawkins, G. (1995) *Incapacitation: Penal Confinement and the Restraint of Crime*, New York: Oxford University Press.

Zinermon v. *Burch* (1990) 494 U.S. 113.

Practical risks

Danger in the penal context

Chapter 5

Calculations of risk in contemporary penal practice

Mark Brown

One of the great paradoxes of the 'dangerous offender' notion is that such a variety of offences qualify individuals for this label. So too do there exist an almost equally great variety of penal responses to the risks and threats such offenders are felt to present. Ironically, then, both the figure of the dangerous offender and the attending ensemble of penal concepts and practices such individuals seem to require have taken on something of a routine appearance in contemporary penality. Risk assessment, cognitive-behavioural therapy, special sentencing strategies, special release mechanisms and so on: each of these represents what might be termed 'growth technologies' in the penal sphere. Perhaps the fastest growing of them all, and one which seems to have captured something of the anxiety and apprehension surrounding dangerousness itself, is the idea of risk. This potentially innocuous concept – one that at another time might never have escaped the discourses of interested professionals – has functioned something like a conduit, however, linking and bringing together a range of otherwise separate lines of thought and practice both within criminal justice and across a wide range of social and scientific disciplines. In relation to the dangerous offender, the concept of risk has become something of a touchstone, an orienting principle around which decisions about appropriate responses to perceived danger are conceived and organised. Yet rather than providing a co-ordinating principle for dealings with the dangerous offender, risk seems instead to have served as a general justifying proposition for the development of different and often conflicting legal and administrative rationalities within the justice system. Risks presented by an offender frequently are calculated in different and often contradictory ways and these differing conceptions of risk are used to justify a set of equally disparate and conflicting responses to the supposedly dangerous individual. It is on the grounds of these different conceptions of risk, therefore, that penal strategies as diverse as three-strikes laws, intensive therapeutic programmes and indefinite sentences find their justification.

   The purpose of this chapter is therefore to examine the way in which the concept of risk has been utilised in relation to the dangerous offender. In contrast to the prevailing approach in the criminological risk literature, however, the aim here is to connect conceptions of risk with penal strategies, working back from the strategies themselves to an idea or model of risk. One of the first things to be revealed by such an approach is that a significant amount of contemporary penal practice grounded in ideas of risk is largely unaccounted for, and untheorised, in the risk literatures of criminology and criminological psychology. This chapter therefore aims to describe two modes of risk calculation – or perhaps better, two ways of thinking about risk – that between them account for much of the great variety of penal practices directed at the dangerous offender. The characterisation of these two approaches will be necessarily brief and the description of their attending penal practices limited principally to the domain of penal sanctions.

The calibration of reoffending risk

The technical notion of risk in criminal justice – the way in which it is most commonly discussed – emerged largely as an artefact of research on prediction of parole success. Beginning with seminal studies in the United States by Hart (1923) and Burgess (1928), this research sought to obtain a better understanding of the association between individual characteristics of prisoners and their subsequent success or failure on release and thus to aid parole decision-makers in making more reliable and better informed judgements. A huge body of subsequent research has attempted both to fine tune the measures of individual characteristics and post-release behaviour and to develop more accurate statistical models of the relationship between individual characteristics and behaviour (for reviews see Champion 1994; Farrington and Tarling 1985; Litwack and Schlesinger 1999; Simon 1971; Gottfredson and Tonry 1987). A recent review of risk assessment and treatment research by Bonta (1996) attempted to bring some order to the history and current status of risk assessment research by proposing three developmental stages. First generation strategies, Bonta suggested, were those grounded in traditional subjective assessments ranging from the professional judgement to gut-feeling or intuition. The parole prediction studies referred to here thus constitute the beginnings of second generation assessment where attempts were made to go beyond intuitive strategies and to quantify the relationship between identifiable characteristics or conditions and particular outcomes. Yet although this second generation research was able to link risk factors with offending outcomes, it failed to describe ways in which risk could be ameliorated. Third generation assessment, therefore, is described by Bonta as those contemporary strategies that bring together measures of offending risk with a linked set of assessments of treatment need. The focus of current risk research is thus not simply upon risk identification but also upon the parallel process of risk management.

Bonta's description of the development and current status of approaches to risk and treatment assessment neatly encapsulates a large and burgeoning field of research. At the same time, however, the presentation of risk assessment strategies as following a linear, generational, developmental path is problematic in a number of respects. Such a representation of risk assessment presumes, for instance, that those intuitive decision-makers now consigned to an historical first generation position in fact conceive of risk in the same fashion as those who construct statistical risk prediction instruments. Linked to this, the generational approach also seems to imply that judgements about risk and danger began in antiquity using the only tools available at the time – gut-feeling, ill-specified professional opinion, intuition – but have since been replaced by the more rational tool of scientific analysis. Bonta reinforces this point, noting that 'It took a millennium to progress to the second generation, fifty years to the third … ' (p.19). While there is a compelling simplicity to this representation of progress in thinking about risk, and while it would be widely accepted in the community of risk assessment scholars, it is ultimately an unsatisfactory approach for it fails adequately to link thinking about risk with penal strategies that deal with risk and to account for the great variation in the way risk is thought of at different points in the criminal justice system at the same time.

Any critical review of responses to risk and danger in contemporary penal practice would have to conclude that risk is not a unidimensional construct in which variations in conceptualisation can be traced to different historical periods of understanding of the phenomenon. Bonta is therefore correct in his identification of different approaches to thinking about risk, but incorrect in his ascription of a linear developmental process. In order to understand contemporary penal practices in relation to the so-called dangerous offender, it will be necessary to invert the assumptions upon which Bonta established his generational classification. Thus, rather than thinking of risk as a phenomenon that has been similarly conceptualised but differently measured, risk could more profitably be thought of as varying in its conceptualisation. Under this view, attention should be directed to the different forms of risk that exist simultaneously within the justice system and to the different practices they serve or give rise to. Such a conceptualisation of risk leads to a system of categorisation that seeks to represent not changes in method but differences in the underlying conception of what can be held to constitute risk. Seen in this light, risk emerges as a label to denote the presence of particular circumstances of interest, circumstances that may differ considerably depending upon what view of the markers of threat and danger are being invoked by the risk assessor.

Two models of risk

A preliminary attempt at such a categorisation of current thinking and practices in relation to the dangerous offender is the aim of the remainder of this chapter. Its main purpose is to view decision making about risk in a broader perspective and to challenge some of the orthodoxies that seem to have calcified thinking in this area. This initial venture into the revision of risk categories reveals two discrete conceptualisations of risk. The first of these, which for the present purpose will be called fluid risk, requires knowledge of the relationship between individual characteristics (or risk factors) and offending behaviour and regards risk so measured as falling upon an identifiable underlying behavioural continuum. The second approach, which will be termed categorical risk, views behaviour instead through its association with established categories of human virtue and character, so that risks, measured in this way, are categorical rather than continuous in nature. Each of these conceptions of risk recognises the existence of the other, yet allows its concepts only peripheral significance in the risk determination. Not surprisingly, each also is central to a set of penal practices and legal or administrative rationalities that produce quite different responses to the dangerous offender.

Fluid risk

The distinguishing feature of fluid risk, and the set of assessment and prediction strategies used to gauge it, is that it is understood as a shifting or changeable entity, constantly evolving in shape and form. Thus, like fluid itself, it is held to have properties that are knowable, that exist in predictable relation to each other, that are measurable and quantifiable and that behave, or produce behaviour, that is explicable and understandable on the basis of an established risk profile. To be sure, the science of this risk assessment and behavioural prediction process is less well developed than that of the physics of fluids, but the essential assumptions about the nature of phenomena and the possibilities of knowledge underlying each are essentially the same.

It is important to recognise also that this description of fluid risk is a description of the fundamental characteristics of risk itself. Discussions of risk in the literature generally do not speak directly to the phenomenon of risk (cf. for example Peay 1982) but instead attempt to sort or categorise 'risk factors' or the assessment and prediction methods used to combine them. Bonta's generational model is one such approach. Another, and one which is perhaps less implicitly judgemental in its ordering of assessment techniques, was advanced by Miller and Morris (1988) and has subsequently been used by a number of writers as a general scheme for classifying risk prediction methods (see for example, Melton *et al*. 1998). Miller and Morris' proposal groups methods into three categories. Actuarial methods utilise statistical means to assess the relationship between individual variables and a specified outcome, which may be simple reoffending or some more complex criterion such as the number of offences, type of offence or type of sanction.

The results of such analyses can be used to develop risk prediction instruments – such as the North American Levels of Supervision Inventory and Wisconsin Risk/Needs instrument (see Andrews and Bonta 1998) or the British Reconviction Predictions Score (see Ward 1987) – which allow new cases (offenders) to be classified into risk categories (often simply high/medium/low) on the basis of their past offence history, demographic characteristics and other factors found in the original research to predict offending. Clinical methods, by contrast, largely eschew statistical reasoning in favour of a range of approaches to the intuitive synthesis of information gleaned about offenders on a case by case basis. The term clinical does not necessarily denote psychological or psychiatric assessments, although it may include them. Rather, clinical assessments of risk involve individual decision-makers selecting, sifting and interpreting information, determining its relevance to the offending behaviour in question and making judgements about how the current case can be understood within the framework of principles and experience drawn upon by the individual decision-maker. Judgements about reoffending risk made by members of the judiciary, probation officers, parole-board members and others who rely upon individual knowledge and expertise rather than statistical tables or prediction instruments fall within Miller and Morris' clinical description. Anamnestic assessments of risk, while also being made by individual decision-makers, draw upon a more circumscribed logic and focus upon the identification of situational determinants of offending behaviour and an assessment of the extent to which these can be expected to reoccur in the future. Anamnestic prediction of offending can thus be thought of as a matching exercise in which the characteristics of past offending circumstances are identified and a judgement made about the likelihood of such conditions holding in the future.

Fluid risk should thus be thought of as something attaching to offenders and the three assessment systems categorised by Miller and Morris as different ways of tapping into the phenomenon of this risk. These three methods can also be thought of as lying on a continuum of methodological rigour, with actuarial assessment clearly being the most well-researched and accurate strategy, followed by anamnestic and then clinical assessment. What is important here, however, is that the existence of risk is recognised by all three systems as something that exists independently of the assessment system itself. Furthermore, although different systems may be used more or less often at different points in the criminal justice process (actuarial assessment, for instance, would rarely be directly drawn upon for sentencing decisions), the risks they reveal are independent also of the sanctions or penal strategies they may have some hand in shaping. Fluid risk, therefore, is held to exist independently both of the systems for its assessment and the penal responses to it. The latter include both traditional penal strategies such as incapacitation and more modern management technologies of rehabilitation and intensive supervision. At the same time, however, understanding of the relationship between risk and the techniques for its management can result in the development of moderating principles. One such example is the research on the relationship between reoffending risk and treatment effectiveness (see Andrews and Bonta 1998) that has revealed a strong positive association between level of risk and treatment success. The resulting Risk Principle now frequently is used as a screen for the selection and allocation of offenders to treatment programmes.

Categorical risk

If fluid risk is in some way described by the scientific or quasi-scientific methods used to reveal and measure it, then categorical risk might equally be characterised as a quality not amenable to scientific modes of analysis. Categorical risk is better understood as grounded in non-scientific (common, philosophical, legal) understandings of human characteristics and the indicative signs of threat and danger. It is therefore upon a metric of human virtue or individual character that categorical risk assessments are made. Yet although judgements of this sort lie at the heart of categorical risk calculation, these judgements often are made, or the conditions for their ascendancy established, in the wider set of social relations within which penality is embedded. Thus, in practice, categorical risk often-times appears in criminal justice as an imputed value or as something determined as much by the methods used to assess it as by any independent characteristic of the person in whom it is thought to reside. Categorical risk is thus a highly complex construction, far more so than the behavioural model of fluid risk, and it will be helpful to examine some examples of its operation in the criminal justice process since often these processes are themselves constitutive of the risk as it is held to exist in the everyday practice of penality.

In the same way that it was possible to identify a continuum of methodological rigour underlying strategies for the assessment of fluid risk, so too it is possible to identify a thread running through the criminal justice strategies operating to produce categorical risk. In this case, however, the connecting element is not scientific method but something like a common/political or legal/bureaucratic rationality. At one end of this continuum lie mandatory sentences wherein risk and danger are imputed by the nature of the offence and sanctions determined on the basis of this fact rather than the character or circumstances of individual offenders convicted of the offence. Perhaps the most well known and roundly criticised of such strategies is the three-strikes model that began in the United States and that, in California, resulted in the well-known 'pizza incident'. In this case, theft of a slice of pizza and the subsequent prosecution of the offence as a felony crime resulted in a third strike conviction and a mandatory sentence of twenty-five years to life for the offender. Toward the middle of the continuum lie strategies like the serious violent offender provisions found in New Zealand's Criminal Justice Act 1985, or the Criminal Justice Act 1991 in England and Wales. These produce a bifurcation of penal regimes on the basis of the seriousness or, conversely, the ordinariness of offending. Under the New Zealand legislation offenders receiving a custodial sentence of two years or more for one of a small, select and apparently arbitrary list of serious offences are defined as dangerous offenders and subject to a different regime of penal conditions (including measures affecting length of time to be served) to those experienced by other prisoners. Finally, at the other end of this continuum, lie strategies of juridical and administrative judgement which eschew scientist constructions and analyses of risk and danger – such as actuarial or clinical assessments – in favour of an avowedly common-sense and intuitive divination of the risks at hand. Such strategies are reflected in frequent judicial pronouncements of the self-evident fact of dangers presented by an offender and given authority by statements of the higher courts. Three Australian cases illustrate aspects of this strategy for establishing risk. In respect of the method by which judgements of appropriate sentence length should be arrived at, the full court of the Victorian Supreme Court provided guidance in *Williscroft* ([1975] V.R. 292). The court explained that:

> ultimately every sentence imposed represents the sentencing judge's instinctive synthesis of all the various aspects involved in the punitive process. Moreover, in our view, it is profitless (as it was thought to be in *Kane's Case*) to attempt to allot to the various considerations their proper part in the assessment of the particular punishments presently under examination.
>
> (p.300)

This view was later reaffirmed in the Appeal Division of that court in *Young* ([1990] V.R. 951). Here Young, C.J. added that schemes designed to structure judicial thinking about sentence 'have no warrant in authority or justification or advantage from a practical point of view' and are 'calculated to lead to error and injustice' (pp.960–1). Guidance on the question of how estimates of risk and danger should best be made can be found in the case of *Attorney General* v. *David* (No. 6823 of 1990, 15 November 1991, unreported), heard before Hedigan, J. in the Supreme Court of Victoria. Justice Hedigan took expert evidence from psychiatrists and acknowledged the vast clinical literature on predicting dangerousness. However, after noting the great difficulty of ever saying what another person might do in the future, he concluded that ultimately 'It does not seem that either psychiatrist or lawyer is more likely to be right than anyone else' (p.33). On this basis he declined to enter the 'serpentine labyrinths' of clinical prediction, preferring instead 'to confine my judgement to an estimation of the risk to public safety and the likelihood of the infliction of personal harm by violence' (p.32). In concluding his opinion Justice Hedigan explained why such a common-sense approach to the problem of dangerousness was necessary:

> the function to be performed is a judicial act to be carried out in accordance with the established precepts and standards that the judicial task connotes. I have steadfastly declined to play amateur psychiatrist or psychologist, and reiterate that I shall decide this application on the whole of the evidence and on no other basis.
>
> (p.92)

In each of these three categorical strategies risk and danger emerge as products of the processes of judgement or definition. As will be described in further detail below, the assessments of character and its link to behaviour occur at very different points for each of these strategies (indeed, for three strikes this point is outside and prior to the penal process). Furthermore, these strategies each find their justification in thinking independent of the behaviourally driven modes of legitimation that seek to evaluate their efficacy by reference to 'independent' measures, such as recidivism or the likely seriousness of further offences (e.g. three strikes – Schichor and Sechrest 1996; serious violent offender provisions – Brown 1996, 1998; judicial decision making – Lovegrove 1997).

Contrasting fluid and categorical risk

It is important to recognise from the outset that the notions of fluid and categorical risk are notions about risk itself. They are not simply either a re-sorting of the methods arrayed by Bonta or Miller and Morris, nor a re-labelling or a different turn upon the rationale for penal strategies such as selective or collective incapacitation. The characterisation of these two forms of risk might best be pursued by clarifying the distinctions between them. It is possible to begin here with an analogy, for there are clear parallels between the fluid/categorical risk distinction and a more familiar binary classification found in the philosophy of science.

Popper's mysticism and logic

In setting forth a case for the primacy of scientific knowledge over other forms of thought, Popper (1966) introduced a binary division of knowledge systems into those that could be characterised by logic and those which relied upon what he could only refer to as mysticism. Science, Popper argued, produced the only defensible form of knowledge and the scientific method stood at its centre. This method Popper referred to as methodological nominalism and he contrasted it with practices based on reasoning and intuition that he referred to as methodological essentialism. The nominalist method draws upon observations of phenomena to reveal empirical regularities in their behaviour which, in turn, allow for the development of universal laws. Such laws describe how things operate and provide causal explanations of the relationship between phenomena. Popper's explanation of the nominalist method accords with the well-known Covering Law model of scientific reasoning and procedure presented by Hempel (1965). Essentialism, in contrast, was characterised by Popper as aiming to describe the true nature of things – their essence – rather than simply the manner in which they worked. In this task, essentialism is aided not principally by systems of observation but by intellectual intuition. Deriving from Platonic thinking, the essentialist method assumes that the essential character of a thing will eventually reveal itself if sufficient intellectual effort is invested in the process. The essential character of a matter or phenomenon is therefore something that may be deduced by the application of thought and reason to a problem. Popper strongly resisted this model of knowledge production for the primacy it gave to intuition and reasoning and for the fact that it produced certainty and closure in its resolutions to questions about the nature of things.

While pure nominalist and essentialist strategies probably exist only as theoretical ideals, the influence of each is widespread and mirrors in many ways the distinctions in assumptions that underpin fluid and categorical risk. The influence of nominalist thinking can be seen in the construction of the concept of fluid risk: here risk is a variable entity, the patterns of risk can be described yet risk itself is nothing more than a description of these patterns, it can change in individuals or populations over time but is predictable by recourse either to statistical or theoretical models and successful predictions of risk will allow an understanding of how other phenomena (such as treatment) can be expected to behave. Similarly, essentialist thought finds reflection in the assumptions underpinning categorical risk: that risk itself is something that can be defined by intellectual means independently of other methods, that the essence of risk or dangerousness in a particular context can be determined by a decision-maker, that the intuitive correctness of such an assessment guarantees the verity of the conclusion and that these conclusions will emerge out of the assembled facts of a case or problem in some kind of 'instinctive synthesis' that defies reductive or mechanistic analysis.

Implicit theories of the person

The contrasting of fluid and categorical risk makes clear not only the way in which they differ in their conception of the abstract notion of risk, it also reveals the existence of a set of quite contradictory assumptions about the individual as offender. In many ways these differing theories of the person are the more important element of the distinction between fluid and categorical models of risk. Fluid risk carries with it a conception of individual behaviour as an at least potentially knowable and manipulable entity, which is why risk is thought of as protean quality and assessment of risk linked with strategies of rehabilitation that should lead to its amelioration. It is also why there exists such great tension in fluid risk assessment between the statistical methods of actuarialism and the clinical approaches which attempt, on the basis of a variety of methods and theories, to produce an understanding of the individual *qua* individual. The assessment of fluid risk thus figures as a small part of a larger project, which is the scientific understanding of human behaviour and the development of generalisable laws – or at the very least, principles – to render that behaviour predictable. The way that fluid risk is thought of and the strategies used to gauge or assess it thus are familiar and well described in the risk literatures of criminology and criminological psychology. Much of this literature tends to represent what is being described here as categorical risk either as something outside the realm of 'real' risk assessment and prediction (the three-strikes response to serious crime for instance) or else as a hopelessly confused attempt at tapping the phenomenon of (fluid) risk by recourse to a set of quite inappropriate strategies (as in judicial determinations of risk).

Such representations are wrong. Underpinning the notion of categorical risk is a complex and not well-integrated ensemble of ideas about qualities of individuals and behaviours. Nevertheless, these assumptions are markedly different from the scientism of fluid risk assessment, bringing to the categorical assessment process a quite different implicit theory of the person. In categorical risk assessments the offender is viewed as an entity at once knowable and unknowable but, more importantly, as bearing the qualities of essential human categories. These include individual qualities – such as kindness, care, vengefulness or evil. They also include, however, what might be called communal qualities which mark off an individual's place in a wider social order – such as moral worth, membership of caste, clan or nation, and so on. The reason why individuals can be viewed at once as both knowable and unknowable is, therefore, that individual relations under this view of the person involve the categorisation of individuals into classes, such as 'the kind' or 'the generous'. But these classes themselves remain ultimately an open quantity, so that one can never know or plumb the depths of kindness nor of other human qualities more commonly found in the justice system such as vengefulness or evil. Categorical risk assessment therefore proceeds as a process of investigating the character of offenders and their crimes in only so much detail as is required to make a categorisation of the individual into a relevant class. Categorical understandings of the person may thus be characterised as a form of common knowledge of the person. Such knowledge should not be thought of or mistaken for naivety, for that construction of common knowledge is one produced by the generational scientism of

Bonta and Popper whose aims are to establish the primacy of scientific knowledge over any and all other ways of thinking. Categorical views of the person do not conform to the ground rules for knowledge laid out in the behavioural science project that spawned fluid risk assessments. But, as will be shown below, categorical thinking does nevertheless operate in a way that sustains and reinforces the social and institutional order from which it emerges.

One of the characterising features of categorical risk and the assessments made to determine it is that different conceptions of the constituent elements or markers of threat and danger may be drawn upon at different times or in relation to different 'types' of dangerous offender. It is in this multiplicity of ways that categorical risk can be established, and in its link with institutional processes independent of individual offenders' behaviour, that this form of risk is made so much more complex than the behaviourally grounded notion of fluid risk. At the same time, however, in the same way that anamnestic and actuarial assessment methods tapped fundamentally the same underlying notion of how fluid risk 'works', so too penal strategies as different as three-strikes statutes and judicial determinations of an appropriate penal response can be seen to draw upon essentially similar views of the person and their relationship to threat and danger.

In the case of three-strikes statutes, for example, communities and legislatures appear to have drawn upon a notion of eligibility to participate in the moral community. The moral claim to mutual respect brought about by the social contract of civil society not only furnishes a justification for punishment of criminals for individual acts of transgression, it arguably also implies a notion of moral capacity and thus moral right that repeated transgressions might progressively erode. The accumulation of qualifying offences that is central to both the three-strikes policy and the baseball metaphor used to convey its logic thus works as a progressive loss of mitigation to claim moral rights to participate in a civil society that has defined the 'three striker' a dangerous person. (Walker (1996) describes a similar rationale for protective sentencing in the British context and Sparks (1996) the role of 'less eligibility' thinking in winding back the quality of prison conditions). Here, in the practical operation of penality, the qualities of risk and dangerousness are imputed by dint of the qualifying offences and need not speak, nor indeed refer in any way, to the person of the individual offender. In this case, whether or not the offender will ever commit another offence – the rationalist criterion that underpins fluid risk – is irrelevant to the determination of risk and danger. Here also, the values and decisions of communities and legislatures, and the creation of three-strike statutes are themselves constitutive elements of the dangerousness determination. The syllogistic logic behind such strategies is simple and compelling: all serious repeat offenders are dangerous and have thus forfeited their right to participate in our community; all three-strike offenders are serious repeat offenders;

therefore all three strikers are dangerous and should be removed from our community.

Yet because categorical risk is so much a product of varying circumstances and organisational arrangements it can also be determined within the penal process with specific reference to the nature of individuals, as in the case for instance of judicial determinations of risk in the context of protective sentencing. While there are many features of judicial determinations of risk in protective sentencing cases that illustrate the development of a categorical risk assessment, there is space in this chapter to address only two of the most salient features. The first flows from the procedural principle of individualised justice and illustrates two related points: that categorical and fluid risk assessments conflict in practice and, thus, that categorical assessments are not simply clouded analogues of the fluid risk assessment process. The second example is the legal notion that expressions or indications of remorse are properly relevant to determination of a penal response to offending, illustrating how a phenomenology of the person grounded in common, legal and moral thought operates as a marker of risk.

Individualised justice

Broadly stated, the principle of individualised justice holds that in order for justice to be done information pertaining to an offender must be specific to that offender and not simply identify the offender, or his or her characteristics, with other known individuals or classes of individual. This principle makes difficult the integration of actuarial risk assessments into the juridical process, for such assessments are based upon a diametrically opposed reasoning and guiding principle. Statistical assessments of risk, and the process of linking an individual case with the statistical reference group, rely upon the principle of extensionality. This principle regards all individual cases as mutually intersubstitutable and knowledge of the individual case relevant only to the extent that it allows identification with the reference group (thus, reference variables such as age, prior offences and so on are relevant while factors such as why the offence was committed and how the individual regards it are not). Although clinical assessment strategies are more likely to provide teleological explanations, their capacity to add knowledge to judicial risk assessments beyond that which refers to psychiatric mental state tends to be limited. Moreover, the lack of consensus among clinical experts and consequently the lack of closure in the assessments they offer invariably leads the judicial decision-maker back to traditional juridical approaches of categorical risk assessment. One such approach is the use of phenomenological markers of the person categories such as kindness or evil discussed earlier.

Remorse as a risk marker

Factors such as the offender's remorsefulness for an offence provide key insights into the more fundamental human qualities that identify an individual as dangerous — as presenting a risk to public safety. Raimond Gaita's (1991) exposition of the essential character of good and evil provides a useful discussion of these two essential human attributes that, on prima facie grounds at least, seem critically important to the categorical risk assessment. From Gaita it is possible to identify at least three ways in which remorse operates not only as a key marker of categorical risk, but also as a marker that is conceptually and practically useful to the judicial risk determination process. First, remorse is useful and important because it is closely tied to the moral discourse within which law is located. In this respect Gaita has argued that the judgement that someone is guilty requires of them a serious response to morality's demands. Since the trial of an offender is predicated upon the assumption that they are (and were at the time of the offence) capable moral actors, the offender's recognition of guilt and response to that guilt in the form of remorse have come to assume an important place in both legal proceedings and the quasi-legal judgements made by parole boards. Morality's claim upon the individual that Gaita speaks of is the recognition and understanding of what it is to have behaved badly and to be that bad person and, moving forward from there, truly to repudiate that behaviour. Remorse thus becomes central to assessing risk because it provides an indication of the extent to which this progression has occurred. Those judging the quality of remorse face a difficult task, however, for the self-knowing which remorse involves is a difficult process and there are many subterfuges to be employed to evade its requirements. Gaita cautions against such strategies, noting 'Remorse is, amongst other things, a disciplined remembrance of the moral significance of what we did — disciplined because it must avoid self deceiving redescriptions and other corruptions peculiar to remorse itself, self-abasement, morbidity, and many others' (1991: 58). If remorse were genuine, however, it would seem to offer a reliable indication of risk particular to the individual offender.

A second way in which remorse is useful to judicial determinations of risk and danger is that it is a state which, in contrast with the fluid risk assessment strategies like actuarial assessment, emphasises what Gaita has termed the 'radical singularity' of the guilty in relation to all other individuals. Although the offender is before the court (or parole board) and can be enumerated among those who have stood in such a position, the genuine recognition of guilt and experience of remorse requires of an offender that they eschew any thoughts of community or fellowship with similarly placed individuals and recognise that their guilt places them outside the common community. That their behaviour and its implications are particular and not part of some common condition. Thus, indications of risk and danger will be given by the extent to which an offender recognises that they cannot claim common cause with other guilty individuals, that both the wrong done and the wrong experienced are *sui generis* and that resolution of this singular position outside the community of others is dependent upon genuine remorse.

Finally, the phenomenon of remorse is important for remorse itself is inescapably tied to the reality of badness and to evil. If evil done and evil suffered is *sui generis* then, as Gaita argues, evaluating remorse 'is fundamental amongst the ethical determinations of human individuality' (1991: 79). Evil as a metaphysical quality is therefore given practical measure not only in the nature and circumstances of an offence but also in the remorse of an offender for the impact of the act upon him or herself and the victim. Seen in this light, the categorical risk assessment is an assessment grounded in the moral evaluations that underpin the legal process. In the absence of access to knowledge of the essential character of the offender, the judicial decision-maker must fall back upon markers logically derived – such as remorse – that provide sufficient indication of what kind of person is before the court and therefore how they might conduct themselves in the future. What connects these logically derived markers of risk with those employed by legislatures considering three-strikes legislation is the recourse in both instances to essential human qualities – of badness and evil, or the moral community of civil society.

Conclusion

Any satisfactory explanation of the way risk operates in contemporary penal practice must account not only for the existence of different strategies and techniques finding their justification in the idea of risk – strategies such as three-strikes statutes, intensive rehabilitative programmes, protective sentences and so on – but must speak also to the theoretical conception of risk underlying these very different practices. The strategy adopted here has involved scrutinising the implicit models of behavioural causation implicit in such practices. This exercise has revealed two quite different forms of causal logic that have been referred to here as fluid and categorical models of risk. The thinking behind these implicit understandings of behaviour seems remarkably similar to the distinction between nominalist and essentialist thought suggested by Popper (1966) and to reflect scientific versus common and philosophical understandings of the characters and virtues of human beings. At the same time, however, an effort has also been made to present these as contemporaneous strategies and not simply as a division between the archaic and the modern. What this points to is the fact that formulations of risk in contemporary penal practice emerge from more than one system of thought and that, as with the concept of dangerousness itself, they are inextricably bound with the methods of their own production. The fact that most writing about risk-based practices in criminal justice focuses upon actuarial or clinical methods reflects nothing more than the preferences and disciplinary affiliations of those who have found a niche in this area. Even cursory examination of the day-to-day operation of courts and administrative bodies like parole boards reveals the myriad and complex ways in which decisions about what an offender 'is like' and what he or she will 'do next' are formulated. The dual taxonomy of risk briefly sketched in this chapter thus represents a first attempt at accounting for such practices and expanding the parameters of risk assessment theory.

References

Andrews, D.A. and Bonta, J. (1998) *The Psychology of Criminal Conduct*, 2nd edn, Cincinnati, OH: Anderson Publishing.

Bonta, J. (1996) 'Risk-needs Assessment and Treatment', in A.T. Harland (ed.), *Choosing Correctional Options That Work: Defining The Demand And Evaluating The Supply*, Thousand Oaks, CA: Sage.

Brown, M. (1996) 'Serious Offending and the Management of Public Risk in New Zealand', *British Journal of Criminology* 36: 18–36.

—— (1998) 'Serious Violence and the Dilemmas of Sentencing: A Comparison of Three Incapacitation Policies', *The Criminal Law Review* October: 710–22.

Burgess, E.W. (1928) 'Factors Determining Success or Failure on Parole', in A.A. Bruce, E.W. Burgess and A.J. Harno (eds), *The Workings Of The Indeterminate Sentence Law And The Parole System In Illinios*, Springfield, IL: Illinios State Board of Parole.

Champion, D. (1994) *Measuring Offender Risk: A Criminal Justice Sourcebook*, Westport, CT: Greenwood Press.

Farrington, D.P. and Tarling, R. (1985) *Prediction in Criminology*, Albany, NY: State University of New York Press.

Gaita, R. (1991) *Good And Evil: An Absolute Conception*, London: Macmillan.

Gottfredson, D.M. and Tonry, M. (eds) (1987) *Prediction And Classification: Criminal Justice Decision Making* (vol. 9, Crime and Justice series), Chicago, IL: University of Chicago Press.

Hart, H. (1923) 'Predicting Parole Success', *Journal of Criminal Law and Criminology* 14: 405–13.

Hempel, C.G. (1965) *Aspects Of Scientific Explanation And Other Essays In The Philosophy Of Science*, New York: Free Press.

Litwack, T.R. and Schlesinger, L.B. (1999) 'Assessing and Predicting Violence: Research, Law and Applications', in I.B. Weiner and A.K. Hess (eds), *Handbook Of Forensic Psychology*, 2nd edn, New York: Wiley.

Lovegrove, A. (1997) *The Framework Of Judicial Sentencing: A Study In Legal Decision Making*, Cambridge: Cambridge University Press.

Melton, G.B., Petrila, J., Poythress, N.G. and Slobogin, C. (1998) *Psychological Evaluations For The Courts: A Handbook For Mental Health Professionals And Lawyers*, 2nd edn, New York: The Guilford Press.

Miller, M. and Morris, N. (1988) 'Predictions of Dangerousness: An Argument for Limited Use', *Violence and Victims* 3: 263–83.

Peay, J. (1982) ' "Dangerousness" – Ascription or Description?', in P. Feldman (ed.), *Developments in The Study of Criminal Behaviour*, vol. 2, New York: John Wiley.

Popper, K.R. (1966) *The Open Society And Its Enemies*, vol. 1, London: Routledge.

Schichor, D. and Sechrest, D. (eds) (1996) *Three Strikes And You're Out: Vengeance As Public Policy*, Thousand Oaks, CA: Sage.

Simon, F.H. (1971) *Prediction Models In Criminology*, London: HMSO.

Sparks, R. (1996) 'Penal Austerity: the Doctrine of Less Eligibility Reborn?' in P. Francis and R. Matthews (eds), *Prisons 2000*, London: Macmillan.

Walker, N. (1996) *Dangerous People*, London: Blackstone Press.

Ward, D. (1987) *Validity Of The Reconviction Prediction Score*, Home Office Research Study No. 94, London: HMSO.

Chapter 6

Criminal careers, sex offending and dangerousness

Roderic Broadhurst

The identification and classification of offenders has been one of the abiding pre-occupations of what has become known as 'administrative criminology'. The search for factors that distinguish habitual and dangerous offenders from others has been the 'Secular Grail' of offender-centred criminologies since the time of the moral statisticians and the Lombrosian school. These quintessential nineteenth-century applications of modernism rationality to the putative irrationalities of crime have persisted. Now the underlying ideological or theoretical perspectives embrace multi-layered and complex narratives of crime causation involving variables and stigmata not visible to the pioneers of criminology. The no less ambitious contemporary goal of classification seeks to identify persistent, serial and high-risk offenders from others in criminalised populations for the purpose of predicting subsequent behaviour (recidivism) rather than to discover causal factors that distinguish between criminals and non-criminals (Farrington and Tarling 1983; Radzinowicz and Hood 1986; Lab and Whitehead 1990; Copas 1995).

The site for investigation remains the individual 'criminal' subject albeit a subject for whom now, in theory, unprecedented datum from birth to death may be assembled. The exponential growth of mass-computerised criminal justice records of individuals linked through time and place have provided criminological research with new opportunities to re-examine the question of differences among offenders. The sheer size of these databases, often containing whole populations, has reduced sampling error for known offenders and enabled precise modelling of the timing of events of interest (arrests, convictions and interventions). Traditional questions about individual differences and the effectiveness of interventions measured by recidivism have been readily adapted to address managerial concerns about risk minimisation.

Specific bio-statistical methodologies have evolved to interrogate these criminalised populations contained in the 'data banks' of individuals known to policing institutions. These statistical or actuarial technologies applied to a criminalised population developed directly from the methodologies that addressed similar questions about patterns of disease. For contemporary scholars the distribution and pathways of disease and the differential propensity of individuals to suffer them was a problem directly encountered in criminal science within the 'criminal career, "career" criminal' paradigm (Blumstein *et al.* 1986; Thornberry 1997). Epidemiological and criminological problems share a common social science in respect to the prevalence, frequency, severity and duration of their respective (and sometimes overlapping) events of interest. The identification of chronic high-risk offenders or career criminals ('dangerous' or habitual) depends on the measurement of these dimensions of the criminalised subject.

In the wake of the new information and statistical technologies the 'virtual' monitoring and surveillance of known offenders has become routine in many jurisdictions. Despite the ubiquity and ordinariness of this information/knowledge it must be harnessed (co-ordinated and linked), structured (into a database) and analysed to address problems of identification, classification and risk. In the 1970s the adaptation of bio-statistical methodologies (Boag 1949) to criminological problems enabled estimation of the *ultimate* probabilities of recidivism (Carr-Hill and Carr-Hill 1972; Maltz and McCleary 1977; Chung *et al.* 1991). Risk assessments based on longitudinal criminal event (acturarial) data are reflexive methodologies capable of continuous re-calibration of estimates of risk for an ever-changing population of offenders and their covariates. These actuarial methods model the crucial timing of events and offer multiple estimates of competing rather than single dichotomous risk (fail) criteria.

The rise of 'actuarial justice' or justice as risk re-distribution maybe theorised but the technology of prediction does not yet allow for a re-distribution such that 'justice becomes a matter of the just distributions of risk' (Erickson and Haggerty 1997: 40). This chapter illustrates the difficulties of risk prediction for the probabilistic estimation of the risk of re-arrest for sex offenders. The extent that a redistribution of the pains of intervention can be determined by notions such as the 'risk principle' and the utility of actuarial prediction are discussed in the conclusion.

The 'criminal career' paradigm and 'dangerousness'

The contemporary focus for concerted research on prediction was the Panel on Research on Criminal Careers (United States National Academy of Sciences Committee on Research on Law Enforcement and the Administration of Justice). Criminal career research in the view of this panel had a variety of important policy uses including:

> identifying variables associated with the most serious offenders (in terms of their criminal careers) so that such information may be used by decision makers, within legal and ethical constraints, to anticipate future

criminal activity by an offender about whom they must make a processing decision.

(Blumstein *et al*. 1986: 29)

Petersilia *et al*.'s (1978: 6) seminal criminal career study also 'sought to illuminate the development of serious criminal careers in the hope of identifying vulnerable times when appropriate interventions by the criminal justice system might best have reduced the offenders' threat to the community'.

Petersilia *et al*.'s (1978) study of the self-reported offending rates of only forty-nine Californian career criminals (selected on the basis of at least one robbery conviction and one prior prison term), reported 10,500 crimes over an average career of twenty years. The group averaged nearly two violent crimes or twelve offences of any kind per annum per person. For this select group there was some evidence of progression to more serious offending but little specialisation and a diminishing rate of offending with age. Diversity in offending was a key finding, and traditional assumptions about habitual offenders as professional or specialists were shown to be too simplistic. Block and van der Werff's (1991) six year follow-up study of 4,026 Dutch criminal careers found the nature of the offence or the mixture of types of crime was not predictive of a criminal career and age was not useful in defining 'high-risk' careers or the length of crime free periods. Concentrating on specialisation was likely to underestimate the number of serious or dangerous offenders found in the offender population. Prior arrest and the speed of re-arrest for a non-trivial offence were more important predictors of dangerous crime than the signal offence. They argue cogently that because identification was possible only after the career had been established, incapacitation was therefore less relevant than prevention of those likely to become career offenders.

High rates of offending by a few persistent persons revived interest in both prediction and the cost-benefits of incapacitation and built on the rudimentary fact established by the Philadelphia cohort study (Wolfgang *et al*. 1972, 1987) that a fraction of all known offenders (chronic offenders) accounted for a substantial proportion of all offending (Shannon *et al*. 1988; Home Office 1985; Moffitt *et al*. 1989). However, 'knowing retrospectively that some individuals are chronic is of little value unless one can identify them by characteristics which can be measured at a very early stage in an offending career' (Blumstein *et al*. 1985: 190).

Blumstein *et al*. (1986) and Blumstein *et al*. (1988) distinguish between research that focuses on criminal careers, as distinct from research on 'career' criminals. They acknowledge the problem of using the term 'career' in describing the behaviour of recidivists (especially in respect to incapacitation policies) and the need to describe the pattern of offending untainted by any presumption of career specialisation or progression to worse behaviour. In this regard they stimulate debate about what constitutes professional, habitual and dangerous offending. Blumstein *et al.* (1986) focus on the frequency or incidence of offending over time and draw an important distinction between *prevalence* (the proportion of offenders in the population or age group) of offending and *frequency* of offending. They found that while the prevalence of offending declines with age the frequency and severity of offending for older active offenders did not. However, as Farrington (1986, 1994) notes there have been several contrary studies and no conclusive picture has emerged about the relationship between frequency of offending and age despite a decline in participation with age. Nevertheless, tracking offenders over time enables the developmental aspects of criminal behaviour to be observed and accounting for all the dimensions of crime (participation, frequency, duration and severity) is relevant to establishing patterns or path-ways useful for prediction (Rolph and Chaiken 1987; Nagin *et al.* 1995). Actuarial estimates of risk of re-arrest are informed by developmental theo-ries of crime that apply empirically rather than theoretically derived criteria (Thornberry 1997; LeBlanc and Loeber 1998; Vold *et al.* 1998).

The criminal career paradigm suggested incapacitation of high-risk offenders was the most effective response to crime but the difficulties of accu-rately predicting prospectively chronic offenders has proved considerable. Consequently incapacitative strategies such as 'three-strikes' laws failed to have the impact theorised because they ignore the environmental contexts which effect recruitment (replacement) and retrospective identification was too late, while prospective approaches both under and over predict risks of offending. These difficulties weakened the salience of incapacitative approaches but nurtured the development of risk assessment, life course and developmental theories of crime. Assessment that ideally was tied to the iden-tified (criminogenic) needs of the offender, especially the career offender. The shift from an absolute standard of risk to a relative standard becomes necessary in a penal climate dominated by fiscal restraint and managerialist approaches.

Risk and the dangerous offender

Homicide, sex, robbery and other violent offenders constitute the imprecise definition of 'dangerousness' for which the term extreme or high risk applies especially to repeat offenders. The most difficult to detect among these offenders are those who relish the role of the criminal and transcend the usual patterns of offending driven by instrumental needs. The popular image of the 'dangerous' offender has been captured by the phenomenon of the serial killer or rapist as the supreme human predators (Jenkins 1994). The serial killer or rapist is portrayed as the archetypal random offender, especially dangerous because they are camouflaged from detection by their very ordinariness and therefore detectable only by the manipulation of the mass data accumulated on all subjects with probable risk.

Studies of serial offenders (Fox and Levin 1998; Keppel 1997) often show prior arrest or contact and certain modal pathways to such extremes of criminal behaviour. Many of the most dangerous of these offenders suffer personality disorders, such as psychopathy for which no specific treatments are known to lower risk (Hare 1991; Rice 1997). The career pathways of these rare serial predatory offenders are often notable for the absence of official records useful for prediction. Although retrospective analysis of their lives frequently shows substantial evidence of well-known risk factors including prior arrest these 'markers' seldom trigger prediction or surveillance (Weiner 1989; Douglas *et al*. 1994). Usually the whole criminal lifetime of the offender is the relevant period for prediction rather than a limited or administrative period for which the 'risk' is required for managerial purposes (bail, diversion and treatment decisions). Consequently only comprehensive 'virtual' life histories are capable of identifying probable candidates for these relatively rare behaviours. New classification and identification systems strive for comprehensiveness and seek to predict and detect probable serial offenders by locating them through the interrogation of databases.

Criminological prediction has three purposes: assessing the potential danger an individual poses to society, ascertaining the level of custody or surveillance required, and determining the therapeutic needs of an offender (Gabor 1986). The appraisal of 'risk' or dangerousness in penal law has been sometimes vague, ambiguous and variously defined. However, most serious sex and violent offences are included in legislative definitions of 'high-risk' offenders and are typical subjects of risk assessment, notification and special release conditions. However, the definition of risk often assumes a specific offence history for which a risk estimate is to be made in the criminal career and this determines the difficulty and accuracy of prediction. For example, there is high validity in predictions of re-arrest for general groups based on sex, race, age and cardinality but less precise the more specific the group and type of risk (offence) being assessed.

Risk and the 'careers' of sex offenders

Estimates of risk based on known sex offenders are criticised because the vast majority of offenders remain undetected (Koss 1996). While this position is cogent, it neglects long-standing evidence that many known sex offenders self-report high rates of sex and other offending often involving dozens or even hundreds of victims and events (Radzinowicz 1957; Groth *et al*. 1982; Abel and Rouleau 1990). The gap (or 'dark figure') between undetected and detected sexual offenders or 'true lambda' may not be as significant as supposed and known sex offenders remain a useful, if imperfect, group for assessing future risk and the effect of interventions upon sex and dangerous offending behaviour.

Statistical 'survival' or 'failure' rate analysis (Broadhurst and Maller 1990, 1992; Broadhurst and Loh 1995; Maller and Zhou 1996) is used to estimate the *ultimate* probability and rate of re-arrest for 2,785 offenders arrested in Western Australia for the first time for at least one sex offence between 1 April 1984 and 31 December 1994. Under half (41 per cent) were re-arrested by the cut off date for any offence, 20 per cent for either a sex or 'against the person' offences and 9.5 per cent for another sex offence but these fractions underestimate the risk because of censoring. Censored cases are those who have not failed at the cut-off date but who may do so, and counting these cases as 'successes' results in underestimates of the probability of re-arrest. An important feature of this method is that it takes account of the bias produced by censored follow-up times. Consequently the ultimate probability of re-arrest is estimated to be much higher at 0.61, for any offence, 0.51 for sex or against the person and 0.33 for repeat sex (see Table 6.1 and Broadhurst and Loh 1998).

Static variables such as Aboriginality, age, bail status, associated prison or community correction event, occupation, offence and offence count were available for every arrest event. Dynamic factors (for example, mental health, family support and drug or alcohol use) often found to be associated with differential risks of re-arrest are not available. The definition of recidivism was varied to include not only the probability of re-arrest for any offence (given at least one sex offence), or re-arrest for repeat sex offence but also re-arrest for another offence 'against the person' (homicide, assault, sex offences, kidnap and abduction, robbery/extortion and others) and constitute a classification of dangerous or violent offending. It was also important for rudimentary distinctions in types of sex offence because it is known that some offenders prefer certain victims and/or sex offences. We classified offences based on the original police charge, however, definitions had changed over the collection period due to the adoption of gender-neutral terminology and other changes. Thus a distinction based on the sex of the victim could not be made for offences against minors. The analysis showed that risk of repeat sex or violent offending did not vary significantly by the type of signal sex offence, although incest tended to have lower risks than other offences.

Table 6.1 summarises the ultimate probabilities and rate or speed of re-arrest for selected covariates and the three definitions of recidivism or 'risk' criteria. Age, Aboriginality, prior record and penalty, varied risks of re-arrest and/or the rate or speed in which offenders were re-arrested. Age varied the ultimate probabilities of recidivism but not the speed of re-arrest, interventions varied the speed of re-arrest but not the ultimate risks and race and prior record varied both the speed and probabilities of re-arrest. For repeat sex, there was little evidence of variation except for age and Aboriginality which differentiate risks for the entire arrest cohort regardless of signal offence (Maller *et al.* 1997). As in other studies young offenders had higher risks irrespective of the type of sex offence (Knight and Prentky 1993; Hagan *et al.* 1994). Thus static covariates and different criteria for 'failure' or risk significantly differentiate the probabilities of re-arrest.

Table 6.1   Summary of the probability and rate of re-arrest by type of re-arrest

Covariate	n	Any offence			Repeat sex			Against person		
		P	rate	n-fail	P	rate	n-fail	P	rate	n-fail
Non-Aborigine	2425	0.56[1]	0.36	883	0.19	0.15	228	0.29	0.24	391
Aborigine	360	0.97	0.71	266	0.27[2]	0.06	45	0.70[2]	0.13	160
All	2785	0.61	0.42	1149	0.33	0.03	273	0.51	0.09	551
Non-Aborigines										
No Prior Record	1635	0.51	0.18	432	0.14[2]	–	157	0.23	0.18	203
Prior Record	790	0.78	0.66	451	0.12[2]	–	71	0.50	0.18	188
Aborigines										
No Prior Record	110	0.98[ns]	0.28	67	0.18[2]	–	14	0.75	0.18	38
Prior Record	250	0.99[ns]	1.02	199	0.42[2]	–	31	0.91	0.18	122
Non-Aborigines Penalty[3]										
CBC	267	0.46[ns]	0.20	66	0.12[2]	–	13	0.36[ns]	0.07	22
Prison	375	0.39[ns]	0.28	69	0.14[2]	–	21	0.27[ns]	0.19	36
None	965	0.47[ns]	0.73	335	0.15[2]	–	111	0.23[ns]	0.88	122
All	1598	0.49[ns]	0.33	470	0.17[2]	–	145	0.30[ns]	0.13	223
Non-Aborigines Sex Offense Group										
Adult	1132	0.58	0.36	387	0.11[2]	–	87	0.41[ns]	0.09	167
Child	397	0.51	0.36	142	0.20[2]	–	58	0.45[ns]	0.09	79
Juvenile	246	0.73	0.36	124	0.05[2]	–	9	0.37[ns]	0.09	40
Incest	75	0.35	0.36	15	0.13[2]	–	6	0.30[ns]	0.09	8
Exposure	476	0.55	0.36	187	0.17[2]	–	60	0.40[ns]	0.09	86
Other	99	0.42	0.36	28	0.09[2]	–	8	0.26[ns]	0.09	11
Non-Aborigines Age Group										
<16	187	0.89	0.42	120	0.20	0.07	16	0.56	0.10	49
16–18	223	0.82	0.42	145	0.12	0.07	12	0.40	0.10	44
18–24	541	0.71	0.42	275	0.22	0.07	48	0.43	0.10	103
24–30	310	0.52	0.42	108	0.28	0.07	33	0.40	0.10	52
30–40	473	0.37	0.42	110	0.24	0.07	41	0.33	0.10	60
40–50	346	0.33	0.42	72	0.33	0.07	41	0.32	0.10	43
50+	344	0.23	0.42	53	0.28	0.07	37	0.28	0.10	40
All	2424	0.56	0.36	883	0.25	0.06	228	0.31	0.07	391

Legend: number of cases (n), the number of cases who fail by the cut-off date (n-fail), the ultimate probability of failure (P) and the rate or speed of re-arrest (lambda). When the model fails the Kaplan-Meier estimator at maximum (KME) or last fail time is substituted (Kaplan and Meier 1958). Note: 1= all P values significant at the p<0.01 level unless indicated by 'ns'; 2=iteration bounded, KME reported; 3=wilful exposure and juvenile offenders excluded from sample; ns=P values not significant, p>0.01; CBC=community-based order.

The slower rate of re-arrest found for offenders under community supervision accords with previous evaluations of the effects of these interventions on recidivism (Polvi and Pease 1991). Namely, that supervision at least delays the reoffending of recidivists. However, studies of treatment programmes for sex offenders have not shown consistent or significant impacts on reducing risks of re-arrest (Marshall 1996; Quinsey *et al*. 1993; Furby *et al*. 1989). Although the type of signal offence varied the probabilities of re-arrest for any offence there was less evidence of differences by offence type in respect to specialisation (repeat sex) or escalation (re-arrest for against the person). A significant relationship between type of sex offence and risks of specialisation and escalation was not found. Thus classification based on only repeating the signal or any sex offence would underestimate a sex offender's risks of 'dangerous' reoffending and the likelihood of general reoffending. However, as in previous studies extra-familial child molesters had higher risks of repeat sex than incest offenders and sexual assault offenders were more criminally versatile (Hanson *et al*. 1995; Quinsey *et al*. 1995; Hanson and Bussiere 1996).

The groups most likely to have higher probabilities of re-arrest, especially for further violence, were those from marginal socio-economic groups: Aborigines, young offenders, 'blue-collar' workers, unemployed and those with a prior non-sex offence arrest. Follow-up studies indicate that sexual recidivism is related to antisociality in much the same way as it is in criminal offending generally (Leib *et al*. 1998). This suggests that sex offending, especially by young offenders, is a form of aggression driven by 'hypermasculinities', low status, chronic and multiple adversity, rather than deviant sexual preferences (Knight and Prentky 1993; Richardson *et al*. 1995; Graves *et al*. 1996).

Absent or incomplete data on 'static' variables, imprecise definitions of different types of sex offending (especially victim status) and the absence of 'dynamic' variables which index behaviour on release, limited the guidance these estimates provide in describing the risks of re-arrest, specialisation and escalation. In addition, the relatively short follow-up time and sparse data indicated the need for longer follow-up and larger samples if more accurate estimates are to be made (Furby *et al*. 1989; Soothill and Gibbons 1976; Soothill and Francis 1998). Too few cases of repeat sex (the usual trigger for special intervention) were available to permit reliable estimation or account for the interactions of covariates. Nevertheless, it is possible to estimate the ultimate risk of re-arrest for another sex or 'dangerous offence' for different types of offenders with a sex offence history. The proportion specialising and/or progressing varied considerably depending on the sub-group so that it was possible to identify, in the crude way provided by static variables, those groups with elevated risks.

Recidivism research, used here as a means of summarising the complex 'careers' of sex offenders showed specialisation was relatively uncommon compared to escalating and general offending profiles. The proposition that sex offenders are driven by sexual preference, is difficult to sustain when the risk of repetition is compared with the risk of re-arrest for general or 'dangerous' offences. However, regardless of how 'failure' was defined or the 'career' summarised desistance was substantial. For example, about 44 per cent of non-Aborigines were never re-arrested, 70 per cent were never arrested for another 'dangerous' offence and 80 per cent were never re-arrested for a repeat sex offence. However, because we estimate *ultimate* probabilities the levels of recidivism are higher than the meta-analysis reported by Hanson and Bussiere (1996). As Leib *et al.* (1998: 100) note:

> the separation of sexual from violent offending makes it more difficult to identify dangerous persons. If the legal concern is only the prediction of sexual offending, the probability of such an event over a particular time will be lower for any given offender than if the probability of either a violent or sexual offence is at issue.

Prediction and the distribution of risk: the 'risk principle'

Copas and Marshall (1998) discern three 'insurmountable' difficulties in the development of a risk assessment instrument based on actuarial data of the kind illustrated above. First, the assumption that reoffending is correlated to reconviction or re-arrest and thus an index or surrogate for actual re-offending is unwarranted. Arrest represents an unknown fraction of true reoffending and variables (such as age, sex and race) which prove to be successful predictors of re-arrest may not be correlated with reoffending, especially certain types of offending or risk. Second, treatment or sentence type may also effect the risk prognosis but an objective estimate of risk is required prior to sentence, and, third, they argue criminal justice data poorly reflects the true sequence of offending due to 'pseudo-reconvictions'. However we do not need a perfectly efficient criminal justice process for prediction to have value. Detected crime can still be of value if the ratio of undetected to detected crime is approximately constant over time, across offences, and among different types of offender (Morgan *et al.* 1998).

Morgan *et al.* (1998) cite the New Zealand study of Fergusson *et al.* (1993) as one of the few Australasian studies to test differential ratios of detected to undetected crime. Self-reports were compared to official arrests and some degree of correlation found. This study confirmed high Maori rates of offending but Maori offenders were more likely to appear in official records than would be expected on the basis of self-reports. The higher risk of offending found for young Maori was explained by socio-economic, family and environmental factors and if taken into account, substantially weakens ethnicity as a predictor of offending. Similar, if less methodologically sophisticated, findings were reported by Cove (1992) for Aboriginal offenders.

In the context of penal managerialism the implications of actuarial risk technologies appear most relevant to the triage problem of allocating scarce penal and surveillance resources to maximise the reduction of risk. Limited resources make it necessary to give attention to those known offenders most likely to reoffend. At this level numerical guidance about probable risk is applied to the decision-making process that allocates different offenders to different levels of custodial or non-custodial supervision, treatment and services. Consequently recidivism (criminal event history) research has been enlisted to compare risks (competing risks) between types of offenders based on their legal liability and inherent characteristics so that a 'risk principle' may be realised.

The application of criminal career and recidivism research to the prediction of risk focuses on the factors (clinically or actuarially derived) that elevate risk, and many of these same factors overlap with the needs of offenders (see p.119). Offender programmes provided on the basis of risk are an efficient way for correctional agencies to deliver scarce services. In general, risk factors are those factors which have been demonstrated to be associated with reoffending, as measured by re-conviction, re-arrest, and self-reported reoffending. A distinction is made between static and dynamic risk factors. Static risk factors are those which are reasonably fixed and include measures of offending history, age, sex or race of the offender used in our example and are included in simple actuarial risk-based instruments. Dynamic risk factors are those which are open to change, and are more commonly found in clinically derived risk instruments. Bonta (1996) for example, includes alcohol and drug abuse, the presence of antisocial friends, quality of marital or family relationships, attitude to offending and financial management skills, and Quinsey et al. (1995) include the Psychopathy Check List, phallometric measures and static factors such as detailed offence history and interventions in the prediction of reoffending.

Andrews et al. (1990) identify three principles of effective intervention which they call the risk, need and responsivity principles. The risk principle asserts priority services are more effective with high-risk cases and that low-risk cases are best assigned minimal service. The need principle is connected with the selection of appropriate treatment targets and the responsivity principle refers to matching 'treatments' to the abilities and needs of the offender. In general, needs and risks are interrelated consisting of static risk factors, dynamic risk factors, criminogenic needs and non-criminogenic needs. Bonta (1996) emphasised the overlap between individual dynamic risk factors and criminogenic needs. In some risk instruments risk and needs are combined, while in others they are kept separate. Dynamic factors such as substance abuse and antisocial attitudes can contribute to the predictive utility of actuarial models of risk assessment based on static variables but are often poorly operationalised in record systems.

The problem of offender needs focuses on the deficits of offenders and the difficulty of discriminating which needs relate to the risk of reoffending. Offenders have many needs and these can be identified differently depending on who is making the assessment: judges, correctional officers, treatment workers, families, and offenders themselves (Lab and Whitehead 1990). Andrews *et al.* (1990) apply the concept of 'criminogenic needs' in order to describe needs which are related to offending behaviour and claim some needs are criminogenic while others are not. Andrews (1996) argues that poor self-esteem and feelings of personal inadequacy are not criminogenic needs, whereas antisocial attitudes, peer associations and behaviour, chemical dependency and poor self-control are related to offending.

The risk principle remains controversial because empirical support based on meta-analytical research for it has been extravagant. The principle relies on arbitrary definition of high and low risk, labels some offenders untreatable and underestimates the role of individual agency (Lab and Whitehead 1990; Losel 1993; Brown 1996; Cumberland and Boyle 1997). Losel (1993) finds support for the effectiveness of programmes that combine all three principles but his review of the relationship between offender selection and programme effectiveness, shows that meta-analyses do not find a consistent effect of offender characteristics on programme outcomes. Offenders learn to adapt (avoid re-arrest) or desist as a consequence of their penal experience or because of changes in circumstance regardless of their risk status and this accounts for desistance even for those offenders with long criminal careers. For example, Brown (1996) found the decision-making processes of New Zealand district parole boards influenced the relative success of paroled, as compared with released, high-risk offenders in avoiding re-conviction. For low-risk offenders there was no significant difference in outcome between parolees and those released unconditionally. He found the most important factor was the board's attitude to high-risk offenders who were motivated to succeed. These prisoners were likely to be released on parole and given access to programmes that helped their re-integration while unmotivated high-risk offenders were unlikely to be released on parole.

Individual agency is therefore relevant, however, it has been difficult to include intangibles (dynamic variables) like motivation, expectations and family support in an 'objective' risk assessment instrument when offenders know that certain responses will be to their advantage and others will not (Morgan *et al.* 1998; Grubin and Wingate 1996). Past behaviour is therefore never a complete guide and can only partly support the complex application of the risk principle. Administratively the demand for such guidance is often limited to the relevant probabilistic rate pertaining to an individual or groups within a specified, often short, time frame and not ultimate risks thus limiting the accuracy of probabilistic estimates and their criminological utility.

Prediction, risk and the re-invention of recidivism

Criminologists have attempted to map the relevant covariates or influences on the development of criminal careers in order to understand what contributes and inhibits the risk of offending. Given the (statistically) uniform nature of age-graded 'transitions' in criminal behaviour focus on changes in the status of dynamic factors such as substance abuse, family support, and employment are observed to effect the type (broadly classified) and frequency of offending. These pathways into and out of criminal behaviour are therefore patterned (Sampson and Laub 1993; Nagin *et al.* 1995). Although age, 'race', sex and cardinality are statistically dominant considerable scope exists for highly accurate estimates of recidivism for groups stratified on other life experience variables. Changes in the status of relevant covariates (indexes of life experience, especially out of age or transitional sequence) are signifiers that can be monitored in longitudinal databases and calibrated to estimate risk. The effect of arrest, surveillance, and incarceration on these pathways and 'careers' is a central but unresolved issue that introduces another factor relevant to the estimation of reoffending.

The re-interpretation of recidivism as risk has helped to revive the promise of correctional and incapacitation goals and shifted concern to a triage based on the probabilities of reoffending (Pratt 1996). Sherman *et al.* (1998), in a review of 'what works' in crime prevention, argued that intervention and treatment programmes designed with attention to risk factors can reduce rates of repeat offending. Thus the use of valid risk assessment is endorsed as a means for identifying offenders for whom 'targeted' intervention maybe effective. Risk assessment thus enables advances to the modest position held in the academy that 'some things work for some offenders' by providing rational means for the matching of offenders to appropriate interventions (Scherest *et al.* 1979).

Because offender data are degrees more extensive, accurate and complete than those available in the past to measure recidivism, they also enable new questions to be addressed by statistical analysis. Perhaps the most important of these is that the timing of events can be more efficiently modelled and risks can be compared by relative rather than absolute standards. However, the availability of such data banks and their concomitant surveillance power do not imply, as some scholars have suggested, that they can be operationalised as a new system of rational or 'actuarial punishments' (Feeley and Simon 1994; Hebenton and Thomas 1996). For practitioners of risk assessment abstract theorising about the (latent) dominance of 'actuarial justice' appears to rest on a wilful exaggeration of the value of such adjunctive techniques despite the qualifications typically stressed. Fundamental problems remain with respect to accurate or valid measures of the actual rate of offending or 'true lambda' and estimations of risk are based entirely on retrospective analysis for similar groups of known offenders and not individuals. Copas and Marshall (1998) stress that risk assessment models provide only a description of the correlates of risk and not an explanation of the causes of risk or predictions about individuals.

Despite these limitations the probabilistic estimation or prediction of risk of reoffending based on the behaviour of a like group of offenders has been regarded as a measure sufficient to meet the conditions implied by categorical if not selective versions of incapacitation theory. The appeal of 'three-strikes', sex offender and related dangerous offenders laws owe in part their existence to the well-supported assumption that repeat or persistent offenders are at higher risk of reoffending than first offenders and that past behaviour is the best predictor of future behaviour. How high-risk offenders develop is now a crucial focus for research on early prevention (LeBlanc and Loeber 1998). Estimates of recidivism (and qualified risk) are also more accurate and the utility of programme evaluation improved but error at the individual level remains significant. That is, those cases predicted to fail and classified 'at risk' but who do not and those not predicted to fail and classified 'not at risk' that do.

The notion of risk contains two elements: the certainty of an event (often a function of chronicity) and the gravity or severity of that event. Risk assessment technologies, in the context of criminal behaviour, attempt to predict the probability of a criminal event and the type or dangerousness of that criminal event often within a specified period (or follow-up). The identification and classification of high-risk offenders is problematic since this is associated with the imprecise notion of 'dangerousness' which in turn reflects everyday concerns about the likelihood of violent criminal events (Floud 1982). Usually it is sufficient to regard crimes against the person as defining the character of criminal dangerousness, however, an assumption is often made that such offenders are dangerous persons. Dangerousness is transformed to a quality or trait of a person not of an act and this is a basic source of conceptual error. A person is considered dangerous on the basis of past record but does not commit a violent reoffence (false positive) while another considered non-dangerous because of his past record does reoffend (false negative). This error and ambiguity can be attributed to the limitations of classifying offenders based on the types of offences (legally defined) in their criminal records and reflects tensions between the classification of *offences* and the classification of *offenders*. It also reflects uncertainty about the extent that official records (the usual basis for classification) reflect true offending, but irrespective of whether known offences index undetected offending, offence 'type' often becomes the substitute for a behaviour or offender 'type'.

Recidivism and criminal career research has shown that repeat offenders are usually generalists and that signal offence does not predict the type of subsequent offending should it occur. However, the criminal careers of persistent or 'chronic' offenders often show offence patterns of preference (or specialisation), escalation (progression to more grave offences), as well as variation in the frequency of offending. These offence patterns or transitions have proven complex and their predictive relevance from one event to the next limited. In practice those subjects with enough arrest, conviction or incarceration events to make the notion of career relevant, form the basis for attempts to predict subsequent criminal behaviour. In risk assessment we are required to deduce the character (dangerous or not) of a criminal career retrospectively and estimate the likelihood of future offending. Prediction is therefore based on the criminal events (and other static and dynamic covariates) observed for designated subjects at a given time or stage in a possible career continuum for whom sufficient numbers of similar subjects reoffend past that point for an estimate (comparison) to be made. Risk technologies estimate what the reconviction or re-arrest rate will be for groups of 'like' offenders who match the individual of interest on the set of variables or factors available.

Statistical methods of prediction, when applied to individuals, entail an inevitable degree of built-in error, since these methods define groups with varying rates of success or failure. In such statistical analysis it is not assumed that all cases will fail or reoffend but clinical prediction attempts to predict for the individual offender and in theory can be 100 per cent successful. However, there is strong evidence that clinical prediction is not in practice as reliable as prediction based on actuarial methods (Monahan 1996; Leib *et al*. 1998). Risk assessments provide a benchmark against which decision-makers in the criminal justice system can test the subjective assessment made in a particular case. Most researchers agree that clinical and judicial predictions can be assisted by actuarial risk assessments, especially if dynamic and static variables can be successfully combined. Risk assessments are not designed to replace but to aid professional judgements of risk. Attempts at establishing principles, although limited, serve to make the criteria for risk-based decisions more transparent and can help realise greater fairness and consistency. Actuarial risk technologies combined with longitudinal data construction, provide a solid foundation for future classification, profiling and risk management but like Cassandra's predictions they are perhaps fated to be disregarded.

References

Abel, G. and Rouleau, J. (1990) 'The Nature and Extent of Sexual Assault', in W.L. Marshall, D.R. Laws and H.E. Barbaree (eds), *Handbook of Sexual Assault: Issues, Theories, and Treatment of the Offender*, New York: Plenum.

Andrews, D. (1996) 'The Principles of Effective Intervention', in A. Harland (ed.), *Choosing Correctional Options that Work*, Thousand Oaks, CA: Sage.

Andrews, D., Bonta, J. and Hoge, R. (1990) 'Classification for Effective Rehabilitation: Rediscovering Psychology', *Criminal Justice and Behavior* 17: 19–52.

Block, C. and van der Werff, C. (1991) *Initiation and Continuation of a Criminal Career*, Deventer: Kluwer.

Blumstein, A., Cohen, J. and Farrington, D. (1988) 'Criminal Career Research: Its Value for Criminology', *Criminology* 26: 1–36.

Blumstein, A., Cohen, J., Roth, J.A. and Visher, C.A. (1986) *Criminal Careers and Career Criminals*, Washington, DC: National Academy Press.

Blumstein, A., Farrington, D.P. and Moitra, S. (1985) 'Delinquency Careers: Innocents, Desisters and Persisters', in N. Morris and M. Tonry (eds), *Crime and Justice: An Annual Review of Research*, vol. 6, Chicago, IL: University of Chicago Press.

Boag, J.W. (1949) 'Maximum Likelihood Estimates of the Proportion of Patients Cured by Cancer Therapy', *Journal of the Royal Statistical Society* BII: 15–44.

Bonta, J. (1996) 'Risk-needs Assessment and Treatment', in A. Harland (ed.), *Choosing Correctional Options that Work*, Thousand Oaks, CA: Sage.

Broadhurst, R. and Loh, N. (1995) 'The Probabilities of Re-arrest for the Apprehended Western Australian Population 1984–1993', *Journal of Quantitative Criminology* 12: 275–90.

—— (1998) 'The Risks of Sex Offender Re-arrest', 23rd Annual conference of the American Society of Criminology, 19–22 November 1997, San Diego, CA.

Broadhurst, R. and Maller, R. (1990) 'The Recidivism of Prisoners Released for the First Time: Reconsidering the Effectiveness Question', *Australian and New Zealand Journal of Criminology* 23: 88–104.

—— (1992) 'The Recidivism of Sex Offenders in the Western Australia Prison Population', *British Journal of Criminology* 32: 50–84.

Brown, M. (1996) 'Refining the Risk Concept: Decision Contexts a Factor in Mediating the Relation between Risk and Program Effectiveness', *Crime and Delinquency* 42: 435–55.

Carr-Hill, G.A. and Carr-Hill, R.A. (1972) 'Re-conviction as a Process', *British Journal of Criminology* 12: 35–43.

Chung, C., Schmidt, P. and Witte, A.D. (1991) 'Survival Analysis: A Survey', *Journal of Quantitative Criminology* 7: 59–98.

Copas, J. (1995) 'On Using Crime Statistics for Prediction', in M. Walker (ed.), *Interpreting Crime Statistics*, Oxford: Clarendon Press.

Copas, J. and Marshall, P. (1998) 'The Offender Group Reconviction Scale; a Statistical Reconviction Score for Use by Probation Officers', *Applied Statistics* (Part 1) 47: 159–71.

Cove, J.J. (1992) 'Aboriginal Over-representation in Prisons: What Can be Learned from Tasmania', *Australian and New Zealand Journal of Criminology* 25: 156–68.

Cumberland, A.K. and Boyle, G.J. (1997) 'Psychometric Prediction of Recidivism: Utility of the Risk Needs Inventory', *Australian and New Zealand Journal of Criminology* 30: 72–86.

Douglas, J.E., Burgess, A.W., Burgess, A.G. and Ressler, R.K. (1994) *Crime Classification Manual: A Standard System for Investigating and Classifying Crimes*, New York: Josey-Bass.

Erikson, R. and Haggerty, P. (1997) *Policing the Risk Society*, Toronto, Ont.: University of Toronto Press.

Farrington, D. (1986) 'Age and Crime', in N. Morris and M. Tonry (eds), *Crime and Justice: An Annual Review of Research*, vol. 7, Chicago, IL: University of Chicago Press.

Farrington, D. (1994) 'Human Development and Criminal Careers', in M. Maguire, R. Morgan and R. Reiner (eds), *The Oxford Handbook of Criminology*, Oxford: Oxford University Press.

Farrington, D. and Tarling, R. (1983) 'Criminological Prediction: an Introduction', in D. Farrington and R. Tarling (eds), *Prediction in Criminology*, Albany, NY: SUNY Press.

Fergusson, D., Horwood, L. and Lynskey, M. (1993) 'Ethnicity, Social Background and Young Offending: A 14-year Longitudinal Study', *Australian and New Zealand Journal of Criminology* 26: 155–70.

Feeley, M. and Simon, J. (1994) 'Actuarial Justice: the Emerging New Criminal Law', in D. Nelken (ed.), *The Futures of Criminology*, London: Sage.

Floud, J. (1982) 'Dangerousness and Criminal Justice', *British Journal of Criminology* 22: 213–28.

Fox, J.A. and Levin, J. (1998) 'Multiple Homicide: Patterns of Serial and Mass Murder', in M. Tonry (ed.), *Crime and Justice: Annual Review of Research*, Chicago, IL: University of Chicago Press.

Furby, L., Weinrott, M.R. and Blackshaw, L. (1989) 'Sex Offender Recidivism', *Psychological Bulletin* 105: 3–30.

Gabor, T. (1986) *The Prediction of Criminal Behaviour: Statistical Approaches*, Toronto, Ont.: University of Toronto Press.

Graves, R.B., Openshaw, D.K., Ascione, F.R. and Eriksen, S.L. (1996) 'Demographic and Parental Characteristics of Youthful Sexual Offenders', *International Journal of Offender Therapy and Comparative Criminology* 40: 300–17.

Groth, A.N., Longo, R.E. and McFadin, J.B. (1982) 'Undetected Recidivism Among Rapists and Child Molesters', *Crime and Delinquency* 23: 450–8.

Grubin, D. and Wingate, S. (1996) 'Sexual Offence Recidivism: Prediction versus Understanding', *Criminal Behaviour and Mental Health* 6: 349–59.

Hagan, M.P., King, R.P. and Patros, L. (1994) 'Recidivism Among Adolescent Perpetrators of Sexual Assault Against Children', *Journal of Offender Rehabilitation* 21: 127–37.

Hanson, R.K., Scott, H. and Steffy, R.A. (1995) 'A Comparison of Child Molestors and Non-sexual Criminals', *Journal of Research in Crime and Delinquency* 32: 308–24.

Hanson, R.K. and Bussiere, M.T. (1996) 'Sex Offender Risk Predicators: A Summary of Research Results', *Forum on Corrections Research* 8: 10–12.

Hare, R.D. (1991) *The Revised Psychopathy Checklist*, Toronto, Ont.: Multi-Health Systems.

Hebenton, B. and Thomas, T. (1996) ' "Tracking" sex offenders', *The Howard Journal of Criminal Justice* 35: 97–112.

Home Office (1985) *Participation in Crime: the 1953 Birth Cohort*, London: HMSO.

Jenkins, P. (1994) *Using Murder: The Social Construction of Serial Homicide*, New York: Aldine De Gruyter.

Kaplan, E.L. and Meier, P. (1958) 'Non-parametric Estimation from Incomplete Observations', *American Statistical Association Journal* June: 457–81.

Keppel, R.D. (1997) *Signature Killers*, New York: Simon and Schuster.

Knight, R.A. and Prentky, R.A. (1993) 'Exploring Characteristics for Classifying Juvenile Sex Offenders', in H.E. Barbaree, W.L. Marshall and S.M. Hudson (eds), *The Juvenile Sex Offender*, New York: The Guildford Press.

Koss, M.P. (1996) 'The Measurement of Rape Victimization in Crime Surveys', *Criminal Justice and Behavior* 23: 55–69.

Lab, S. and Whitehead, J. (1990) 'From "Nothing Works" to "The Appropriate Works": The Latest Stop on the Search for the Secular Grail', *Criminology* 28: 405–17.

LeBlanc, M. and Loeber, R. (1998) 'Developmental Criminology Updated', *Crime and Justice: Annual Review of Research*, vol. 23: 115–98.

Lieb, R., Quinsey, V. and Berliner, L. (1998) 'Sexual Predators and Social Policy', *Crime and Justice: Annual Review of Research* vol. 23: 43–112.

Losel, F. (1993) 'The Effectiveness of Treatment in Institutional and Community Settings', *Criminal Behaviour and Mental Health* 3: 416–37.

Maller, R., Morgan, F. and Loh, N. (1997) 'An Analysis of the Effects of Offenders' Ages on Re-Arrest Probabilities in the Western Australian Population', unpublished research report, Nedlands: Crime Research Centre, University of Western Australia.

Maller, R. and Zhou, S. (1996) *Survival Analysis with Long Term Survivors*, Chichester: Wiley.

Maltz, M.D. and McCleary, R. (1977) 'The Mathematics of Behaviour Change', *Evaluation Quarterly* 1: 421–38.

Marshall, W.L. (1996) 'Assessment, Treatment and Theorising about Sex Offenders', *Criminal Justice and Behavior* 23: 162–99.

Moffitt, T.E., Mednick, S.A. and Gabrielli, W.F. (1989) 'Predicting Careers of Criminal Violence: Descriptive Data and Predispositional Factors', in D.A. Brizer and M. Crowner (eds), *Current Approaches to the Prediction of Violence*, Washington, DC: American Psychiatric Press Inc.

Monahan, J. (1996) 'Violence Prediction: The Past Twenty Years and the Next Twenty Years', *Criminal Justice and Behavior* 23: 107–21.

Morgan, F., Morgan, N. and Morgan, I. (1998) *Risk Assessment in Sentencing and Corrections* (report to the Australian Criminology Research Council, project 22/95–96), Nedlands: Crime Research Centre, University of Western Australia.

Nagin, D.S., Farrington, D.P. and Moffitt, T.E. (1995) 'Life-course Trajectories of Different Types of Offenders', *Criminology* 33: 111–39.

Petersilia, J., Greenwood, P. and Lavin, M. (1978) *Criminal Careers of Habitual Felons*, Santa Monica, CA: Rand Corp.

Polvi, N. and Pease, K. (1991) 'Parole and It's Problems: A Canadian-English Comparison', *The Howard Journal of Criminal Justice* 30: 218–30.

Pratt, J. (1996) 'Reflections on Recent Trends Towards the Punishment of Persistence', *Crime, Law and Social Change* 25: 243–64.

Quinsey, V.L., Harris, G.T., Rice, M.E. and LaLumiere, M.L. (1993) 'Assessing Treatment Efficacy in Outcome Studies of Sex Offenders', *Journal of Interpersonal Violence* 8: 512–23.

Quinsey, V.L., Rice, M.E. and Harris, G.T. (1995) 'Actuarial Prediction of Sexual Recidivism', *Journal of Interpersonal Violence* 10: 85–105.

Radzinowicz, L. (1957) *Sexual Offences*, London: Macmillan.

Radzinowicz, L. and Hood, R. (1986) *A History of English Criminal Law: Emergence of Penal Policy*, vol. 5, London: Stevens.

Rice, M.E. (1997) 'Violent Offender Research and Implications for the Criminal Justice System', *American Psychologist* 52: 414–23.

Richardson, G., Graham, F., Bhati, S.R. and Kelly, T.P. (1995) 'A British Sample of Sexually Abusive Adolescents: Abuser and Abuse Characteristics', *Criminal Behaviour and Mental Health* 5: 197–208.

Rolph, J. and Chaiken, J. (1987) *Identifying High-Rate Serious Criminals from Official Records*, Santa Monica, CA: Rand.

Sampson, R.J. and Laub, J.J. (1993) *Crime in the Making: Pathways and Turning Points Through Life*, Cambridge, MA: Harvard University Press.

Scherest, L., White, S. and Brown, E. (1979) *The Rehabilitation of Criminal Offenders: Problems and Prospects*, Washington, DC: National Academy of Sciences.

Shannon, L.W., McKim, J.L., Curry, J.P. and Haffner, L.J. (1988) *Criminal Career Continuity: Its Social Context*, New York: Human Sciences Press Inc.

Sherman, L., Gottfredson, D., Mackenzie, D., Eck, J., Reuter, P. and Bushway, S. (1998) *Preventing Crime: What Works, What Doesn't, What's Promising*, Washington, DC: National Institute of Justice.

Soothill, K. and Francis, B. (1998) 'Reviewing the Pantheon of Sexual Offending', paper presented to the 12th International Congress of Criminology, 24–9 August, Seoul, Korea.

Soothill, K., Jack, A. and Gibbons, T.C.N. (1976) 'Rape: A 22 Year Cohort Study', *Medicine, Science and the Law* 16: 62–9.

Thornberry, T.P. (1997) 'Introduction: Some Advantages of Developmental and Life-course Perspectives for the Study of Crime and Delinquency', T.P. Thornberry (ed.), *Advances in Criminological Theory*, vol. 7, New Brunswick: Transaction Publishers.

Vold, G.B., Bernard, T.J. and Snipes, J.B. (1998) *Theoretical Criminology*, 4th edn, New York: Oxford University Press.

Weiner, N. (1989) 'Violent Criminal Careers and "Violent Career Criminals": An Overview of the Research Literature', in N. Weiner and M. Wolfgang (eds), *Violent Crime, Violent Criminals*, Newbury: Sage.

Wolfgang, M.E., Thornberry, T.P. and Figlio, R.M. (1972) *Delinquency in a Birth Cohort*, Chicago, IL: University of Chicago Press.

—— (1987) *From Boy to Man, From Delinquency to Crime*, Chicago, IL: University of Chicago Press.

Chapter 7

Risk and blame in criminal justice controversies

British press coverage and official discourse on prison security (1993–6)[1]

Richard Sparks

In Britain in recent times the penal realm has been an arena of marked contention and political controversy. During the 1990s the passions and anxieties that surround the punishment of offenders have often been apparent in acute forms. At first sight there is nothing new in this, nor exclusive to that country. The politicisation of punishment is an antique and recurrent, even in some versions of the argument a *cyclical*, phenomenon. However, as I will seek to show here with reference to a particular sequence of events that seem to me to crystallise and condense some contemporary concerns quite illuminatingly, each such iteration or recycling also includes new elements that are more specific to their time and circumstances. Thus while the story that I relate in this paper concerns one of the most 'classic' varieties of prison controversy, namely a series of dramatic escapes, their representation and reception within the public culture of Britain in the 1990s also betrays some particular features of the surrounding conceptual and ideological environment. Among these figurations are two that are expressly marked as 'new' in much current commentary, namely the so-called 'new penology' and the 'new managerialism' (or 'new public sector management').

I outline certain aspects of each of these 'new' sightings on the penal landscape as they can be said to have infiltrated the practice and politics of imprisonment in Britain in the 1990s in slightly more detail below. Let us simply note briefly at the outset that insofar as they are indeed 'new' their novelty resides, or at least *emerges*, primarily at the level of *technique* (of the specialist knowledges deployed by and expected from penal professionals). Yet the changes that they might herald in the nature, scope and political sensitivity of penal practice may be much more far-reaching than this would initially seem to suggest. Thus, if there is indeed anything substantially novel and different about the 'new penology' it would lie in the claims made by penal practitioners to be able reliably to anticipate and to forestall offender risk. During a period when some of the older claims of the penal system to do something useful (to resettle or rehabilitate on the one hand, or to deter on the other) looked threadbare and vulnerable such a promise might begin to displace them as a major rationale for its operation. Such a posture might emerge only *faute de mieux* and in a spirit of some pessimism – if the penal system can do nothing else it can at least contain and supervise those who bear intolerable quotients of risk. Nevertheless its dynamic would be expansionist. It would urge longer sentences for many, and *indeterminate* confinements for some, of those who entered the orbit of the penal apparatus. And when it broke the bounds of the specialist jargons and practices of the professionals and entered public consciousness it would tend to do so in the form of slogans and sound-bites promising (if nothing else) some shreds of safety and protection through eliminative confinement of the risk carriers – 'Three Strikes and You're Out', 'Prison Works!'. In so doing it would have a further effect. It would re-focus attention to the legitimating principles of the penal system squarely upon its effectiveness in delivering what it would chiefly promise, namely confinement and the security of its perimeters. Among the questions I want to explore in this essay, therefore, are: To what extent does this thumbnail sketch capture important features of British penal controversies in the 1990s? But at the same time in what ways do such novelties also share the turf with other perhaps older, perhaps even ostensibly incompatible passions, anxieties, principles and demands?

Addressing penal politics

The main bones of contention in recent British public debate are in outline quite familiar, and by no means exclusively 'new'. They include both the capacity of the penal system to deliver justice (however defined by the contending parties) and its capacity to contribute to the safety of an uneasy public. Some of the main lines of controversy, especially in the period 1993–7 when the then Home Secretary Michael Howard and senior members of the judiciary often stood in open confrontation over matters of sentencing and the release of prisoners, are matters of record and the positions are well known. The points of difference between Mr Howard and, among others, the late Lord Taylor, Lord Bingham and Lord Woolf and with the distinguished retired such as Lords Ackner and Donaldson (and some of his own predecessors in office) have been widely aired in the press as well as receiving increasingly comprehensive scholarly attention (Windlesham 1996; Rozenberg 1997). I will largely try to avoid re-telling the more familiar features of this story here.

However, not all aspects of the penal politics of Britain in the 1990s – even were we to draw a line under 30 April 1997 and the sweeping election victory of Tony Blair's New Labour – appear to have been equally well understood. Here I draw attention to one or two of these less remarked (or at least less readily resolved) questions. I have three kinds of issues in mind. These are broadly questions of: (i) political culture; (ii) developments in penal practice and administration; and (iii) some open conceptual problems in understanding processes of change in the penal realm. I want to approach these issues through a concrete example, namely the press and official reactions to the escapes from Whitemoor and Parkhurst prisons in 1994/5. These were very *visible* events, and their immediate aftermaths (culminating in the dismissal of the then Director General of the Prison Service, Derek Lewis) were also acutely controversial. Yet it seems arguable that their longer-term significance lies in much less visible arenas, namely in the reconstruction of major aspects of prison management and regimes. Perhaps something similar may be said for other issues in penal policy and policing too; in which case my little story might be a cautionary tale with a certain exemplary value. I suggest that most academic commentators have lately rather ducked the challenge of thinking through how such contingent events, and the low politicking that surrounds them (i.e. the kinds of occasions when penal questions enter the sphere of press interest and public controversy) pose problems for the ways in which we think about the position and condition of the penal realm in contemporary Western societies.

This lack of interest has two sides. First, the question of what happened to English penal politics in the early and mid 1990s appears too obvious to warrant much further reflection. In other words there is a standard story: the Home Office fell into the hands of an ambitious and opportunist right-wing politician; it did so during a period of political difficulty for the incumbent party which (in the time-honoured manner of regimes menaced by economic problems and lack of popularity) sought to arouse and play upon the resentments and anxieties of the populace; this was accentuated by external pressures such as the Bulger murder and the acute public prominence of criminal justice questions that ensued; moreover the rising popularity of the then opposition, successfully claiming political ground on law and order questions, ratcheted up the pressure to provide clear demonstrations of toughness. End of story. This version of events seems to me to be both true and inadequate. It fails to pose some major questions such as – why exactly was the penal realm the arena on which so much prestige and importance in terms of political legitimacy and authority were staked? what in detail were the affinities between the specific measures proposed and the predominant social and political beliefs and outlooks of the period? why is this so much more a *British* story (in parallel with some rather similar American stories) than, say, a German or Swedish one?

Second, I think it can be argued that for many criminologists and students of penality the action was elsewhere. They were much more interested in what they saw as the longer-term, infrastructural developments in the criminal justice and penal systems to detain themselves for long over passing headlines and platform rhetoric. We have become much more preoccupied with questions of 'managerialism', the rise of the 'audit culture', the privatisation of former public monopolies and with transnational tendencies in police co-operation and so on than with the ebb and flow of penal debate, short-run fluctuations in the prison population and other such episodic matters.

For many academics, therefore, the question of the politicisation of punishment is both rather obvious (old-hat even) and of secondary importance. I think both these views (if we could find anybody to put their hand up to subscribing to them) would be mistakes. What enjoins the exercise of sociological imagination is rather the task of attempting to think through the relationship between some quite local, momentary and even accidental events (such as a prison escape) and the larger landscape on which they occur, some of whose features moreover are revealed in sharper perspective by looking in some detail at those minutiae. In other words I want to argue that if we wish to understand what has been happening in penal politics and penal policy over this period and if beyond that we want to grasp some important features of the position of the penal realm in the larger play of political and ideological conflicts in contemporary societies then we need to think seriously about events and processes that escape the control of the key actors (however much they seek to manipulate them and turn them to advantage). We need, that is to say, a sociology of (as Mary Douglas puts it) the 'dirty side' of the subject. We continue to need, therefore, a *sociology of the scandal*.

Managerialism, populism and risk

Tony Bottoms (as is often the case) sums up some of the peculiarities of the recent politics of punishment concisely. On the one hand we see a preoccupation with management systems, administrative structures, performance indicators and so on. These are features that Bottoms terms 'systemic managerialism'. On the other hand there is the tendency for politicians and moral entrepreneurs to reach over the heads of the professionals to the feelings and intuitions of voters and newspaper readers. This is what Bottoms terms 'populist punitiveness' (Bottoms 1995). These tendencies seem somewhat disparate and in tension. I will argue, using the illustration of the escapes, that we can see ways in which they directly affect one another. Before entering on a discussion of the escapes I want to make a brief excursion into some of the theoretical issues that arise here.

One well-known starting point is Feeley and Simon's (1992) thesis that an emergent 'new penology' could be discerned which had begun to shift the balance of penal practice increasingly towards the prediction and management of offender risk using 'actuarial' techniques (as distinct from either clinical or social work principles as traditionally understood). There are numerous developments in the British criminal justice and penal systems that might plausibly be fitted under this kind of description, though they have only recently begun to be explored using this vocabulary (see variously Garland 1996, 1997; Hebenton and Thomas 1996; Kemshall *et al*. 1997).

The new penology is in the first place a theory of professional and expert discourses and practices. Like much other work that in some degree aligns with the views of the later Foucault (1991) on 'governmentality', it is primarily concerned with how responsible authorities construe and periodi- cally reappraise the objects of their concern and the expert systems that they institute in order to govern their more obdurate and troublesome features. Work in this vein is also concerned with how certain political 'rationalities' (in the present case that of 'neo-liberalism') select and indeed generate novel forms of government. It has been quite rapidly recognised (not least by Feeley and Simon themselves) that there are many aspects of contemporary penal developments which this perspective leaves unilluminated. These notably include the often intense emotional investments that people continue to make in questions of punishment and the symbolic weight that punishment still carries in the culture and politics of our times (see e.g. Sarat 1997). Penal issues retain (and have perhaps indeed intensified) their historic proximity to the questions of legitimate authority, competence, trust and consent (Simon and Feeley 1995).

This has marked implications for how we should theorise 'risk' in relation to the penal realm. This recognition does not necessitate the abandonment of the new penology perspective or of cognate views that have regard mainly to the managerial and calculative aspects of criminal justice practice, but neither does it leave them untouched. Nor can we rest content with a sepa- ratist division of labour between those whose interests lie in the infrastructure of penal practice (where developments redolent of the 'new penology' indeed seem to continue apace) and those who are principally interested in public discourse and overt politics. Rather I am preoccupied by the question: how do the professional (calculative, pragmatic, results-led) and public (rhetorical, performative) 'faces' of the penal question intersect, and with what consequences for each? For example, it seems readily apparent that practitioners in prisons, probation or parole know themselves to be working in an arena characterised by marked political risks. Their work comes into unwelcome focus when 'mistakes' or 'accidents' occur. This knowledge constrains the range of choices that they can feasibly make and influences the systems they institute for coping with their work. Risks arising in one arena (the media politics of punishment) direct activity in another (calculating and managing offender risk). Sometimes the political risks become so large that almost any risk-taking by practitioners comes to seem unaffordably foolhardy. In this paper I demonstrate a case in point, namely how trouble incurred at the political level (a dispute over account- ability for two somewhat exceptional prison escapes) contributed to a marked alteration in mundane practice (an intensification of security and control measures throughout the prison system).[2]

There is here a conceptual problem. If analysts of criminal justice and penality deploy a concept of risk that is unduly self-limiting they will be unable to address the interface between the public-political and backstage-professional worlds. That question requires attention to the ways in which risks are *communicated* and how they are *politicised*. Among the most eloquent explorations of this point known to me is that proposed by Douglas in *Risk and Blame* (1992). Douglas comments wonderingly on the 'innocence' of those who seem to suggest that risk can be domesticated, kept strictly within the bounds of probability calculations. In Douglas' view our rationalities of risk-management exist to *address* dread, danger and catastrophe; they do not thereby eliminate them nor drain them of their meaning. Moreover, Douglas argues, risk comes into public focus in 'forensic moments' – i.e. when the question of accountability arises (is someone to blame?).

In the wider literatures on the social nature of risk (i.e. largely outside the domain of current criminology) there have been numerous attempts to tease out the implications of this sort of position. This is perhaps most evident in studies of industrial accidents and environmental threats. There it is increasingly recognised that technological risks generate not only corresponding forms of expert technical assessment and management but also chronically give rise to public controversies, including passionate feelings of anger, anxiety and recrimination (cf. Beck 1992a, 1992b). While there are advocates of 'hard science' positions who remain apt to interpret all such public responses as manifestations of irrationality and sources of interference with the dispassionate business of risk assessment others insist that the questions of *how* awareness of risk enters public consciousness, *how* it is communicated and deliberated and how *decisions* on risk acceptability are made are intrinsic and permanent issues for any risk domain (see on this Rayner 1992; Kasperson 1992; and the debates collected in Hood and Jones 1996).

Many of these debates have clear analogues in the fields of crime and punishment. The long and often rather stymied debate on the rationality or otherwise of the fear of crime is one (Sparks 1992; Walklate 1997), the closely related question of the depiction of crime and law enforcement in mass media is clearly another. Indeed both the literatures of risk-communication and criminology have quite independently developed notions of 'amplification' (Kasperson 1992; Cohen and Young 1974). In studies of crime in the media the position most directly germane to Douglas' cultural theory of risk is probably that developed by Ericson *et al.* (1991). Ericson *et al.* argue that stories of deviance, incompetence and failure are integral to the representation of order and that the processes of blame-allocation that follow are integral to activities of reform and repair in legal and administrative contexts. In other words *personalised* and *dramatised* narratives of particular *events* have an intrinsic and recursive relation to *systemic* processes and the varieties of continuity and change that are apparent therein.

Brecht says somewhere that in the modern world 'we gain our knowledge of life in catastrophic form'; and this seems resonant both with the literature of technological hazards and with the lessons of studies of crime in the media. It suggests to me that concepts of risk that are too one-dimensional (where programmes of risk regulation are seen as unfolding by their own inner logic without a detailed understanding of their cultural and political contexts) leave too much unilluminated. It would also seem to suggest that *particular* events, stories and controversies can in their aftermaths exercise profound effects, both at the level of popular consciousness and of political, legislative and system-level change. In the United States one can point to certain names and stories that have taken on totemic status – Willie Horton springs to mind; so too in a different way does Rodney King; and differently again do Megan Kanka, Kimba Reynolds and Polly Klaas. In Britain the killing of Jamie Bulger and the enormity of Dunblane were events that have marked the whole ethos of penal politics in the 1990s. So too, I will argue, in a further and less immediately obvious way, were the escapes that took place from Whitemoor and Parkhurst prisons in 1994 and 1995.

Is there then a theoretically relevant similarity between (in the present case) a prison riot or escape and the kinds of accidents, hazard inquiries and so on that more often occupy social scientists interested in the public perception of risk (cf. Wynne 1992)?[3] In addressing this question I use a brief illustrative case study of the press coverage of the escapes from Whitemoor and Parkhurst prisons in 1994/5 and their aftermaths both for the *dramatis personae* most directly concerned *and* for the subsequent conduct of prison management.

Why am I claiming that such a case study (of such exceptional episodes) is relevant to the theoretical assessment of criminal justice as low-visibility risk-management? There are two main reasons. First, the more strongly the credibility or authority of an institution is staked on a capacity to protect the public from risk the more scandalous demonstrated cases of its failure to do so are, and the more drastic their impacts are likely to be. In this respect instances of system failure are not sharply separable from the particular political projects that animate them (O'Malley 1992), nor from the degrees of trust invested in them (Nelken 1994), nor from other features of their surrounding political culture (Melossi 1993, 1994).

Second, because such special administrative systems as prisons almost *only* come to public notice under conditions of scandal, and because they do so within the regimes of representation characteristic of mass media, it would be inadequate to argue that 'managerialism' and 'populist punitiveness' (Bottoms 1995) merely co-exist as elements of contemporary penality. The relationship between them is more dynamic and recursive than this. It seems more likely that the techniques of risk management and their episodic representation in popular culture engender new compromise formations. Systems of punishment therefore necessarily hybridise curious and ostensibly contradictory elements (elements that only exist in pure form in their ideal-typical models).

I therefore want to try to indicate some ways in which the political culture of 1990s Britain conditioned the representation and reception of two major breaches of prison security in 1994/5 and the struggles over interpretation and accountability that ensued. The intense press reaction to breaches of prison security which I outline below provides a clue, I will argue, to the analysis of the structures of feeling that characterised British public discourse about crime and punishment at this time. And the nature of the official reaction to those breaches indicates the state's sensitivity to their importance.

The escapes, the press and the aftermaths

In September 1994 six Irish Republican prisoners briefly escaped from the Special Security Unit (SSU) at Whitemoor prison in Cambridgeshire. In the course of their recapture a prison officer was shot and wounded in the stomach. The shot was fired from a gun that had been smuggled into the prison in pieces and reassembled. A second gun failed to fire.

In January 1995 three inmates escaped from Parkhurst dispersal prison on the Isle of Wight.[4] They remained at large for a number of days. This event coincided almost exactly with the suicide in his cell at Birmingham prison of Frederick West.

In each case substantial inquiries were initiated – by Sir John Woodcock (former HM Chief Inspector of Constabulary) in the case of Whitemoor (Woodcock 1994) and General Sir John Learmont in respect of Parkhurst (Learmont 1995). The interval between the escapes and the publication of the Woodcock and Learmont reports gave both stories an extended life. This was particularly true in the case of Parkhurst because the appearance of the report precipitated the dismissal by the Home Secretary of the Director General of the Prison Service, Mr Derek Lewis. Indeed, this was really the *culmination* of the story and attracted more coverage and editorial comment than the escape itself. The stories thus passed through certain distinct phases. There was the initial scandalised reporting of the events. This was followed almost immediately by an accusatory phase (including a series of exposé accounts of life in each prison, and in other prisons, some of it of, at best, indirect relevance to the main plot). This period was provisionally 'closed' by the commissioning of the inquiries. The stories then went into a latency period, only to re-emerge with renewed prominence on publication of the reports. The reports were to prove somewhat fateful, in differing ways, for both the main protagonists. More importantly, they were also profoundly consequential for the subsequent development of prison regimes. This, however, was much less fully reported.

In both cases the press' quest for the location of personal blame began almost immediately. The Whitemoor escape was the 'Fiasco of the "Colditz" breakout' (*Observer*, 11 September 1994). A subsequent discovery of explosives among prisoners' property engendered 'Fury' (*Guardian*, 23 September 1994). Although the first few days' reporting was principally preoccupied with the mechanics of the escape (*Observer*, idem; *Today*, 12 September 1994) and secondarily with the insecurity of Mr Lewis' position, by the following weekend Mr Howard's role was also closely in question. Thus in the *Observer* (18 September 1994):

HOWARD'S LAW AND DISORDER

HOME SECRETARY FAILED TO ACT ON IRA JAIL WARNING

As all parties sourced the press, accusations ran up and down the Prison Service hierarchy. John Bartell for the Prison Officers' Association laid the blame on Mr Howard and Mr Lewis alike: 'They are responsible for the policies which resulted in staff cutting corners vital to security' (*Today*, 12 September 1994). Meanwhile, unnamed sources riposted: 'Authoritative sources confirmed that the escaping prisoners began by climbing a ladder in the only video surveillance "blind spot" in the unit compound. "How did they know?", one source said' (*Observer*, 18 September 1994).

The second main strand of reporting, arguably of more tangential relevance to the escape itself, concerned the 'luxurious' conditions enjoyed by the SSU prisoners. It was suggested that at Whitemoor the relatively privileged conditions of confinement in the SSU (a confined space in which the prisoners passed the whole of their time), combined with the unvarying staff rota, had enabled a process of 'conditioning' of the staff and the psychological dominance of the prisoners. (This suggestion was taken up with alacrity by Sir John Woodcock in the report of his inquiry.) For some papers this became a primary interest, in a way that extended far beyond the Whitemoor SSU to encompass prisons at which no recent security lapses had occurred. For the *Sunday Times* (18 September 1994) the issue was high living in high-security jails. Although none quite matched the concision of the *Sun*'s earlier:

JAIL PERVERTS LIVE IN LUXURY

The theme took on an energy of its own. Hence Mr Howard took the opportunity to distance himself publicly from such 'abuses': 'I want to see privileges earned, not handed down as a right' (*Sunday Express*, 18 September 1994). In terms of Woodcock's subsequent recommendations, and their effect on routine practice throughout the prison system, this avowal turned out to portend perhaps the most significant outcome of the whole drama.

Many of the same formal features of press coverage were repeated in the case of Parkhurst. The main additional elements were:

1   That because the prisoners remained at liberty for an extended period the exposure of the public to danger loomed larger. 'Killers on Run after Top Jail Breakout' (*Mirror*, 4 January 1995); 'Three Danger Men Flee Jail' (*Express*, 4 January 1995). Several papers printed profiles and mug-shots of the escapers, emphasising their dangerousness.

2   That because the escape followed the earlier one (and coincided with the West suicide) it could be represented as part of an *ongoing* security 'crisis' (*Guardian*, 4 January 1995). This sense of escalation was crucial to the reporting, and arguably instrumental in Mr Lewis' dismissal.

3   That several newspapers prominently named the Governor of the prison and identified him strongly with the 'lax', 'cushy' regime in operation there. The allocation of individual blame was thus further complicated, and the dispute between Howard and Lewis crystallised partly around their differing postures on the Governor's fate. This dispute ultimately raised the question of whether the escape resulted from an 'operational' failure or from defects of 'policy'. As a result the public reception of these events became transfixed by a morally charged form of single combat, and their profound implications for the structural problems of the prison system and its management of security passed relatively unremarked.

But in what ways does this sorry story inform theory? It seems at first sight to stand at some remove from the dispassionate calculation attributed to the 'new penology', or even from the higher statecraft outlined by Garland (1996). Conversely, does one need the resources of cultural theory, or any other account of *risk*, in order to interpret its shabby details? I suggest that this story is in fact rather laden with such implications and that theory is necessary to winkle them out. Here I can only sketch some responses.

Ironically, the conflict has its very origins in developments redolent of the 'new penology', or more precisely its cousin the 'new managerialism'. The prison service became an 'executive agency' in 1993, with a brand new Director General, the same Mr Lewis, appointed from industry on a fixed-term contract including a substantial performance-related component. Among the more immediately visible signs of the new managerial style were a series of documents setting out the terms of the new dispensation.[5] One of the more important of these, the *Corporate Plan*, introduces a series of 'statements', adding to the existing 'statement of purpose' those on 'vision', 'goals' and 'values'. Progress towards the realisation of goals was to be monitored using measurable 'key performance indicators' (KPIs) covering escapes, assaults, crowding, sanitation, 'purposeful activity', time out of cell, visits and costs. In other words, the division of accountabilities between the Director General and Home Secretary was precisely the product of a managerialist initiative, premised on a view of prisons as in most respects similar to other organisations, and designed to remove their day-to-day management from direct political control (see further Sparks *et al*. 1996).

However, the escapes provided one of those liminal moments which revealed the intrinsic *dis*similarities between prisons and most non-controversial businesses or bureaucracies (at the same time as perhaps suggesting their resemblances to some other risk-containing and emotive places, like nuclear plants and military installations). At critical moments the limits of the managerialist paradigm become apparent and the capacity of prisons to evoke anxiety and passion returns to the surface of discussion.

Moreover, while the escapes would have been newsworthy and controversial at any time, in the penal climate of 1993–95 they were especially so. Not only did they raise difficult questions about the division of responsibility between the Home Secretary and the Director General in the new agency, but they also followed hard on the heels of a renewed and very deliberate politicisation of penal affairs initiated by the Home Secretary himself. This prior stance – and the general tenor of retrenchment and increasing severity that went with it – seem to have conditioned the nature of the official response to the Whitemoor and Parkhurst incidents. 'Prison Works' as a doctrine expressly brought together an emphasis on the instrumental, risk reducing, aims of incapacitation and deterrence and a sharp, morally toned, stress on austerity (hence on the desirability of retrenchment in prisoners' privileges). That raised the stakes, and made all breaches of security potentially scandalous. But *both* elements of the strategy were placed in jeopardy by the revelations surrounding the escapes.

Responding to these difficulties, Sir John Woodcock's report on Whitemoor reiterated the connection between managerialist risk-reduction and the propriety of austerity. Woodcock interprets the escape as arising *exclusively* from the failure of managerial supervision and control (see also Sparks 1996). Woodcock diagnoses an absence of supervision and searching, in a climate of compromise and the 'relentless' erosion by prisoners of proper levels of staff dominance and surveillance. He therefore calls for more intensive use of CCTV, extra searching, standardisation of privilege levels, 'volumetric control' of private possessions[6] *and*, most importantly, an incentives-based structure of 'earnable and losable privileges' which is to provide the future basis for good order and security.[7] Sir John summarises his views thus:

> It is imperative that the supervisory and leadership elements, notable by their absence to date, should be established in the SSU at Whitemoor to provide a firm but fair regime where the 'dog' wags the 'tail', and not the reverse.

It is readily apparent that this departs sharply from the tone of much earlier English official discourse on control in prisons, especially that articulated as recently as 1991 by Woolf in response to the Strangeways siege of April 1990 (Woolf 1991; Sparks and Bottoms 1995; Sparks *et al.*, 1996). Woodcock thereby confirms Mr Howard's view of prisoners' *entitlements* ('decent but austere … ' – an expression by now also included in the prison service's own *Corporate Plan*) and supplements it with a parallel view of the best *method* of institutional control. For these reasons, the escapes have catalysed developments throughout the prison system, and in ways much wider than the conventional understanding of perimeter security. Under *Instruction to Governors 74/1995* (IG 74/95) schemes for 'earnable and losable privileges' become *required* in prisons in England and Wales. IG 74/95 states that the systematic introduction of these will encourage 'responsible behaviour', 'hard work' and 'progress through the system' and will serve to create 'a more disciplined, better controlled and safer environment' for prisoners and staff. IG 74/95 requires establishments to introduce incentive systems with 'basic', 'standard' and 'enhanced' privilege levels, each reflecting the individual's 'pattern of behaviour' over a certain period of time. To qualify for privilege levels above the 'basic' (roughly equivalent to Woolf's 'threshold quality of life'), prisoners are required to demonstrate 'good and responsible' behaviour. IG 74/1995 also insists that all privileges must be 'acceptable to reasonable public opinion' and 'justifiable in the face of informed criticism' and '*Above all* … not bring the Prison Service into disrepute' (Annex A, para. 17, emphasis added).

Accidents will happen, but politics frames the dominant responses to them. Because of the environment in which the escapes occurred, the manner of their public representation and the domain assumptions that governed the policy diagnoses that ensued, managerialism and penal populism are now thoroughly hybridised in official discourse on prison security. This is in some part what I take Douglas' account of risk and blame to predict. By the same token, however, it was never *enough*, from the point of view of the press response, to attribute the escapes to a purely systemic or managerial problem, nor to a human failure at a relatively low level of the organisation. From an early point the press became preoccupied with ferreting out the liabilities of one or both of the main protagonists – a moral structure that made it more or less inevitable that those two would find themselves in a struggle for survival. The forms of risk reduction promised by the institution in question necessarily engender their own blaming system (Douglas 1992: 15–16). Similarly the manner of the press reporting betrays the media's characteristic interest in the representation of order through the discovery of deviance or incompetence (Ericson *et al.* 1991). But none of those general observations capture the particularities of the *moment* in which the escapes occurred and which helped to constitute their political and cultural significance (in which the ironic but not unfamiliar way in which such momentary events contribute to the long-term reconfiguration of policy resides).

Conclusion

Most uses of notions of 'risk' in current criminological and penological work connote some sense of long-term conceptual and technical change (in the ways implied by the terms 'new penology', 'managerialism' and 'governmentality'). Yet, protestations to the contrary notwithstanding, there remains something of an analytic hiatus between these ideas and the detail of policy change (and politicisation) in specific cultural and political environments (cf. O'Malley 1997 for a parallel discussion of developments in policing). Many of the practices that promise risk reduction and containment (especially when expressed in such graphic forms as 'three strikes') in fact seem 'drenched in' (Hebenton and Thomas 1996) impassioned and emotive language, and pregnant with implications for the legitimacy and trustworthiness of institutions. This would seem to be the point of connection between Garland's account of *sovereignty* (1996) and Douglas' argument about the refusal of risk to 'shed its ancient moral freight'. Similarly herein lies some sort of reconciliation between Ericson and Haggerty's (1997) emphasis on the infrastructure of police-work in the risk society and Ericson *et al.*'s (1991) earlier discovery that crime and deviance enter public communication in episodic, personal, dramatised and scandalous ways.

There is a certain tradition in the sociology of the scandal (from Smelser 1962 to Fine 1997) which precisely attempts to describe the confluence between the event, its antecedent conditions and subsequent struggles for mobilisation and the control of meaning. The scandals of criminal justice (escapes, mistakes, aberrant sentences and so on) would seem ripe for this kind of analysis. The history of imprisonment, for example, is in a certain sense littered with 'new' penologies and replete with moments in which new techniques, institutions, regimes and management systems have been promoted in the promise of extending supervisory capacity or perfecting security. But these have rarely been *purely* intellectual or technological developments. Rather the record of advances and retrenchments in penal technique is scarcely separable from the dirtier and less visible history of riots, escapes, scandals, crises and inquiries that accompanies and in part animates it. The 'mutinies' at Chatham and Dartmoor in the early 1860s met their answer in the rigorous and calculating severity of the Carnavon Commission (Sim 1990; Radzinowicz and Hood 1986). Similarly a century and more later neither the debates on the 'concentration' and 'dispersal' of security risk prisoners in the 1960s and 1970s nor those in the 1980s on the development of special provision for 'difficult' or 'control problem' prisoners (Bottoms and Light 1987; Sparks *et al.* 1996) are properly intelligible outside the context of the turbulence that prefigured them and the risks of erosion in public and political confidence and legitimacy that were thereby incurred.

Perhaps what we observe in the episodes set in train by the escapes in the

1990s is indeed a system marked by many features of the 'new penology' and of 'managerialism'. But its model of business as usual is placed in jeopardy by disturbing events, especially those touching the most basic of its legitimation-claims, namely the ability to maintain secure custody. Among that system's responses were the desire to achieve closure over the episode. This is perhaps what the Woodcock and Learmont diagnoses appeared to offer. It was an objective for which the reception and estimation among relevant audiences of the adequacy of the system's response was crucial. However, in the manner of the return of the repressed to consciousness, the critical moment also permits the resurgence of some of the more antique aspects of punishment emphasised by Garland (1990, 1996). The escapes were singular moments. But they betrayed a confluence between a highly personalised and recriminatory low politics conducted in the full glare of media publicity and a political programme centring on the function of deep custody as an impregnably effective form of public protection from offenders seen as incorrigibly and virulently dangerous (a promise of protection whose credibility they placed in jeopardy). What resulted was a retrenchment of prison regimes involving thematics whose moral and imaginative basis went far deeper than questions of perimeter security as such and whose effects upon the routine operation of the prisons in future extended far further.

There are indeed therefore distinctively novel features in the conceptual and organisational basis of penal arrangements in Britain in the 1990s. But they are not conjured out of thin air, and neither do they have the field all to themselves. Instead in their practical realisation the new strategies of risk prevention and control enter a field that is already structured by its history – its long accretion of problems and contradictions – by the prevalence of certain characteristic public anxieties and their ready interpolation by the standard formats and condensing slogans of the press and by the contingencies (simultaneously both particular and familiar) of political competition. What followed in the present case was a translation of new penological and managerial themes from their pristine, ideal-typical forms into a brutal study in low politics whose instruments were the living conditions and prospects of all those working in and incarcerated in British prisons.

Notes

1 My work during the preparation of this paper has been supported by a grant under the Economic and Social Research Council's 'Risk and Human Behaviour' research programme (award no. L211252026). I gratefully acknowledge this support. I am also very grateful to those who have commented on aspects of the argument. They include David Garland, Roger Hood, Tom Horlick-Jones and Les Levidow.
2 Hebenton and Thomas (1996) have outlined a similar view on the question of how known sex offenders are 'managed' 'in the community' – another topic of the most acute press and public interest and controversy. They suggest that a prevalent contemporary 'cultural repertoire' of views of sex offenders connects

'in a reflexive way with official (criminological) discourse' – or in other words that specialised language blurs into everyday understandings (and vice versa). Hebenton and Thomas follow Ewald (1991) in arguing that in current public policy dilemmas 'risks' are problems for which there are no unambiguous solutions. These are arenas in which there exists an intrinsic capacity for insecurity and for conflicts over blame and in which problems chronically arise over disparities between expert and lay opinions. These conditions provide great scope for lobbies (notably those connected with the victims' movement) to mobilise, not least because their knowledge of the matter is 'drenched with experience' and is more readily communicable through mass media than the desiccated calculations of professional risk assessment and management (1996: 441).

3   It is not my wish to over-argue these analogies, only to draw attention to the numerous formal similarities between certain criminological problems and issues in the social analysis of risk in other domains. Differences remain, for example over the nature of the accountabilities in question or the precise extent of state obligation involved. Not least there is the *volitional* character of the criminological/penal questions (unlike the radiation the prisoners can plot, plan and struggle to get out).

4   'Dispersal' prisons are those between which 'Category A' adult male prisoners (i.e. those whose escape is deemed to represent the most serious risk to the public) are 'dispersed' (in a ratio of about 1:5 with 'Category B' prisoners). They are the maximum security sector of the English prison estate. Two of those who escaped from Parkhurst (using a copied key) were 'Category A' at the time. Special Security Units, as their name implies, supposedly build in yet higher levels of surveillance and physical security and are reserved for the few dozen men reckoned most dangerous and most capable of escape. Thus, although they were recaptured almost immediately, the breach of the perimeter at Whitemoor by this group of prisoners, with access to firearms, was especially controversial.

5   See, for example, the 1993 HM Prison Service document *We Are Now an Agency* (which, perhaps wittily(?) recalls a remark of Mrs Thatcher's on becoming a grandparent), as well as successive versions of the *Corporate Plan* and *Business Plan*. On the new Prison Service management more generally see King and McDermott (1995: 47–57).

6   This means that prisoners will be able to bring into prison only such possessions as will fit into a container of a standard size.

7   A more extended critical commentary on Woodcock is provided in Sparks *et al.* (1996).

References

Beck, U. (1992a) *Risk Society*, London: Sage.
—— (1992b) 'Modern Society as a Risk Society', in N. Stehr and R. Ericson (eds), *The Culture and Power of Knowledge*, New York: de Gruyter.
Bottoms, A. (1995) 'The Philosophy and Politics of Punishment and Sentencing', in C. Clarkson and R. Morgan (eds), *The Politics of Sentencing Reform*, Oxford: Oxford University Press.
Bottoms, A. and Light, R. (1987) *Problems of Long-Term Imprisonment*, Aldershot: Gower.
Cohen, S. and Young, J. (eds) (1974) *The Manufacture of News*, London: Constable.
Douglas, M. (1992) *Risk and Blame: Essays in Cultural Theory*, London: Routledge.

Ericson, R.V., Baranek, P. and Chan, J. (1991) *Representing Order*, Buckingham: Open University Press.

Ericson, R.V. and Haggerty, K. (1997) *Policing the Risk Society*, Toronto, Ont.: University of Toronto Press.

Ewald, F. (1991) 'Insurance and Risk', G. Burchell, C. Gordon and P. Miller (eds), *The Foucault Effect*, London: Harvester Wheatsheaf.

Feeley, M. and Simon, J. (1992) 'The New Penology: Notes on the Emerging Strategy of Corrections and its Implications', *Criminology* 30(4): 449–75.

Fine, G.A. (1997) 'Scandals, Social Conditions and the Creation of Public Attention', *Social Problems* 44(3): 297–323.

Foucault, M. (1991) 'On Governmentality', in G. Burchell, C. Gordon and P. Miller (eds), *The Foucault Effect*, London: Harvester Wheatsheaf.

Garland, D. (1990) *Punishment and Modern Society*, Oxford: Oxford University Press.

—— (1996) 'The Limits of the Sovereign State', *British Journal of Criminology* 36(4): 445–71.

—— (1997) ' "Governmentality" and the Problem of Crime: Foucault, Criminology, Sociology', *Theoretical Criminology* 1(2): 173–214.

Hebenton, W. and Thomas, T. (1996) 'Sex Offenders in the Community: Reflections on Problems of Law, Community and Risk Management', *International Journal of the Sociology of Law* 24(4): 427–44.

HM Prison Service (1993) *We are Now an Agency*, London: HM Prison Service.

Hood, C. and Jones, D. (1996) *Accident and Design: Contemporary Debates in Risk Management*, London: UCL Press.

Kasperson, R. (1992) 'The Social Amplification of Risk: Progress in Developing an Integrative Framework', in S. Krimsky and D. Golding (eds), *Social Theories of Risk*, New York: Praeger.

Kemshall, H., Parton, N., Walsh, M. and Waterson, J. (1997) 'Concepts of Risk in Relation to Organisational Structure and Functioning within the Personal Social Services and Probation', *Social Policy and Administration* 31(3): 213–31.

King, R.D. and McDermot, K. (1995) *The State of our Prisons*, Oxford: Oxford University Press.

Learmont, Sir J. (1995) *Review of Prison Service Security*, London: HMSO.

Melossi, D. (1993) 'Gazette of Morality and Social Whip', *Social and Legal Studies* 2: 259–79.

—— (1994) 'The Economy of Illegalities; Normal Crimes, Elites and Social Control', in D. Nelken (ed.), *The Futures of Criminology*, London: Sage.

Nelken, D. (ed.) (1994) *The Futures of Criminology*, London: Sage.

O'Malley, P. (1992) 'Risk, Power and Crime Prevention', *Economy and Society* 21(3): 252–75.

—— (1997) 'Policing, Politics and Postmodernity', *Social and Legal Studies* 6(3): 363–81.

Radzinowicz, L. and Hood, R. (1986) *The Emergence of Penal Policy in Victorian and Edwardian England*, London: Stevens and Sons.

Rayner, S. (1992) 'Cultural Theory and Risk Analysis', in S. Krimsky and D. Golding (eds), *Social Theories of Risk*, New York: Praeger.

Rozenberg, J. (1997) *Trial of Strength*, London: Richard Cohen Books.

Sarat, A. (1997) 'Vengeance, Victims and the Identities of Law', *Social and Legal Studies* 6(2): 163–90.

Sim, J. (1990) *Medical Power in Prisons*, Buckingham: Open University Press.

Simon, J. and Feeley, M. (1995) 'True Crime: the New Penology and Public Discourse on Crime', in T. Blomberg and S. Cohen (eds), *Punishment and Social Control*, New York: Aldine de Gruyter.

Smelser, N. (1962) *Theory of Collective Behavior*, New York: Free Press.

Sparks, R. (1992) *Television and the Drama of Crime*, Buckingham: Open University Press.

—— (1996) 'A System in Contra-flow', *Criminal Justice* 14(1): 4–5.

Sparks, R. and Bottoms, A. (1995) 'Legitimacy and Order in Prisons', *British Journal of Sociology* 46(1): 46–62.

Sparks, R., Bottoms, A. and Hay, W. (1996) *Prisons and the Problem of Order*, Oxford: Oxford University Press.

Walklate, S. (1997) 'Risk and Criminal Victimization: a Modernist Dilemma?', *British Journal of Criminology* 37(1): 35–45.

Windlesham, Lord (1996) *Responses to Crime: Legislating with the Tide*, vol. 3, Oxford: Oxford University Press.

Woodcock, Sir J. (1994) *Report of the Enquiry into the Escape of Six Prisoners from the Special Security Unit at Whitemoor Prison on Friday 9 September 1994*, London: HMSO.

Woolf, Lord Justice (1991) *Prison Disturbances April 1990*, London: HMSO.

Wynne, B. (1992) 'Risk and Social Learning: Reification to Engagement', in S. Krimsky and D. Golding (eds), *Social Theories of Risk*, New York: Praeger.

Part IV

Violence, danger and modern government

The future

Chapter 8

Naturalising danger
Women, fear and personal safety

Elizabeth Stanko

When visiting the United States in the autumn of 1998, I noticed an advertisement in *The Village Voice* for a personal security device. The product – Defender DNA – boasts that it is the 'smallest' personal protection device. It has the special advantage of combining an alarm with a probe. This probe – when jabbed into the skin of an attacker – collects skin particles, the advert claims, that can be analysed as 'an identifying' DNA sample. An enclosed box tells readers that the FBI has opened a DNA data bank 'to apprehend criminals'. The device was offered 'on sale', for $69.95 (or $119.95 for two). Accompanying the text are three pictures of women, two of which depict the same woman with a man – in one picture she is under attack, in the other, escaping with the attacker shown grasping his head. The third picture shows another woman jogging with the device in her hand. Presumably, this device gives her the freedom to enjoy her exercise. Awareness about the potential danger of men's violence to women has grown rapidly over the past three decades. Its depiction as a potential encounter for any woman has now become normalised. Its solution is commodified in the form of protection devices such as rape alarms or mobile phones, or particularly in the US, handguns.

The women's movement in the 1960s became the catalyst for speaking about the violence women experienced at the hands of men. The research about and challenges to men's violence and its particular salience in women's everyday lives placed violence against women on local, national and international agendas. In terms of interpersonal violence, research consistently shows that largely men who are familiar and familial endanger women (in terms of physical, sexual, and emotional violence and abuse). Conceptualising risk to women of men's violence as arising from strangers, who must be fended off in public space, as the above advert shows, is fundamentally flawed. These recalcitrant images of stranger danger and 'woman-at-risk' hold fast, despite volumes of evidence to the contrary. It is this very conceptualisation, however, that has continued to dominate public imagery, public discourse and the private fears of women. Such fears have become sales opportunities. Safety devices are big business and are sold to assuage women's anxiety.

Academic and intellectual discourses about the nature of modern and post-modern society have proposed a major shift in the way we define and conceptualise the nature of risk in contemporary life (Beck 1990; Douglas 1992). It has been suggested that we conceive of risk as something very different now. This shift, many influential thinkers argue, has led to nothing short of fundamental changes to the way we locate ourselves in the world: it affects how we engage with political democracies and with everyday life. I seek here to interrogate to what extent our knowledge about what endangers women has been altered in any way by this fundamental shift in thinking about the nature of danger and risk in modern life.

This chapter is organised to take a look at what we know about the dangers of men's violence from the research on the victimisation of women and women's fear of crime. The way in which this knowledge is translated into discourses of crime prevention is the subject of the next section. The fourth part examines and critiques both the knowledge gained from feminist research as well as that underlying crime prevention advice. In particular, the difficulties feminist research on men's violence and crime prevention has in generating so-called guidance to women are founded, I suggest, in the contradictions of what it means to be 'at-risk' to men's violence. Finally, I suggest an approach to re-conceptualising the danger to women from violent crime. In an effort to forward debates about men's violence to women, we must eschew theoretical frameworks that naturalise women's victimisation *and* men's violence.

A spotlight on men's violence

Awareness of the commonness of men's violence in women's lives is due to the women's movement. The commonness of men's violence was indeed noted by many feminist campaigners in the 1800s and throughout the twentieth century. As historians have shown, women's experiences of violence have always been much more prevalent than official records recognise (see, for instance, Allen 1988; Clark 1987; D'Cruze 1999; Gordon 1988). Yet it was the development of the so-called second wave of feminism in the 1960s that provided the continuous backdrop in challenging men's entitlement to power in contemporary society. Women demanded changes in their work, leisure and private lives. Prominent in the discussions about women's private lives was the violence women faced at the hands of men. Debates, articles, television programmes and public forums aired the growing understanding about how violence impacts women's lives, from birth throughout their life course.

As women began to speak about the forms of violence they experienced at the hands of men, feminist activists established self-help groups and safe refuges that assisted women in coping and surviving the aftermath of such violence. Support for those who had been raped or sexually abused as children or adults, battered by boyfriends and/or husbands, sexually harassed by clients, colleagues and bosses, and threatened or assaulted on the streets grew organically from this mass of experience. In many local areas around the world, women's refuges, rape crisis centres, legal advice centres and community safety schemes sought to meet the needs of many abused women. Women organised globally. Violence against women is now recognised as a violation of women's human rights in UN Resolution 48/104 (December 1993). Men's violence is now named as a public, collective harm to women.

Arising from the work of self-help groups and feminist research, an approach to conceptualising the potential of encountering men's violence coalesced around rethinking the nature of women's risk from violent crime. In effect, the experience of self-help activists taught us that any woman was at risk from men's violence; being a woman meant being a target of men's violence (Stanko 1985). What is important to my discussion here is the way in which theorising about risk, and perceptions about that risk and the nature of danger, became cornerstones to the feminist debates about men's violence to women. If men's violence to women is a common phenomenon, then placing men's violence at the heart of the debate about women's oppression is crucial to women's liberation.

In the area of violence against women, the 1970s and 1980s were dominated by debate – at times vitriolic – which was driven by the need to establish the prevalence of violence in women's lives. Crime surveys were criticised for the crude methodological approach in defining women's experiences of men's violence (Stanko 1988). What feminist activists learned in their day-to-day work with abused women was that women's way of understanding men's violence was linked to their relationships with and to men. This understanding – though not universal nor shared by all women in the same way – was affected by how women saw their lives and experiences of violence intertwined with marriage, courtship, family, friendship and working relationships. Feminist researchers began to question the language and approach of survey research that failed to use women's own meanings about the violence they experienced. These feminist researchers challenged the framework of criminal law, outside of which, it was argued, women managed most of men's violence. Moreover, these same feminist critics also assailed criminal justice and other service institutions for failing to offer service and support to women whose needs should be anticipated given the commonness of men's violence.

Sexual violence – ranging from sexual threats to rape – is common in women's lives.[1] Research exploring physical violence in adult, married women also clearly demonstrates the pervasiveness of violence in heterosexual partnerships. Approximately one in ten women report experiencing domestic violence in any current year, and one in three or four during a lifetime of partnerships (Johnson and Sacco 1995; Mirrlees-Black 1999; Stanko *et al.* 1998). Violence against children, particularly sexual violence, shows that the perpetrators of violence are those familial and familiar with the abused children. No doubt, many surveys, which explore the extent of violence against women in the general population, are important, in that they consistently demonstrate how widespread violence against women is.

Feminist work links the *potential* of violent victimisation to women's relationships with men. In so many ways, however, violence – its impact, its origins, and its motivations – is *naturalised*. Deeply embedded in our thinking about violence are assumptions that unproblematically associate violence and its threat as based in the biology or the psychology of its perpetrators. The way in which violence is and can be imagined appears to be taken for granted as the vagaries of individual evil, disease or weak character. Such assumptions about women similarly included explanations for victimisation that are fashioned to the violence we experience. Indeed, discourses of blame were prominent in thinking about violence to women. We women were held responsible for men's violence to us (see Girard 1986). Victimised women, according to this thinking, provoked, invited, or enticed their own harm. Feminist research, in re-conceptualising men's danger to women, sought to challenge this natural order of things.

To do so, feminist research challenged contemporary criminology. Where the threat to women is greatest, even official statistics tells us, is within women's intimate relationships. Feminist research has emphasised the instrumental impact of serial, intentional, and directed violence by men on women in intimate settings (Dobash and Dobash 1979; Hoff 1990).[2] Studies of violence between intimates (or former intimates) argue that it is men's sense of entitlement to women's services which feeds sources of conflict leading to violent events. Dobash and Dobash (1992) propose that the nature of relations between men and women, men's consequent demands and expectations of wives, support for the prerogatives and power of husbands, and cultural beliefs that sustain individuals' attitudes of marital inequality, combine to such an extent that collectively women are more at risk of violence in intimate relations than in public spaces. Men use violence against women in domestic situations as a result of men's possessiveness and jealousy; an expectation concerning women's domestic work; a punishment for women for perceived wrongdoing; and as a prop to men's authority (Daly and Wilson 1988; Dobash and Dobash 1992). What contemporary criminology may now acknowledge as constituting most violent *crime* to women, though, has not led to an overturning of popular conceptions of the nature of violence.

It is very difficult to question a so-called natural state – heterosexual union – and label it as dangerous. Discourses about violent men highlight the individual pathology or shortcomings of the violent offender. With woeful regularity in the media and elsewhere, women's experiences of encountering violence are reduced to simple accounts of being a woman who encounters an evil or sick man. The heterosexual union – and in particular the often unequal power over women men have in many such couples – seldom comes under scrutiny. That women are most likely to be assaulted or killed by known men is still explained as a *natural* course disaster of some intimate relationships. What is not part of the explanation are the findings of many of the feminist-inspired studies: men's control, not natural conflict, looms large in women's experiences of physical and sexual violence. Time and time again, feminist surveys underscore the evidence collected by feminist activists: those who endanger women and children are by and large not strangers to those they abuse. Shifting our understanding of violence to the danger of heterosexual intimacies remains difficult. We continue to separate the danger of known men from that of the so-called dangerous stranger. Violence against women is *qualitatively and quantitatively* different from the violence experienced by men at the hands of men (and for that matter at the hands of women). Violence for women is largely embedded in wider networks of authority, power and kinship. It is relational.

And women, in the way these relations with men are central in our own lives, naturalise the existence of violence too. Women's identities are given meaning by and through personal and family relationships. Violence experienced here can so easily be taken for granted within the domain of the private. In part, the power of the imagery of violent-man-as-stranger is its separation from women's sense of their own identities (see Connell 1999). One place to explore this in greater depth is to examine why women say they feel at greater risk in public places. The imagery of the bush-lurking rapist or the unpredictable stranger dominates the conceptualisation of women's abusers. Such imagery is not only dominant in the media, it is held in our own heads (Holland *et al*. 1998; Madriz 1997b). This is because, I suggest, the framework of violence as criminal assault by a stranger looms large in common sense, legitimised in the work of criminologists, legislatures, courts and other institutions. Our fear of crime, as we shall explore in the next section, is a glaring example of the intractable discourses in our thinking about violence: its origins lie in biology or psychology, not the social.

Criminology's spotlight: men's violence and fear of crime

During the 1960s, the social science tools of criminology developed the victim survey, the first examples of which were carried out on behalf of the US 1967 comprehensive review of law enforcement and criminal justice (President's Commission 1967). The victim survey documented how much crime was not reported to the police. Also, it asked people about experiences of victimisation, moreover, the survey created a measure to assess people's perceptions about their risk from personal crime. The criminological concept – fear of crime – was born and has since generated volumes of research (Hale 1996). While there is no overall consensus among researchers about a definition of fear of crime, there are basic components of fear of crime upon which many researchers would agree.

Generally, fear of crime is taken to represent individuals' diffuse sense of danger about being physically harmed by *criminal* violence. It is associated with concern about being *outside* the home, probably in an urban area, alone and potentially vulnerable to personal harm. The most popular question, which appears on victimisation surveys, is: How safe do you feel walking alone in your neighbourhood (in this area) after dark (or at night)? In responding, interviewees are assumed to be thinking of their personal safety with regard to criminal violence. This is the question used in most large-scale victimisation surveys. Individuals may be asked to assess their probability of encountering, say, a burglary, robbery or rape within the next twelve months. It is from this perspective that an analysis is made as to respondents' evaluation of their risk of being a victim of crime. Finally, information is collected about actual (that is, reported to the researchers) victimisation.

Beyond any doubt, the gender differential is the most consistent finding in the literature on fear of crime (Stanko 1995). Women report fear at levels that are three times that of men, yet their recorded risk of personal violence, especially assault, is, by all official sources, lower than men's. Indeed, there is a mismatch between women's and men's *reported* risk of violent criminal victimisation and their fear of falling victim to such violence. Those who admit feeling safest, young men, reveal the greatest proportion of personally violent victimisations. While there have been a number of criticisms about how the concept of fear of crime is constructed, the concept itself and what it is presumed to represent – here women's anxiety about crime and disorder – is treated as a social problem in its own right.

The above description of the creation of a tool for 'measuring' people's anxiety about crime does not problematise the way in which this survey has become the mechanism for assessing attitudes toward crime. Left out of any discussion is the way in which narratives about the danger of crime intersect with the narratives of the danger of contemporary life. So the kinds of questions criminologists ask are: Why do women say they feel unease, and admit more to fearing the potential danger of encountering assailants in public, when they are 'safer' from violence, at least according to crime surveys? Indeed, women's imagery about criminal danger seems to match that of men's. The women Madriz (1997b) interviewed, for instance, reveal strong imagery of criminals, characterising them as 'beasts, irrational and violent' (Madriz 1997b: 98). As Pain (1993) found, despite disclosing a variety of domestic and intimate assaults, her interviewees spoke of potential violence as 'stranger danger'. Such concern about danger begins early in life. Schoolchildren interviewed for a recent study took safety precautions to avoid encounters with potential violence, especially with strangers. Girls took more precautions than boys did (Goodey 1994). My research on safety and violence avoidance strategies of adult women illustrates how early lessons in danger become part of a lifetime of negotiating danger, inside and outside the home (Stanko 1990). So when women are asked about danger, their fears translate into concerns about hazards lurking in the physical environment: parking lots, public stairwells and public transit,[3] places where 'beasts' or 'uncontrolled' men prowl.

What is taken for granted in studies of fear of crime is the absence of commentaries on structures of inequalities or historical analyses of discourses about violence that embrace the naturalness of violence from certain types of people. Any wider context of women's lives – which is intertwined with and negotiated through systems, practices, ideologies that continue to privilege male power – is ignored. Drawing here on the work of Holland and her colleagues' ten-year study of young people and sexuality, I suggest that the logic used to project imagery of danger to women reveals the enduring strength of male power in dominating the lens though which danger is constructed. Holland *et al.* (1998) demonstrate convincingly in a study of young people's sexuality that heterosexual practices are negotiated on and through men's needs. Such imagery about so-called real criminals, I suggest, also reflects the power to preserve 'men' as safe in sexual partnerships and dangerous outside such partnerships or other familiarity (that is supposed 'to protect'). Many of us do negotiate and safely resist and challenge the normative image of men as the embodied protector of our respectability. Men's violence can of course be resisted. Not all men are violent to women. This fact challenges the *naturalness* of men's violence. However, the standard for judging appropriate resistance behaviour – and for women's safety this includes their public and private behaviour – remains firmly within discourses about violence that place the origins of the violence of the man to be resisted in nature or in individual psychology. Consequently, 'real' femininities and masculinities, socially constructed within heterosexuality as embodied practices, meanings and institutionalised power relations, are 'drawn into making masculinity powerful' (Holland *et al.* 1998: 30). And this power becomes part of a natural order (see, Yanagisako and Delaney 1995). When this theorising is applied to an understanding of women's fear of crime, the logic of fearing the stranger rather than the intimate is more fully understood. But what is missing is an analysis of what makes some masculinities dangerous. It is in the space of these contradictions – some men are dangerous and others are 'safe' – where the so-called naturalness of men's violence can be challenged. What is also missing is the challenge to the way that women who experience violence are separated into categories of deserving and undeserving victims.

Criminologists' explanations for why women might harbour anxiety about their personal safety, though, converge around a number of key issues, ignoring this context and power of institutionalised heterosexuality. Greater physical and social vulnerability (Skogan and Maxfield 1981) and women's fear of sexual assault (Maxfield 1984; Warr 1984) dominate these explanations. Gordon and Riger (1988) even name women's fear of rape as 'the female fear'. Limiting the explanation of women's fear of crime to the fear of rape, as some criminologists have, directs our attention to the worst scenario of sexual violence, the violent invasion of rape. By categorising rape as the only understandable, abhorrent sexual intrusion that could reasonably frighten women, ordinary events, such as receiving sexual comments on the street or from co-workers, experienced as threatening, often private encounters, are overlooked as part of a wider continuum of men's control over and treatment of women. The irony is of course that most women experience these 'little rapes'. But even when women do encounter sexual threat and danger, it is most likely the danger arising from men they know. The study of fear of crime therefore allows us, on an institutional basis, to retain the dominance of a discourse about violence that naturalises it as based in the biology or psychology of the perpetrator. By excluding the domestic and familiar settings from collective worry, we give more power to myth of the dangerousness of stranger violence. The majority of men's and women's experiences of violence however contradict this mythology.

Danger to women: crime prevention and discourses of risk

How has feminist knowledge about the potential of violence – whether from known or unknown men – been managed as a problem for crime prevention? In a previous article, I explored women's techniques of risk assessment, arguing that women's crime prevention is as much about the regulation of self as a respectable woman as it is minimising crime (Stanko 1997). Women's narratives about having to 'stay safe' anticipate negative judgements about their respectability. Women with whom I spoke displayed an acute awareness of social hierarchies and social expectations of others. The intersection of the discourse about violence and the discourses about appropriate femininities converge to demonstrate how inequalities structure even mundane aspects of women's lives. Women rely on different resources drawn from different cultural and social wells. Our understanding of our ability to manoeuvre away from the impact of violence is strongly framed within our relationships to the men who abuse us. The discourses of crime prevention, however, reflect the state's concern about the danger of strangers.

In Britain, crime prevention has become the dominant framework driving government policy in the 1980s and 1990s. Garland's (1996) analysis of these developments suggests that crime prevention mobilises those outside government to aid in the fight against crime. This responsiblisation strategy, as Garland terms it, seeks to encourage individuals and non-state agencies to work in 'partnership' to increase awareness about how to avoid crime, to identify suspicious people, and to join a civic movement to combat crime. Key to this strategy, moreover, is the use of the Home Office and the police as the distributors of appropriate advice about how best to avoid victimisation (Stanko 1997). Women are a critical target audience for this information. As crime surveys reveal, women are far more concerned about their personal safety, hence, the 'natural' audience for crime prevention advice. (This choice of target audience may be curious. This constituency is, according to their own data, of lower risk to interpersonal violence. Young men, by all accounts, should have been the prime audience for advice about avoiding violence.) Crime prevention literature did begin to recognise domestic violence as a common experience for women in danger and thus within its remit. However, there continues to be a clear separation between domestic violence and stranger violence, keeping very much alive the illusion that fear of crime is directly linked to women's perceptions of being at risk to unknown, uncontrollable men.

The persistence of the image of the dangerous criminal should however come as no surprise. As Sparks (1992) has argued, there is no simplistic link between fear of and risk of crime. Deeply embedded cultural signifiers about the nature of crime, fear, danger, blame or responsible citizenry haunt the debates about risk (Douglas 1992; Luhmann 1993), and I suggest, lurk within any discussion of violence. All too often, these complexities are marginalised by contemporary criminological debates. As Walklate (1997) argues, fear of crime has great value in popular cultural portrayals of good/evil (Sparks 1993; Madriz 1997a). Linking fear to violence retains a hold on the discourses of biology and psychology, thereby naturalising it. The imagery used for selling safety devices or within advice literature shows men to be menacing, lurking in dark alleys or unkempt. Women's accounts of danger, on the other hand, often include stories about abusive men's behaviour which feature men when they are 'loving' and otherwise 'not violent'. The practical consequences of these contradictions in our holistic accounts of dangerous relationships, however, regardless of whether our fear stems from actual crime or its risk, are that we are expected and are encouraged by crime prevention literature to be literate about avoidance of stranger danger *and* about how to seek redress for domestic violence. This inclusion of domestic violence within crime prevention literature acknowledges its embeddedness in intimacy. What kind of literacy is being displayed through this literature? Seeking redress for domestic violence assumes that we have already managed its fear, its contradictions (the man is both dangerous and loving), and its damaging consequences. The burdens of this literacy are seldom recognised. Nor are the contradictions. Women who do not leave violent men are characterised as enjoying the abuse, or as bad mothers, or even as weak and defeated victims by many service providers. Women who experience violence may also be silenced by the dissonance that accompanies labelling a 'loved one' as violent. Women's agency – the creative strategies we employ to minimise the impact of violence on our lives and the lives of our children – is also excluded from this advice literature. As O'Malley (1992) argues, the burden of responsibility for minimising the risk of crime has shifted, from that provided by the state via its criminal justice apparatus to the shoulders of its citizenry, in the form of self-help crime prevention.

But this crime prevention advice incorporates innumerable contradictory assumptions into this self-help literature for women. As it stands, it sets out a number of suggestions for women to avoid violent men in public. To avoid the dangerous, lurking male menace (the other), we are advised how to travel locally ('with petrol in our car') and afar, how to dress, how to walk, how to talk to a potential intimidator, how to appear assertive and in control of our modern lives (Stanko 1990; Gardner 1988). At the same time, these precautionary strategies for minimising men's violence are practices that display an awareness of the relationship women have to men – the dangerous 'other'. This awareness of our relational insecurity *vis-à-vis* men is not restricted to crime prevention advice; it is already embedded within our routine consciousness about being respectable in contemporary life. What is *at risk* for women in an encounter with any potentially violent man, is a sullied self. And while risk is normalised (Walklate 1997), the dangerous *other* – the criminal – becomes more vilified. But only the villain 'outside' becomes potentially dangerous. The self-help advice about domestic violence treats violence as if it 'could happen to any woman', but also that this private danger has no 'collective' predictability. How do we advise women that heterosexual partnerships can be the source of danger and not protection?

The evidence about women, violence and victimisation is overwhelming; its implications about danger give rise to contradictory discourses about women's risk, women's responsibilities and men's accountability for such danger. Only beasts hurt women; but 'intimates', who retain separateness from beasts, perpetrate most violence against women. The research suggests that women lead more restricted lives and use greater caution when out in public, despite the overwhelming evidence of the *collective harm against all women* of domestic violence and abuse. How is it that women can remain safe from men's violence?

Perhaps one location of the contradictory discourses within the advice literature revolves around the way the term 'safety' is used. Safety has become a fundamental value – in health, in finance, in sex, in employment, in environmental risks, to name only a few. Risk in this context is ever present. We are bombarded by evidence about the risk of contracting cancer, losing our job, experiencing the death of a child and so forth. The problem is as we learn more about potential risks, we learn less about ways to avoid successfully these known risks – not all people who smoke contract cancer, not all of those who contract cancer are smokers. But the fact that the risk exists at all means that we begin to act in ways to avoid the knowable. What does this mean when thinking about women's risk of men's violence? Knowing that known men constitute the greatest danger does not assist us in knowing which men are dangerous, and which men are not violent. As radical feminists have argued, the discourse that underpins men's violence is social, institutional and personal power (for a useful discussion of the discourses and wife abuse, see O'Neill 1998). Giving women more access to this power, perhaps, might minimise the risk of men's violence to women. Yet as the work of self-help activists and analyses of public service records attests, no particular category of woman is immune from men's violence. Defining risk in this context places all women at potential risk to men's violence. Safety for women becomes defined as problematising the actions of violent men, not advising women how to move about or form relationships which might be safer than others. While safer, no woman is ever outside the category, though, of being at risk to men's violence. Men's violent behaviour must be challenged in order for women to be safer.

If we were to explore crime prevention advice for the assumptions about what 'at risk' means for women, we might see different discourses at work. In the literature listing women's 'safe' actions in public, there is an assumption that such actions will deter all but the pathological offender. Women then are expected, as part of active citizenship, to be responsible for their own safety. Self-governance, in the form of acting like appropriate 'feminine' women, provides the 'right' signals to those non-pathological men not to abuse women. State programmes that address men's domestic violence, in addition, as a problem of learned behaviour or dysfunctional families, fail to extend the prevention to the potential problem of all men. That problem remains, as Holland and her colleagues so eloquently describe, as a problem of male power (Holland *et al.* 1998).

So despite over twenty years of sustained campaigning, feminist work has not shifted attention in criminology away from thinking about the danger of strangers. We are still being told about being careful walking on the streets at night. Even highly publicised cases of random murder against women have given rise to media commentary that 'no woman alone is safe in public'. Observations from such feminist commentators as Caputi (1987) or Cameron and Fraser (1987), who argue that sexual murder is not just an unfortunate event, but part of systematic violence against women, are not to be found in these public comments. Problems, however, remain for both approaches to challenging men's violence to women. On a collective and individual basis, the responsibility for avoiding violence seems to fall squarely on the shoulders of individual women. Such advice about how to avoid men's violence also arises within the growing arena of advice to avoid all kinds of hazards. This advice rarely accounts for the diversities among people, the differential resources – financial, social and personal, and indeed differential ways in which women might indeed be more likely targeted for abuse than other women. It is to an argument for this diversity that I now turn.

Naming the danger of men's violence: the resources of diversity and women's agency

The collective naming of men's violence as a key element in the social control of women is the cornerstone of confronting the myths about danger to women. The interwoven links among our private and public identities, our experiences of threat (whether as individuals through physical or sexual harm or as a collective, in terms of the diffuse sense of anxiety many of us speak about), and the public discourses about crime combine to give strength to conceptualisations of violence that locate its explanations in the discourses of biology and psychology. From the crime prevention literature to its media coverage, myths about danger to women continue to coalesce around stranger danger. The fact that we women are most at risk to the violence of men closest to us or with access that disarms us by friendship, authority or kinship demands that we ask why myths about stranger danger continue to prevail in today's contemporary society.

Has our 'modern consciousness' altered during this new era of awareness of danger and risk? Many of us prepare ourselves to avoid men's violence as an 'impending disaster'. Such preparation has become a routine and expected part of being a woman (Stanko 1990; Stanko 1997; Madriz 1997a). As a consequence of this state of alert, we police ourselves by restricting public activities because of the anxiety about potential violence and we use more safety precautions than men do (Gardner 1995; Stanko 1997). The routines of precaution, though, become an invisible commentary about the unspeakable: it is largely men who are supposed to be the protectors, the intimates, the sources of support, who are the source of danger.

If we conceptualise men's violence as inevitable or as natural, we fail to see how its meanings articulate with other inequalities that are supposedly structured by other 'natural' differences. Sexuality, race, nation, religion, ethnicity, family and so forth intersect with our experiences of men's violence. The stories we tell about managing danger reveal far more about the discourses that naturalise men's danger. Our narratives about safety – whether they are in relation to avoiding the potential of violence or managing its consequences – display overlapping links between power and desire (Holland et al. 1998). For many women, a wider web of sexual desire mediates the fact that men known to us may pose danger. But sexual desire is not fixed, nor immutable. Resisting the trappings of heterosexuality is a task for all women, 'straight' and 'not-straight' alike. The debate about sexualities and its impact on identities is one area where lessons can be gleaned to challenge the discourses about the dangers of men. This intersectionality of gender and sexuality, for instance, allows a display of a discourse 'on the edge'. Yanagisako and Delaney suggest:

While institutions and cultural domains of meaning have a profound impact on shaping ideas and practices, people do not necessarily organise their everyday actions according to these divisions. Rather, people think and act at the *intersections* of discourses.

(1995: 18)

Interrogating the intersectionality of the dangers men pose to women though is often muted by the discourses of biology and psychology as explanations for the violence of men and by the association of men's violence with *criminal* harm. The harm of criminality must be attributed to the actions of an individual. Differences though may allow us to fall back on a discourse that so easily explains why this man in this situation is violent and another, in a similar situation, is not. (If only nagging women are battered, and all women are potential nags, why does one man batter and another not?) Such diversities of identities create difficulties in conceptualising violence to women from known men as both a collective and an individual experience. The intersectionality of difference, Crenshaw (1994) observes in challenging domestic violence, is difficult to achieve when one is interested in gaining widespread support. So portraying the 'victim' of domestic violence as a middle-class, white, heterosexual may engender the sympathy of the majority in any particular population, but may confine that sympathy and support to some categories of women who experience abuse. In exploring homophobic violence, Smith (1992) has warned queer activists in particular that in the process of negotiating safety for the 'non-straight', both campaigners from homophile organisations and police essentialise, as well as de-essentialise, identities. Inevitably, using diversities among women as a resource in challenging debates about violence without confronting the discourses which naturalise violence, may have the effect of separating the evils of particular men, or the failure of women to exercise appropriate judgement about avoiding the violence of these particular men. Diversity among women and our agency – the ability to choose a non-violent course of action – become the sustenance for separating violent men using discourses of biology and psychology (thus eschewing the lessons of the collective responsibility of all men in the social control of women). We women who struggle to avoid the 'inevitability' of men's violence are sorted into 'deserving' and 'undeserving' victims. Violent men are confined to short-comings of biology or to weakness of character.

And so it is possible to retain the aura of the nature of men's violence to women as something outside the remit of our contemporary social order. The experience of self-help activists attests to the persistence of our own ability to rationalise men's violence in terms of our own behaviour and/or in terms of individual men's failings. The 'male in the head' (Holland *et al.* 1998) continues to have a strong influence on our sense of ourselves and our so-called duty to manage men's violent behaviour on our own. At the same time, institutional responses focus on attributing blame for encountering violence or perpetrating it on an individual basis. The discourses of family-centred social policy, moreover, resist the association of men's violence with normal, family life. These logics embrace a naturalised social order and assist in the disarming of challenges to social inequalities. Welded to these logics is a lack of understanding of how violence works for a myriad of women, mediated through and by other social inequalities. Violence then becomes divorced from additional dangers of such inequalities. Danger is left to be negotiated individually or through the social agents such as the police who are best able, it is believed, to target the evil stranger.

In many respects, I worry about the lack of transformation in the discourses about violence. Perhaps the risks of modern life have changed, but the discourses about violence remain firmly welded to the dangers of strangers. The portrayal of men's violence to women has altered little in public and popular discourse. Of course, there are changes in the discrete recognition of domestic violence. Indeed, some of the daily work of state and social institutions has altered through the pressure of feminist lobbying to challenge what we know about the danger to women. No doubt, feminists have offered new discourses about men's danger to women. But there is little evidence that the forces that give sustenance to men's violence have altered. Women's narratives about the violence of men highlight the way men use such violence to control, to assert authority or to punish. The challenge in the twenty-first century – as many who have occupied positions of less power demand transparency in the decisions of the state and in the so-called benefits of Western progress – is to find a way to debate the impact of violence. Not only is violence important to our lives as women, but so too many men's lives are indeed blighted by the so-called naturalness of the violence they experience (see Stanko *et al.* 1998). One way forward is to refuse to accommodate the discourses of violence based in biology or psychology. To extend the debate by eschewing simple explanations about why violence occurs may be the first step in unmasking the unnatural impact of violence. Using women's experiences of danger is just one of many steps in this stage of transparency.

Notes

1 Russell's study of sexual assault, heralded as the first large-scale survey of sexual violence from a feminist perspective, documented a wide range of men's acts which women defined as coercive and damaging (Russell 1982). From sexual abuse and rape during childhood, courtship coercion and violence to wife rape and battering, Russell's survey revealed the commonness of men's violence for a sample of US women living in the San Francisco area. One in six of the women reported some form of incestuous abuse before aged eighteen. Nearly one in two of the women reported experiencing some form of sexual abuse at any point in their lives. One in seven reported being raped by their husbands. This survey prompted a number of studies of prevalence of sexual abuse around the world.

The most cited is the 1993 Statistics Canada survey which found that 39 per cent of the women reported sexual assault; one in three of all women questioned reported physical threat or assault at the hands of men (Johnson and Sacco 1995). Koss and her colleagues revealed high levels of sexual coercion on US university campuses. Over half of college women, according to her survey, have experienced some degree of sexual coercion (Koss *et al.* 1987). One in four of these women reported an experience of rape or attempted rape. Most of those sexually assaulted knew their assailants, many of whom assaulted women during courtship. DeKeseredy and Kelly's (1993) study of Canadian postsecondary school courtship found that 45 per cent of the women reported some form of abuse since leaving high school.

2 Women are most likely to be injured, raped and receive medical attention in assaults from known assailants (Mirrlees-Black *et al.* 1996). Further evidence shows that men do not sustain the same level of serious injuries at the hands of intimates (unless they are killed, often in self-defence, by women they batter). Women (or those acting on behalf of women) ask police for help in 90–95 per cent of requests for assistance in domestic violence.

3 Community safety audits collected by campaign groups or local crime prevention initiatives.

References

Allen, J. (1988) *Sex and Secrets*, Sydney: Allen & Unwin.

Beck, U. (1990) *The Risk Society*, London: Sage.

Cameron, D. and Fraser, L. (1987) *The Lust to Kill*, Cambridge: Polity.

Caputi, J. (1987) *The Age of Sex Crime*, Bowling Green, OH: Bowling Green State University.

Clark, A. (1987) *Women's Silence, Men's Violence*, London: Pandora.

Connell, P. (1999) 'Theorising Woman Abuse Through Identity: The Experience of Black British Women', unpublished Ph.D. thesis, University of Cambridge.

Crenshaw, K.W. (1994) 'Mapping the Margins: Intersectionality, Identity Politics and Violence against Women of Color', in M. Fineman and R. Mykitiuk (eds), *The Public Nature of Private Violence*, London: Routledge.

Daly, M. and Wilson, M. (1988) *Homicide*, New York: Aldine de Gruyter.

D'Cruze, S. (1999) 'Sex, Violence and Local Courts: Working-Class Respectability in a Mid-nineteenth Century Lancashire Town', *The British Journal of Criminology* 39(1): 39–55.

DeKeseredy, W.S. and Kelly, K. (1993) 'The Incidence and Prevalence of Woman Abuse in Canadian University and College Dating Relationships', *Canadian Journal of Sociology* 18: 157–9.

Dobash, R.E. and Dobash, R.P. (1979) *Violence Against Wives*, New York: Free Press.

—— (1992) *Women, Violence and Social Change*, London: Routledge.

Douglas, M. (1992) *Risk and Blame*, London: Routledge.

Gardner, C.B. (1988) 'Access Information: Private Lines and Public Peril', *Social Problems* 35: 384–97.

—— (1995) *Passing By*, Berkeley, CA: University of California Press.

Garland, D. (1996) 'The Limits of the Sovereign State: Strategies of Crime Control in Contemporary Society', *British Journal of Criminology* 36(4): 445–71.

Girard, R. (1986) *Scapegoat*, Baltimore, MD: The Johns Hopkins University Press.

Goodey, J. (1994) 'Fear of Crime: What can Children Tell Us?', *International Review of Victimology* 3: 195–210.

Gordon, L. (1988) *Heroes of their Own Lives*, London: Virago.

Gordon, M. and Riger, S. (1988) *The Female Fear*, New York: Free Press.

Hale, C. (1996) 'Fear of Crime: A Review of the Literature', *International Review of Victimology* 4: 79–150.

Hoff, L.A. (1990) *Battered Women as Survivors*, London: Routledge.

Holland, J., Romazanoglu, C., Sharpe, S. and Thomson, R. (1998) *The Male in the Head: Young People, Heterosexuality and Power*, London: The Tufnell Press.

Johnson, H. and Sacco, V. (1995) 'Researching Violence against Women: Statistics Canada's National Survey', *Canadian Journal of Criminology* 37(3): 281–304.

Koss, M., Gidycz, C.A. and Wisniewski, N. (1987) 'The Scope of Rape: Incidence and Prevalence of Sexual Aggression and Victimization in a National Sample of Higher Education Students', *Journal of Counselling and Clinical Psychology* 55: 455–7.

Luhmann, N. (1993) *Risk: A Sociological Theory*, New York: Aldine de Gruyter.

Madriz, E. (1997a) *Nothing Bad Happens to Good Girls*, Berkeley, CA: University of California Press.

—— (1997b) 'Images of Criminals and Victims: A Study on Women's Fear and Social Control', *Gender & Society* 11: 342–56.

Maxfield, M. (1984) 'The Limits of Vulnerability in Explaining Fear of Crime: A Comparative Neighbourhood Analysis', *Journal of Research in Crime and Delinquency* 21: 233–50.

Mirrlees-Black, C. (1999) *Domestic Violence: Findings from a New British Crime Survey Self-Completion Questionnaire*, London: Home Office.

Mirrlees-Black, C., Mayhew, P. and Percy, A. (1996) *The 1996 British Crime Survey Issue 19/96*, London: Home Office.

O'Malley, P. (1992) 'Risk, Power and Crime Prevention', *Economy and Society* 21(3): 252–75.

O'Neill, D. (1998) 'A Post-structuralist Review of the Theoretical Literature Surrounding Wife Abuse', *Violence Against Women* 4(4): 457–90.

Pain, R. (1993) 'Crime, Social Control and Spatial Constraint', unpublished Ph.D. thesis, University of Edinburgh, Edinburgh, Scotland.

President's Commission on Law Enforcement and the Administration of Justice (1967) *Task Force Report: Crime and Its Impact*, Washington, DC: US Government Printing Office.

Russell, D.E.H. (1982) *Rape in Marriage*, New York: Free Press.

Smith, A.M. (1992) 'Resisting the Erasure of Lesbian Sexuality: A Challenge for Queer Activism', in K. Plummer (ed.), *Homosexualities*, London: Routledge.

Skogan, W. and Maxfield, M. (1981) *Coping with Crime*, London: Sage.

Sparks, R. (1992) 'Reason and Unreason in Left Realism: Some Problems in the Constitution of Fear of Crime', in R. Matthews and J. Young (eds), *Issues in Realist Criminology*, London: Sage.

—— (1993) *Television and the Drama of Crime: Moral Tales and the Place of Crime in Public Life*, Buckingham: Open University Press.

Stanko, E.A. (1985) *Intimate Intrusions: Women's Experiences of Male Violence*, London: Routledge.

—— (1988) 'Hidden Violence against Women', in M. Maguire and J. Pointing (eds), *Victims of Crime: A New Deal?*, Milton Keynes: Open University Press.

—— (1990) *Everyday Violence: How Women and Men Experience Physical and Sexual Danger*, London: Pandora.

—— (1995) 'Women, Crime and Fear', *The Annals* 539: 46–58.

—— (1997) 'Safety Talk: Conceptualising Women's Risk Assessment as a "Technology of the Soul"', *Theoretical Criminology* 1(4): 479–99.

Stanko, E.A., Crisp, D., Hale, C. and Lucraft, H. (1998) *Counting the Costs*, Uxbridge, Middlesex: Centre for Criminal Justice Research, Brunel University.

Walklate, S. (1997) 'Risk and Criminal Victimisation: A Modernist Dilemma?', *British Journal of Criminology* 37(1): 35–46.

Warr, M. (1984) 'Fear of Victimization: Why are Women and the Elderly More Afraid?' *Social Science Quarterly* 65: 681–702.

Yanagisako, S. and Delaney, C. (1995) *Naturalising Power: Essays in Feminist Cultural Analysis*, London: Routledge.

Chapter 9

Drugs and dangerousness

Perception and management of risk in the neo-liberal era

Adam Sutton

Toward the end of 1998 *The Age*, one of Australia's premier broadsheet newspapers, ran a series of articles on the 'heroin problem' in Melbourne. The focus of one story – a sequel to a news item on commercial television the preceding evening – was a specific dealer. What made this entrepreneur newsworthy was that she was a mother. Indeed as both *The Age* and *Channel 10 News* were at pains to emphasise, her infant was present during at least one transaction. Cameras portrayed the baby cradled for an instant in the arms of a user-client, as the mother retrieved the product.

Reviewing the article, it is apparent that for both the journalist and potential readers, the perils in this situation were so self-evident as to require no elaboration. The bulk of the story in fact was devoted not to detailing or moralising about behaviour 'exposed' but to providing reassurance: that relevant authorities had been informed; that already they were assessing whether the child should be 'taken into care'. To this reader, however, the item served another purpose: as a reminder of the extent to which illicit drugs, their suppliers and, to a lesser extent,[1] users continue to be demonised in contemporary Australia and many other Western countries. Why, despite the absence of any real evidence of abusive behaviour, does the mass media find it so easy to portray a 'woman who deals' as posing inherent threats to her own child – dangers greater, even, than those traditionally posed by females whose sexuality is not 'properly' constrained and controlled?[2] Why, in late-modern, post-industrial economies whose viability depends on high levels of consumption, should one category of goods and services be taboo? Why, in an increasingly globalised economy, should commodities such as heroin, cocaine, amphetamines and even cannabis continue to bear the taint of the 'dangerous other'?[3]

The current chapter explores these issues. In doing so, it interrogates an important seam of theory on relationships between crime policy and broader systems of control. Drawing on Foucault (1979), Beck (1992) and Rose (1990), criminologists such as such as O'Malley (1994), Feeley and Simon (1992, 1994), Pratt (1997) and Garland (1996) have argued that modern and late-modern approaches to crime need to be understood in the context of the ways in which power is exercised and social risk defined and managed. According to these theorists, recent changes to law and policy – including the resurgence of attempts to identify and incapacitate 'dangerous' offenders, and a rekindling of interest in prevention – are products of a shift toward 'neo-liberal' (or 'post-Keynesian') modes of governance. Under such regimes, the emphasis is on ensuring individual (and local community) responsibility for social control and risk management. 'Care of the self', rather than direct support from the state, has become the dominant theme.

The starting point for this chapter is that theories about contemporary modes of governance and risk management are useful for helping to understand the various ways (which range from drug crime, property crime and sex crime) in which 'dangerousness' is conceptualised. Nonetheless, I also will contend that key aspects of illicit drug policy in Australia, the United States and other contemporary Western democracies are difficult to reconcile with these perspectives. Ongoing prohibition of substances such as cannabis, amphetamines, heroin and cocaine seem fundamentally inconsistent with doctrines of control at a distance, which has been a central tenet of neo-liberal analyses (see Miller and Rose 1990). In fact, rather than facilitating 'governance of the self', most states devote considerable resources to direct, coercive interventions which exacerbate difficulties drug users encounter as they try to assess and manage relevant risk. None of this seems compatible with neo-liberal models of power, and associated theories of dangerousness.

This chapter therefore suggests that theory needs to be modified to account for this anomaly. In particular, it needs more fully to acknowledge contradictions inherent to late capitalism. Following Jordan (1996), I will argue that while economic rationalism may emphasise *individual* choice, its practical consequence often has been to force people to act on *collective* bases. Health, education, housing and other key social needs now often are best satisfied by people 'clubbing together', to share costs and manage relevant risks. Such associations are more likely to be viable, however, if they rigorously exclude those who 'cannot be trusted' to conform and contribute. In this context, preference patterns in relation to psychoactive drugs – always important cultural markers – are assuming even greater significance. This, it will be argued, helps explain why taboos on psychoactive substances – often assumed to be relics of 'irrational' traditionalism (Morris and Hawkins 1970) – continue to exert force today.

An underlying theme of this chapter is that economic, political and broader social discourses within late-modern societies often are in tension. Such tensions, not always acknowledged in discussions of neo-liberal modes of governance, are of central relevance to contests over criminal law and crime policy. They are also of critical importance for understanding how Australia and other countries construct and try to deal with the 'dangerousness' of illicit drugs.

Governance, dangerousness and illicit drugs

First, however, to the theoretical perspectives which provide the starting point for the current discussion. Can concepts of danger be related to economies of power and systems of social control? John Pratt's *Governing the Dangerous* (1997) – an historical analysis of dangerousness in English-based jurisdictions[4] – argues that they can. Drawing on materials from the late eighteenth century onwards, he contends that in any specific era there are correlations between legal and popular concepts of dangerousness and dominant modes of governance.

Pratt points out that ideas about dangerousness have varied markedly from the mid nineteenth century to the present. Initially in England and Europe, the concern was with the 'dangerous classes': displaced and impoverished agrarian or urban workers. From the 1870s onward, however, such anxieties subsided. Twentieth-century modernist states provided citizens with a 'right to life' (Foucault 1979) and 'protection from risks which were thought to endanger [its] quality' (Pratt 1997: 1). In this context, threats to order were seen as emanating from recidivist individuals.

Even within modernism, however, there were shifts in the criteria for determining which criminals posed the greatest problems. Early in the twentieth century, focus was on repeat property offenders. After the 1930s, many countries witnessed a 'sexualising' of dangerousness with an emphasis on paedophiles, homosexuals and other 'deviants' who now fell into this category. By the 1960s, with welfarism at its height, and many Western governments prepared to provide comprehensive assurance against health and other life risks, a preoccupation with dangerousness receded, to be replaced with a concern for 'managing' those whose repeated offending was seen as symptomatic of 'personal inadequacy'. The final thirty years of the twentieth century have seen a marked decline in state interventionism. With comprehensive welfare no longer sustainable, neo-liberal rationality has shifted 'the general burden of risk management away from the state and its agencies and onto the self, in partnership with non-state forms of expertise and governance' (Pratt 1997: 133). One consequence has been that private citizens and organisations have been encouraged and expected to take greater responsibility for their own security. Another has been renewed legal and other discourses about dangerousness. Much of this has concentrated on sexual and violent offending: seen as violating individual rights to self-governance, choice and participation in the 'new economy of bodily pleasures' (Pratt 1997: 140). Most Western countries – Australia included – have seen a general increase in punitiveness, which has been reflected in tougher sentences and higher prison populations. Drawing on Beck (1992), Pratt sees this also as symptomatic of insecurities inherent to the era of neo-liberal governance: 'if [this] now helps to make the horizons of life seem infinite and exciting ... then it also creates new fears and uncertainties through the dismantling and erosion of traditional support structures' (1997: 151).

Pratt's account does not extend to Western government policies on psychoactive drugs. While understandable,[5] this also is regrettable. As theorists such as Manderson (1993, 1995) point out, the history of debate and legislation in countries such as Australia suggests that such substances often serve as metaphors for danger. At key stages, moreover, this history seems out of step with progressions presented in *Governing the Dangerous*.

There is no evidence, for example, that over the last three decades Australia has been shifting away from direct state involvement in the regulation of illicit drugs. If anything, the neo-liberal era has seen Federal, State and Territory governments become more interventionist. As Manderson points out, it is now a hundred years since Australian policy emphasised 'self governance':

> a hundred years ago, legislative structures and social attitudes relating to drugs were radically different from those now in place. Their use was left to individual choice, rather than being subject to strict medical control or even prohibited by law. The lines between medical and non-medical use, or between use and abuse, now so clear and bright, were indistinctly drawn. The addict was defined as neither diseased nor evil, and the label was not yet a way of pigeon-holing a whole person.
>
> (1993: 10)

Since the early 1970s, penalties for production and distribution of substances such as cannabis, amphetamines, opiates and cocaine have escalated, to the point where trafficking even in cannabis may attract a prison sentence of up to thirty years.[6] Use of these drugs also continues to be prohibited, even in the context of medical trials. Financial and other resources dedicated to supply reduction by the Federal, State and Territory governments now total at least A$500 million per annum, with vastly more being spent on enforcement than on treatment and other user-support.[7] None of this is consistent with policies of self-management – indeed current Australian laws and enforcement practices can make it extremely difficult for users to assess and manage relevant risk.

The most dramatic evidence is the trend in deaths due to drug overdoses – mainly heroin related – which in Australia have doubled over the last eight years. Research by Australia's National Drug and Alcohol Research Centre (Darke *et al.* 1999) suggests that for many of these fatalities, lack of knowledge about drug purity was a major contributor. Older and/or less frequent users – particularly those returning to the scene after a period of abstinence – were unable to cope when the quantity normally purchased contained a higher than usual dosage.[8] Of course, stringent penalties for trafficking, which oblige those in the supply chain to make their work inconspicuous and provide powerful incentives for keeping retail transaction times to a minimum, render provision of accurate and comprehensive product information unlikely.

Other ways those associated with illicit drugs can try to manage associated hazards include making sure that they use in environments which are supportive (e.g. in company, in supervised injecting rooms), that they employ proper equipment (e.g. clean needles), and that they give preference to suppliers who mix and transport products hygienically. Users also, of course, can try to take drugs in ways which are intrinsically less problematic (e.g. smoke or snort rather than inject) and to opt for less hazardous (even if still illegal) drugs (e.g. cannabis rather than crack cocaine). Again, research suggests that prohibition undermines the capacity for such choices. Recent data from two of Australia's largest cities (Maher *et al.* 1997; Fitzgerald *et al.* 1999) indicate that vigorous police presence makes it far more likely that users will shoot up hastily and/or alone, in unsanitary venues (e.g. laneways, stairwells and public toilets) and share needles (thereby increasing exposure to blood-borne hepatitis C and HIV infection).[9] Almost inevitably, intensive street level surveillance makes it difficult or impossible for the average user to be 'choosy' about the ways drugs are supplied. The Sydney study (Maher *et al.* 1997) found that retail dealers in one area of high intensity policing carried heroin 'caps' in the mouth or nose, to facilitate rapid disposal if apprehended. By (even temporarily) drying up supplies of some types of product, successful supply reduction also inadvertently can help steer providers and clients toward more risky substances. Hamid (1991) for example argues that successes by New York police in disrupting Rastafarian trade in ganja (cannabis) effectively shifted dealers and users toward crack cocaine. Finally, because prohibition helps make illicit drugs more expensive, it increases the likelihood that users will adopt less safe modes of administration (e.g. injecting), which yield better 'value for money'.

Such data highlight the fact that in complex neo-liberal societies, consumer freedom – the capacity to exert choice in a marketplace – is the key to effective risk management. By undermining such freedom, prohibitionism renders 'governance of the self' more difficult. Many advocates of market-oriented policies – including such luminaries as Milton Friedman – are aware of this, and favour drug law reform. The fact remains however, that few countries even have tried to translate such economic rationality into political programmes. The United States, largest and most influential of the 'free enterprise' democracies, remains adamant in its 'just say no' (or be arrested) policies: not only this, but drug use in some states is considered sufficiently serious to activate 'three-strikes' provisions where available. Countries such as Australia have deviated somewhat from this line – for example by endorsing policies that give priority to minimising drug-related harms rather than to supply reduction *per se*, by introducing needle exchanges and other user-support initiatives, and by putting (theoretical) emphasis on treating rather than punishing those with a habit. Basically however, Australia also views the trade in illicit drugs as an evil that must be suppressed. Of all the Western democracies, only the Netherlands, with its philosophy of 'normalising' drug use and comparative tolerance not just for users but for some aspects of supply (Grapendaal *et al*. 1995: 5–13), has taken steps toward a policy regime consistent with neo-liberal models of governance. However Holland's steadfast refusal to endorse the 'war on drugs' renders it isolated, even among the Western European democracies. Despite the Netherlands' comparative success in containing relevant harms, no other Western country seems able to countenance the idea of showing some tolerance toward illicit drug markets – even though this may well be the key to ensuring that users can be saddled with greater responsibility for 'care of the self'. Direct police and other state intervention, not 'control at a distance', has been the guiding principle in Australia, the United States and most other post-industrial democracies.

The fact that the drug policies of most Western countries are inconsistent with neo-liberal models of power and risk management has major implications for associated theory about dangerousness. Pratt, for example, suggests that in addition to stressing individual responsibility, neo-liberal governance holds sacred the right to participate in 'new economies of bodily pleasure'. Like David Harvey (1989, 1996), he is conscious that late capitalism thrives on the 'creative destruction' of tradition and the ceaseless generation of new commodities and lifestyles. In this context Pratt argues that in the neo-liberal era, activities and individuals are more likely to be construed as dangerous if they threaten rights and capacities to consume. However, how can this be reconciled with the fact that the majority of late capitalist economies continue to proscribe many substances employed in the pursuit of hedonism, and continue to characterise as 'menaces to society' those involved in producing and distributing them? Again, illicit drug policies seem fundamentally at odds with the logic of market-based economies.

Using drugs as a case in point, this section has argued that concepts of dangerousness cannot be explained purely in terms of the overt rationalities of neo-liberalism. Relevant laws and policies are in conflict with dominant principles of governance and economics. Opponents of current legal regimes may be wont to portray the prohibition of substances such as cannabis, amphetamines, heroin and cocaine as a moralistic relic of tradition, but this is one relic which stubbornly resists dissolution in the acid bath of late modern consumerism and competition (Beck 1992: 94). The remainder of this chapter explores why this aspect of culture should exhibit such resilience. In my view the key lies in developing the other part of Pratt's thesis – that is, in locating the 'dangerousness' of illicit drugs in the broader context of current 'fears and uncertainties'. Such reassessment must start by briefly reviewing the ways societies and cultures make use of psychoactive substances.

Drugs, culture and society

If mass media are to be believed, consumption of drugs is a 'problem' unique to the late twentieth century. Reality, of course, is more complex. As Sherratt (1995a: 26) points out, archaeological and ethnographic data suggest that all 'human societies are more likely than not to have discovered the psychoactive properties of the plants in their environment and to have canonised their usage in culturally characteristic forms of consumption and ritual'. Alcohol in the form of beer and wine has been in use for at least 8000 years, tobacco was introduced into Northern America more than two millennia ago, and there is evidence that the opium poppy was cultivated by the first Neolithic groups in central Europe. While early uses of drugs seem mainly to have been religious or medicinal, there is evidence of wine being the preferred drink among Mesopotamian elites at the beginning of the first millennium, and of coffee, tea, chocolate and tobacco being mass consumed in many parts of Europe by the mid 1720s.[10]

Throughout much of this history, moreover, there have been tensions between drugs as consumer commodities and their more selective employment as markers of cultural and political boundaries. Disdain for alcohol is a case in point. Reinforced by law in many contemporary orthodox Islamic states, this taboo has its origins in political struggles in the Near and Middle East which culminated in a fundamental shift in the balance of influence around 700AD. Prior to then, the region had been dominated by urban civilisations centred in small areas of intensive cultivation and characterised by wine production, consumption and trade. Their sovereignty was displaced by nomadic tribal groups who controlled the desert trade routes. Such groups' rejection of wine reflected both cultural preference and an explicit attempt to supplant the values and practices of a previous elite (Sherratt 1995b: 22–3).

The capacity for psychoactive substances to be endowed with profound cultural and political significance is not difficult to understand. Drugs have played critical roles in the formation and maintenance of religious cults, with ritualised consumption helping to intensify communion and shared mystical experience.[11] In less concentrated ways such principles also are at work in ceremonies of hospitality, where willingness to 'lower the guard' and partake in the drug of preference can both symbolise and help cement affinities.

As the history of Islam and alcohol demonstrate however, to those outside the 'charmed circles', such practices also can present as exclusionary. Indeed at times of intense political or economic conflict, they are apt to be read as sinister, with even the possibility of acceptance among the 'other' characterised as a threat. In Australia, the classic example is racist media and other responses to opium smoking by Chinese people during the mid to late nineteenth century. Although initially forced on China by British mercantile interests, opium smoking had become a characteristic mode of recreational drug use. When large numbers of Chinese workers were imported to Australia to help meet labour needs generated by the gold rushes, their presence and capacity to compete successfully for low-paid work was resented by locally born labour. Populist media outlets such as the *Bulletin* magazine, whose banner at the time proclaimed 'Australia for the white man', helped amplify the hysteria, exemplified by the following extract from an 1886 edition:

> Disease, defilement, depravity, misery and crime – these are the indispensable adjuncts which make Chinese camps and quarters loathsome to the senses and facilities of civilised nations .... Wherever the pig-tail pagan herds on Australian soil, they introduce and practise vices the most detestable and damnable – vices that attack everything sacred in the system of European civilisation.
>
> (Manderson 1993: 19–20)

For the Bulletin and its followers 'opium dens' posed an extreme threat – not just of general 'social pollution' but more specifically of the seduction of 'innocent white girls'.[12] Absurd though these fears may now seem, they were catalysts not just for criminalising opium use – completed throughout the country by 1908 – but for the enactment in 1901 of 'White Australia' immigration policies.

Moral panics such as this highlight the ways specific substances and ways of consuming them can be fetishised, as symbols not just of problems perceived to emanate from particular groups, but of more deep-seated concerns about disruption to an established order. Most, if not all, societies use both food and drugs as elements in complex systems of non-verbal communication (Goodman *et al.* 1995). In *Purity and Danger*, her seminal review of ideas about pollution in 'primitive' cultures, Mary Douglas (1966) points out that qualities of impurity, uncleanliness and 'danger' tend to be attributed to substances which are 'out of place' in relation to the dominant structure of classifications. Constant denunciation of the 'dirtiness' of opium smoking attests to the relevance of her ideas for more 'developed' societies:

> Down from the fan-tan dens are stairs leading to lower and dirtier abodes: rooms darker and more greasy than anything of the ground floor: rooms where the legions of aggressive stinks peculiar to Chinamen seem ever to linger. Yet the rooms are not naturally repulsive, nor would they be so when occupied by other tenants; but the Chinaman has defiled their walls with his filthy touch; he has vitiated what was once a reasonably pure atmosphere with his presence, and he has polluted the premises with his disgusting habits; and so it is that nought save suggestions of evil, incentives of disgust and associations of vice, now

seems to move in the fetid atmosphere. The very air of the alley is impregnated with the heavy odour of the drug.

(Manderson 1993: 24)[13]

Clearly, this form of drug use struck powerful dissonances with the prevailing cultural order – even though opium itself was widely used in other (e.g. medicinal) contexts.[14]

Late nineteenth-century Australian responses to immigrant Chinese smokers of opium provide a relatively straightforward example of a dominant system striving to 'maintain boundaries' against perceived external threat. It should be noted, however, that not all cultural taboos can be understood in terms of this simple model. As Douglas points out, concepts of pollution and danger are also often invoked in situations of *intra-societal* conflict: when a system is 'at war with itself' (1966: 141–59). In my view, this latter idea helps better explain why prohibitionist impulses continue to dominate Western drug policies. Historical analysis of prohibitionism suggests that while attempts to ban psychoactive substances may have gained initial impetus from specific inter-group conflicts, their ongoing strength derives from tensions within the cultures of capitalism itself.

The first great campaign of the modern era of course, was that of the United States Temperance Movement, which culminated in a fourteen-year ban on alcohol during the early years of this century. As Gusfield (1986) points out, this undoubtedly had its origins in inter-cultural conflict. Alcohol prohibition was the goal of a status group desperate to use politics to reaffirm a leadership role and the supremacy of its way of life and beliefs in a society that no longer bent to its ideals. For this group – rural Protestants whose temperate, abstinent lifestyle derived almost directly from that of the Puritans who had forged the first European settlements in New England – recreational drinking jarred fundamentally with a culture of self-control, industriousness and impulse renunciation. Enactment in 1919 of legislation proscribing alcohol production, sale and distribution provided symbolic reassurance that ascetic values could continue to hold sway in the face of encroaching urbanisation and industrialisation.

As an example of 'boundary maintenance', prohibition was, of course, at best only a fleeting victory. Alcohol consumption did not cease, and by 1933 relevant legislation had been repealed. Politically, as well as economically and socially, abstentionism ultimately was compelled to give way to more catholic lifestyles where activities of consumption were almost as important as those associated with production, and a resort to alcohol to 'switch off' for relaxation was seen to be as legitimate as the use of tea or coffee to 'switch on' for work (see Mugford 1992). Indeed, from the vantage point of post-1970s consumerism, attempts to perpetuate a cultural order devoid of reliance on psychoactive substances now can appear merely eccentric, proof of the futility in an ever-changing world, of attempts to cling to absolute values.

Such dismissal hardly does justice, however, either to the complexities of contemporary drug policies or to forces underlying the prohibitionist exercise. While it is true that, in the West at least, the battle to banish alcohol has been lost, there is ample evidence that fronts against other drugs are maintained with unabated vigour. Moreover the concerns which motivated Gusfield's 'symbolic crusaders' live on, albeit in transmuted form, in the late-modern era. The Calvinist ethic rejected 'pleasures of the flesh' because they could distract attention from the most fundamental imperative: to discover one's eternal fate through systematic engagement with the material world (Weber 1976). Attempts to ban alcohol were prompted by profound inner concerns about life's potential to divulge whether or not one was a member of the 'elect'. Contemporary consumerism has not extinguished such anxieties, rather it has universalised them. No less than the Calvinist ethic, neo-liberal governance confronts every citizen with responsibility for establishing the 'meaning' of his or her own existence (Beck 1992). In predominantly secular societies the 'here and now' – the present life – has become 'all there is'. Quite rightly, Pratt points out that neo-liberalism's infinite possibilities create unique stresses. To this I would add that the inner uncertainty which haunts many of our attempts to deal with such dilemmas bears testimony to what Weber saw as Christian asceticism's most profound legacy to the spirit of capitalism.

Given such tensions, it is not difficult to understand why neo-liberalism, like most other forms of governance, exhibits profound ambiguities in relation to psychoactive substances. Undoubtedly, writers such as Mugford (1992) are correct when they argue that the pressures of a contemporary lifestyle can make access to drugs as commodities seem essential: critical aids in dealing with life's constant shifts in pace and demand. Simultaneously however, such pragmatism tends to be undermined by anxieties associated with the need to 'maintain the proper balance' of roles and activities – for example to combine career and personal relationships with discerning consumption and an ongoing capacity to present a healthy, attractive body. These concerns can reinforce tendencies to utilise drugs in quite different ways: not as commodities, but as critical components in an unspoken cultural syntax which provides cues about individual and social stability, and about potential 'threats to order'. Popular stereotypes of those associated with illicit drug production, distribution and consumption bear direct witness to the importance of this symbolism. 'The addict' for example, exemplifies the individual who has lost all capacity to maintain, not just life-equilibrium, but even a healthy body, falling victim instead to obsessive consumption. 'Pushers' stand for those who, purely for self-interest, lure others down this path to self-destruction. 'Mr Bigs' represent remote, immensely powerful and manipulative outsiders who in the era of globalisation are burdening us all with unmanageable change, while remaining indifferent to its consequences. As Manderson (1995) points out, the very thought of use of a substance such as heroin 'is feared as a challenge to the mighty boundaries we have constructed between mind and body, reason and emotion, self and other'. While offering relief from the pressures of everyday life, drugs simultaneously evoke 'disgust at the notion of hedonism, distrust of unearned pleasure, and distress at the thought of living exclusively in the present' (1995: 807). In these respects, the cultural values of the late-modern period exhibit symptoms of a system 'at war with itself'. Moreover these conflicts – and associated preoccupations about danger, disorder and drugs – may well be exacerbated by neo-liberal modes of governance.

Discussion

While conceding that psychoactive drugs may seem essential commodities for post-industrial societies, the preceding section has argued that not even mass consumerism has been able to obliterate their significance as cultural markers. This helps explain why readers of *The Age* and viewers of *Channel 10 News* and no doubt channels of the news media in other countries find it so easy to infer danger in any scenario that juxtaposes an infant with illicit drug users and dealers. Such stories evoke visceral responses about the need for children to be protected from exposure to chaos, lack of balance and lack of control. In our society the 'drug dealer' is feared like the carrier of a plague – as someone who, by the merest contact, can inculcate a virus of self-destruction. What hope can there be for any child who for protection must rely on such a figure?

Discussion of the roles drugs play in culture also helps understand why Western policies on such substances often seem resolutely to defy neo-liberal principles of governance. While empirical evidence may indicate that the 'dangerousness' attributed to illicit drugs often is arbitrary and exaggerated, this cannot obscure the fact that such assessments are the product of a need – to be found in all societies – for shared non-verbal understandings about order. There is little reason to believe that the 'rationality' of any system of power will easily rearrange such deep structures. In Australia and other Western countries, 'control at a distance' in relation to illicit drugs only will be achieved once relevant substances and activities associated with their production, distribution and consumption no longer are demonised within relevant cultures. With the exception of the Netherlands, however, there is little evidence that political systems are even beginning to address this issue.

In exploring contemporary drug policy as a major 'exception case', my argument is not that no relationships can be found between neo-liberal modes of governance and contemporary crime policies and practices. Undoubtedly, theorists such as Feeley and Simon (1992, 1994) are correct when they argue that risk assessment and management principles exert profound influence over the ways correctional and other criminal justice systems are administered in most late capitalist societies. What legislative and policy-trends on drugs highlight, however, is that it is by no means certain that this technocratic approach will be able to dominate all cultural systems (including mass media) and political strategies. Fiscal constraints may make senior politicians and bureaucrats yearn for the day when victimisation has become merely an 'everyday risk to be managed like air pollution and road traffic', and a compliant public finally has accepted 'erosion of one of the foundational myths of modern society: that the sovereign state is capable of providing security, law and order and crime control' (Garland 1996: 4). However, even as the 'iron logic' of power and economics seems to dictate that politics and policy be reshaped in this way, the 'soft architecture' of culture continues to constrain other relevant discourses from moving in the required directions.[15]

The fact is that late capitalism is a system which tends permanently to be 'at war with itself', and the apparent 'irrationality' of illicit drug policies is an almost eradicable symptom of that conflict. Already, this chapter has discussed ways these contradictions can be reflected within individuals, as they strive to strike the right balance of roles, responsibilities and pleasures. To complete the picture, it is useful finally to discuss the broader structural dimensions of this 'war' — because again it helps understand why some substances retain importance within culture as significant markers of danger and disorder.

The most basic problem is that strategies of governance that emphasise individualism and strategic, self-interested behaviour always run the risk of becoming self-defeating. Rather than assisting each player to achieve optimum outcomes, such systems can result in the majority receiving minimal benefits. This is because, as Dryzek (1995) and others point out, social interactions based on these principles become characterised by high levels of distrust. The problem can be resolved only if some or all participants are able to break through the 'prisoner's dilemma' impasse, and establish empathy and co-operation. Clearly, shared culture — including shared non-verbal systems of communication — is likely to be of critical importance in this context.

This structural tension is exacerbated by the fact that in neo-liberal governance even 'fundamental' needs — for example for housing, education, health and other social insurance — are complex, and likely to make significant resource demands. In practical terms, this means that if forced by these principles of governance to become more self-reliant, many individuals, groups and families will adopt the strategy of joining one or more 'clubs' with others who share similar needs and expectations (Jordan 1996). Such decisions make considerable sense, from a self-interested point of view. By joining with others in a health insurance association, a housing estate or a private school, participants can minimise their own outlays while at the same time sharing in the benefits of a major investment. Such 'clubs' can only be effective, however, if members both feel confident in committing to one another on the basis of trust and at the same time are able rigorously to exclude those unlikely to 'fit in' – whether through inability to make relevant financial and other contributions, or because they are likely to put excessive demands on the shared resource.

Ultimately, then, at the level of structure as well as of the individual, neo-liberalism is characterised by warring principles: of co-operation and competition; of trust and distrust; of inclusion and exclusion. Just as in the 'primitive' societies cited by Mary Douglas, concepts of danger and taboo – in this case applied to some psychoactive drugs – both reflect these tensions and provide mechanisms for helping deal with them. A key to the ongoing symbolic importance of drugs in contemporary societies may well lie in their usefulness as part of the armoury of techniques which can be brought to bear in making critically important judgements about whether to co-operate with, or to exclude, specific individuals or groups. This suggests that, albeit in complex ways, contemporary stereotypes about illicit drugs reflect not just the fears and uncertainties of neo-liberalism but also its operational needs.

Notes

1 I say 'to a lesser extent' because in Australia, attitudes towards users of illicit drugs are ambiguous. In some contexts users are portrayed as dangerous – part of the alleged threat for the infant in *The Age* article was that, albeit fleetingly, it was left in the clutch of a 'drug user'. Parents who use 'hard' drugs also tend routinely to be portrayed by the mass media as endangering and neglecting their children (see for example the *Herald Sun*, *The Age*'s tabloid competitor, which on 18 February 1999 carried a front page picture of, and editorialised about, a young woman using intravenously in a public park while her baby 'looked on' from a pram). Against this, however, both political and media debates in contemporary Australia now are tending to argue that it is traffickers and dealers who constitute the main danger, with users – their 'helpless victims' – best dealt with by means of treatment.

2 Testimony to the continuing 'threat' posed by undomesticated female sexuality is the fact that Victoria's current sex industry legislation – 'reformed' in 1994 – continues to forbid sex industry work within 200 metres of 'churches, hospitals, schools, kindergartens or any other place where children may be' (Prostitutes' Collective of Victoria, undated: 2). Current laws also favour discreet, segregated brothel and escort industry-based enterprise over more conspicuous 'street work'.

3 Responding to ongoing media campaigns about illicit drug trading and use, the then Premier of Victoria stated that the focus should be on 'dealing with those bastards who bring the stuff in' (*The Age*, 19 February 1999). Among other things, Victoria's Chief Commissioner of Police has suggested that chemical and biological warfare be used to reduce production of heroin in 'source' countries such as Burma, Thailand and Laos (*Herald Sun*, 20 February 1999).

4 That is, the United Kingdom, the United States, Canada, Australia and New Zealand.

5 An ambitious attempt such as Pratt's to analyse shifts in crime policy over two centuries in five countries cannot avoid being accused of overgeneralising and/or of significant omissions.

6 In South Australia, the maximum penalty for possessing cannabis or cannabis resin in a 'school zone' for the purposes of sale, supply or administration is one million dollars or thirty years in prison. In other Australian States maximum prison sentences for cannabis-related offences range from ten to twenty years.

7 A recent report for the Australian State of Victoria (Victorian Premier's Drug Advisory Council 1996) estimated that law enforcement accounted for 74 per cent of all expenditure in relation to illicit drugs. MacCoun and Reuter (1998: 233) estimate that the United States spends $US30 billion per annum on drug control – again with the great majority dedicated to supply reduction.

8 Of course, even a customary dosage may have toxic effects on a heroin user who has been abstinent for some time (Whelan 1998: 23). This reinforces the point that for users to manage risk they need precise information on drug type and purity.

9 On the basis of syringes retrieved from needle disposal units in an inner-city suburb of Melbourne, Fitzgerald et al. (1999) estimated 1200 injections in public toilets during a one-month period.

10 For general histories see Goodman et al. 1995; Lang 1998. The reference to tobacco is from Von Gernet 1995.

11 An exotic example is the peyote cult, a messianic movement based on a hallucinogenic cactus. First recorded ritual use of peyote was by the Aztecs at the time of the sixteenth-century invasion of Mexico. Subsequently, it was incorporated in Catholic ceremonies. After suppression in South America by the Inquisition, ritual use was adopted by some American Indian cultures. Peyote is now widely used by members of the Native American Church (see Lang 1998; Sherratt 1995b: 16).

12   A European girl lay as if under the soporific influence of hell, opium, or the Chinese drugs, nude, or nearly so; yes, dear reader, there she lay on the same bed or couch, three adult and lascivious Chinamen lay around her; they were to me, so many fiends exulting 'oer the deadened, inert, opiumed, drugged woman or girl aforesaid.
(Manderson 1993: 25 – the extract is from 'Humanity', *Sketches of Chinese Character*, Beacham, Castlemaine: 1878)

13 This extract is from 'The Chinese in Australia', *Bulletin*, 21 August 1886.

14 At the turn of the century Australia was the largest per capita consumer in the world of patent medicines, many of which (e.g. Mrs Winslow's Soothing Syrup, Bonnington's Irish Moss, Godfrey's Cordial and Ayers' Sarsparilla) contained strong dosages of opium (see Manderson 1993: 52–3).

15 In passing, it should be noted that drugs is by no means the only area of contemporary crime policy which is resisting rationalist incursions. Close assessment of the ways Australian and other Western governments have gone about implementing crime prevention, whose ongoing 'rediscovery' since the early to mid 1980s has been cited (e.g. by O'Malley 1994; Garland 1996; Pratt 1997) as primary evidence of the influence of neo-liberalism, in fact suggests that funding and other priority is being given to 'community development' schemes aimed at achieving idealised notions of social order and stability rather than to risk management projects based on theories of 'situational' prevention (see O'Malley and Sutton 1997).

References

Beck, U. (1992) *Risk Society: Towards a New Modernity*, London: Sage.

Darke, S., Ross, J., Zander, D. and Sunjic, S. (1999) *Heroin-related Deaths in New South Wales: 1992–1996*, National Drug and Alcohol Research Centre, Sydney: University of New South Wales.

Douglas, M. (1966) *Purity and Danger: An Analysis of Concepts of Pollution and Taboo*, London: Routledge and Kegan Paul.

Dryzek, J. (1995) 'Critical Theory as a Research Program', in S White (ed.), *The Cambridge Companion to Habermas*, Cambridge: Cambridge University Press, pp.97–119.

Feeley, M. and Simon, J. (1992) 'The New Penology: Notes on the Emerging Strategy of Corrections and its Implications', *Criminology* 30: 449–74.

—— (1994) 'Actuarial Justice: the Emerging New Criminal Law', in D. Nelken (ed.), *The Futures of Criminology*, London: Sage.

Fitzgerald, J., Broad, S. and Dare, A. (1999) *Regulating the Street Heroin Market in Fitzroy/Collingwood*, Melbourne: VicHealth and The University Of Melbourne.

Foucault, M. (1979) *The History of Sexuality*, vol. 1, London: Allen Lane.

Garland, D. (1996) 'The Limits of the Sovereign State: Strategies of Crime Control in Contemporary Society', *British Journal of Criminology* 36(4): 445–71.

Goodman, J. (1995) 'Excitantia: Or, How Enlightenment Europe Took to Soft Drugs', in J. Goodman, P.E. Lovejoy and A. Sherratt (eds), *Consuming Habits: Drugs in History and Anthropology*, London and New York: Routledge.

Goodman, J., Lovejoy, P.E. and Sherratt, A. (eds) (1995) *Consuming Habits: Drugs in History and Anthropology*, London and New York: Routledge.

Grapendaal, M., Leuw, E. and Nelen, H. (1995) *A World of Opportunities: Lifestyle and Economic Behaviour of Heroin Addicts in Amsterdam*, Albany, NY: State University of New York Press.

Gusfield, J.R. (1986) *Symbolic Crusade: Status Politics and the American Temperance Movement*, 2nd edn, Chicago, IL: University of Illinois Press.

Hamid, A. (1991) 'From Ganja to Crack: Caribbean Participation in the Under-ground Economy in Brooklyn, 1976–1986. Part 1. Establishment of the Marijuana Economy', *The International Journal of the Addictions* 26(6): 615–28.

Harvey, D. (1989) *The Condition of Postmodernity*, Oxford: Oxford University Press.

—— (1996) *Justice, Nature and the Geography of Difference*, Oxford: Blackwell.

Jordan, B. (1996) *A Theory of Poverty and Social Exclusion*, Cambridge: Polity Press.

Lang, E. (1998) 'Drugs in Society: A Social History', in M. Hamilton, A. Kellehear and G. Rumbold (eds), *Drugs in Australia: A Harm Minimisation Approach*, Melbourne: Oxford University Press, pp.1–13.

MacCoun, R. and Reuter, P. (1998) 'Drug Control', in M. Tonry (ed.), *The Handbook of Crime and Punishment*, Oxford: Oxford University Press, pp.207–38.

Maher, L., Dixon, D., Swift, W. and Nguyen, T. (1997) *Anh Hai: Young Asian Back-ground People's Perceptions and Experience of Policing*, Sydney: University of New South Wales Faculty of Law.

Manderson, D. (1993) *From Mr Sin to Mr Big: A History of Australian Drug Laws*, Melbourne: Oxford University Press.

—— (1995) 'Metamorphosis: Clashing Symbols in the Social Construction of Drugs', *The Journal of Drug Issues* 25(4): 799–816.

Miller, P. and Rose, N. (1990) 'Governing Economic Life', *Economy and Society* 19: 1–31.

Morris, N. and Hawkins, G. (1970) *The Honest Politician's Guide to Crime Control*, Chicago, IL: University of Chicago Press.

Mugford, S. (1992) 'Policing Euphoria: The Politics and Pragmatics of Drug Control', in P. Moir and H. Eijkman (eds), *Policing Australia: Old Issues, New Perspectives*, Melbourne: Macmillan.

O'Malley, P. (1994) 'Neo-liberal Crime Control: Political Agendas and the Future of Crime Prevention in Australia', in D. Chappell and P. Wilson (eds), *The Australian Criminal Justice System: The Mid 1990s*, Sydney: Butterworths.

O'Malley, P. and Sutton, A. (eds) (1997) *Crime Prevention in Australia: Issues in Policy and Research*, Sydney: Federation Press.

Pratt, J. (1997) *Governing the Dangerous: Dangerousness, Law, and Social Change*, Sydney: Federation Press.

Prostitutes' Collective of Victoria (undated) *The Hussey's Handbook*, Melbourne: Prostitutes' Collective (also available from the Victorian Department of Justice).

Rose, N. (1990) *Governing the Soul*, London: Routledge.

Sherratt, A. (1995a) 'Introduction: Peculiar Substances', in J. Goodman, P. Lovejoy and A. Sherratt (eds), *Consuming Habits: Drugs in History and Anthropology*, London: Routledge, pp.1–10.

—— (1995b) 'Alcohol and its Alternatives: Symbol and Substance in Pre-industrial Cultures', in J. Goodman, P. Lovejoy and A. Sherratt (eds), *Consuming Habits: Drugs in History and Anthropology*, London: Routledge, pp.11–46.

Victorian Premier's Drug Advisory Council (1996) *Drugs and our Community: Report of the Premier's Drug Advisory Council*, Melbourne: Government of Victoria.

Von Gernet, A. (1995) 'Nicotean Dreams: The Prehistory and Early History of Tobacco in Eastern North America', in J. Goodman, P. Lovejoy and A. Sherratt (eds), *Consuming Habits: Drugs in History and Anthropology*, London: Routledge, pp.67–87.

Weber, M. (1976) *The Protestant Ethic and the Spirit of Capitalism*, trans. Talcott Parsons, London: George Allen and Unwin.

Whelan, G. (1998) 'The Pharmacological Dimension of Psychoactive Drugs', in M. Hamilton, A. Kellehear and G. Rumbold (eds), *Drugs in Australia: A Harm Minimisation Approach*, Melbourne: Oxford University Press, pp.14–29.

Chapter 10

Dangerous states

Nils Christie

Danger is one of the central themes in criminology. Dangerous men and women. Monsters hiding in the shadows, or even more dangerous, living among us camouflaged as ordinary beings. Much energy and ingenuity is spent on identifying these individuals, on changing, eventually neutralising them, and on explanations and understanding of the phenomena of dangerous persons.

What a comfortable, tranquillising perspective on a globe filled with dangerous states! Dangerous for other states. But also, in what will be my perspective, dangerous for their own citizens.

Violent death

I was back from Moscow a few weeks ago, back to life as normal in my little country, back to write this long since overdue chapter on dangerous people. But there were some problems in concentrating on the scientific agenda. The theme in Moscow had been prison conditions. I had been there before, so I knew the basic: one million prisoners, that is 685 per 100,000 inhabitants, a prison population roughly similar to the one in the United States, which again means about ten times as many prisoners as in Scandinavia and eight times as many as in most Western European countries.

What was new was hunger. After the economic crisis last summer, the Russian state is out of money. At present, the state gives away two-thirds of a rouble per day per prisoner. This amount is also for medicine. Twenty roubles are at present equal to one dollar. While the West still is eagerly discussing the Holocaust occurring in Europe sixty years back, a catastrophe is emerging in the East, but quietly, with no serious attention raised in the West.

What is also new, at least in its dimensions, is the tuberculosis. Among the one million prisoners, 92,000 are estimated to have this disease. Some have received treatment, but it has been inadequate. Ordinary TB has developed into multi-resistant TB among 20,000 of these sick prisoners. A sentence of imprisonment means a sentence with heavily increased risk of TB and death, or in the words of Farmer (1998), this is a situation with

'Drug Resistant Tuberculosis as Punishment'. Imprisonment before being sentenced is particularly dangerous. The Moscow Centre for Prison Reform (1998) gives this description of the conditions in the prisons for those waiting for trial – the SIZO-prisoners, as they are known as in Russia:

> In the SIZOs of larger populated areas each prisoner is allocated less than 1 sq.m. of space, in some cells it is less than 0.5 sq.m. Prisoners have to sleep in turns. There is no place for all inmates to sit there. Conditions in SIZO cells are extremely harsh: lack of oxygen, dampness, stench. Many inmates have bloody ulcers and legs swollen from long standing, many are infected with scabies and other skin diseases. Their bodies are perspiring and nothing can dry due to the humidity. There is practically no light that enters through the heavily barred window. Two or three-tier beds are fastened to the walls. Any cell, be it for 10 or 100 inmates, has one sink and one toilet.
>
> (1998: 31)

I would not have believed it, if I had not been there myself, seen it, smelled it. The description need only be combined with our knowledge of tuberculosis: in the closed and non-ventilated rooms, often for more than 100 prisoners, inevitably some will be among the infected and cough out their tuberculosis.

It is of poor comfort that Western Europe has succeeded with the task of forcing Russia to abolish the use of the death-penalty. If Russia and its neighbours do not stop executing their prisoners, the state will not get access to the European Council. Russia has succumbed to that pressure. No one is executed in Russia these days. They just die.

The United States has the same relative number of prisoners. They have also to some extent rooms filled with sixty to eighty prisoners living extremely close together. But they also have the other extreme. The Maxi–Maxi electronically governed prisons mean the utmost of isolation. Single room with your own shower, your own toilet, your own balcony for fresh air and exercises, and in addition sufficient food. All this in total isolation from any other human being. A system which only gives its prisoners room space of one square metre would be considered violent by most of us. But such words might also be used on systems which for years force humans to be completely barred from other human beings. What we have is a different economy of violence – physical suffering is kept to a minimum, while the mental one is at the maximum.

Death is also a reality in the US prisons, but then a different death. Compared to the Russian, a prolonged one. A sentence for life might mean life until death. Little by little, some of the US prisons are transformed into geriatric institutions these days. Human beings are sent to prison to die, just at a slower pace than in the Russian ones.[1] But of course, in addition, the US system also kills by intention: 500 have been executed since 1977, more than 3000 are now on death row. What a pity that the United States is not an applicant for membership in the European Council, so we could have forced them to stop their use of the death penalty.

The problem

Hopefully, the contours of my approach are visible by now. A picture of dangerous people must be supplemented with a picture of dangerous states. In foreign policy, the image of the dangerous state is one much in use. But that type of danger is not my theme here. Mine is an essay in criminology. *I am interested in the danger that national states represent in their penal law approach towards their own citizens.* I look at the state as a potentially dangerous body. We ought to know what sort of states are dangerous to their citizens according to various types of danger, if it is possible to differentiate between states in that regard, and also if it is possible to come up with answers as to how dangerous states might be controlled and eventually changed.

Doing this, I will take the institution of penal law as my central unit for analysis. Penal law has to do with delivery of pain. This pain is said to be necessary to counteract other unwanted phenomena. But we know that unwanted behaviour also can be met with other reactions than penal ones. And we do also know that modern states vary enormously in volume and forms of punishments. These variations cannot be explained by variations in crime. To purify my approach, I will therefore ignore the question of 'effects of punishment', and concentrate all attention on the penal system as an instrument for creating suffering among prison inhabitants.

Some major variables in the evaluation of states

There are five general categories which might prove useful in an attempt to describe the amount of danger a state represents to its own citizens.

Size of the penal system

Since punishment means intended use of pain, it seems sensible to suggest that states with a profile of a large volume of penal law activities come closer to a pattern where they represent an exceptional danger for their citizens than do states with a low volume. One major dimension is the sheer volume of control activities linked to punishment. Is the state one which interferes much with punishment in the life of its citizens, or is it a state that is restrictive in its use of punishment? This might be measured by the size of the prison populations, or by the amount of fines applied each year. Another possible measure might be to make a count of the total volume of all encounters between the general public and all those working within the framework of the institution of penal law. Still another approach would be to make a count of all persons who worked within the institution of penal law, and compare their number, status, tasks and total costs with those working within alternative institutions such as health, social services and education. Some states would show a dominance within the area of penal law, some within the other areas. All these indicators might change over time. A 'life study' of dangerous states can be made in this way.

More suffering is created in big systems than in small by the simple fact that more people are in this system created for delivery of pain (Christie 1981). A big penal system is therefore more dangerous to a state's population than a small penal system. Russia with 1 million prisoners, and the United States with 1.7 million have both close to 1 per cent of their adult population in prison at any time. Most of these will be relatively young males. Among black and Hispanic males in the United States, 20 per cent will be in prison at any time. Among black men between eighteen and thirty in cities such as Washington and Baltimore, more than half are at any time in prison or on parole or probation. In other words: if you belong to these categories in the United States, you are in severe danger of being hurt by the state. It is also the case in Russia. If you come from one of the Eastern Republics in the former USSR, you have a heavily increased risk of being in prison.

The penal system is not restricted to use of imprisonment. Probation and parole are important instruments in many countries. Four million inhabitants are under that type of control in the United States these days. If those four million are added to the prison figures, and if we again only look at the youngest half of the adult male population, my estimate would be that 8 per cent of them are under control of the penal apparatus at the end of 1999.

The size of the prison population also has indirect consequences. Those close to prisoners might share sorrow and shame, and might also be directly hurt by husbands and partners taken away – or simply by limited access to find partners. For young black females in Washington or Baltimore, it has created a sort of war situation. They live in a society with a deficit of males. In addition there is the problem that those available might be less attractive due to damage created through earlier stays in prison, by the values and habits imprinted during life in captivity, by later handicaps at the labour market, and also by health problems acquired during the stay in prison. This last point is of course particularly dominant among a great number of prisoners released from Russian prisons, coming home to their families with active multi-resistant tuberculoses – if they come home at all.

Size is also of importance in another way: the greater the size of the penal system, the greater are the difficulties in creating personalised relationships. In a small prison – and here I talk about small in the Norwegian tradition where 50–100 prisoners is a normal size, and where 350 is the biggest prison in the country – there are possibilities to preserve at least a minimum of normal standards for interaction. It is difficult (but still possible) *not* to see the other person as something more than just a prisoner or a guard. In the large systems, the possibilities for monster-creating are considerable. In large prisons, where the inmates are living under degrading physical conditions, where they are so many that they only become numbers to the guards and also to some extent to each other, or where the prisoners are kept in a situation of complete segregation from the guards by the help of all sorts of electronic devices – in such prisons the conditions created are coming very close to those that in the past made concentration camps possible.

Amount of control of growth

But also in another way, prisons, or the whole prison system, might be closed off from the general society. The prison system might become a state within the state. It becomes so big or so important to the general society, that it moves out of control. The Californian prison system is an example of this. The economic contribution from the correctional organisations to the politicians from both major parties become so important that the prison-organisations can influence the size of the prison system. But they are not alone, as I have described in my book *Crime Control as Industry* (Christie 1994) and later described by Schlosser (1998) in his article on 'The Prison Industrial Complex'. He gives an example from upstate New York:

> in addition to the more than $1.5 billion spent to build correctional facilities, the prisons now bring the North Country about $425 million in annual payroll and operating expenditures. That represents an annual subsidy to the region of more than $1000 per person. The economic impact of the prisons extend beyond the wages they pay and the local services they buy. Prisons are labour intensive institutions, offering year round employment. They are recession proof, usually expanding in size during hard times. And they are non-polluting – an important consideration in rural areas where other forms of development are often blocked by environmentalists. Prisons have brought a stable, steady income to a region long accustomed to a highly seasonal, uncertain economy.
>
> (p.58)

The chances for unlimited growth of the prison system might be increased if the political system is organised in a way that makes it particularly difficult to resist that sort of pressure. Systems where judges as well as prosecutors are up for election every fourth year are of course more vulnerable to all sorts of moral panics than systems where both groups are given their positions for life and where there also exists a sort of cultural acceptance of the independence of these positions. Systems with backdoors out of the prisons – parole boards with integrity and authority – also have possibilities for keeping growth under control. The Russian system is an example of one where amnesties are one of the few possibilities for keeping numbers under control. But also in Russia, crime is one of the major themes in the media. The Tsars could declare amnesty. In the Duma (the Russian legislature) they have for months discussed a proposed amnesty for 100,000 prisoners, but even facing a pending hunger catastrophe among the prisoners, no decision has been made. It is not a popular decision with the electorate.

Life qualities within the penal institution

At the bottom-line comes the question of physical safety. Is life endangered by being committed to prison? Is that the case with all prisons, or only a few? Is it non-intended danger created by sickness under bad external conditions, or is it, as we also often find, dangers from violence by prison guards or fellow inmates? And again, is this violence a non-intended consequence of prison life, an unwanted result of the organisation of the prison, or is it intended, designed to increase suffering or exhort information? What is the annual ratio of death in prison – or sub-groups of prisons – compared to what we find in similar populations outside of prisons?

Of great importance for the life qualities in prisons are questions such as: who runs the prison, guards or prisoners? If it is the prisoners, is it a terror-regime, a caste system, or one with some minimum of mutual concern? Is it a system where it is possible to keep self-respect, or is it one where most people leave, if they leave at all, as badly hurt human beings? Are the guards placed on external watchtowers, or do they day in and day out mingle with the prisoners, giving both parties possibilities to meet the other as relatively ordinary human beings? For the service as a whole, does it belong to the military system, the ministry of interior, or the ministry of justice? It is a reasonable hypothesis that the system will gain more civil qualities the closer it comes to the ministry of justice. The Russian system has just moved from the ministry of interior to the ministry of justice. It gives some hope. Several countries have a circle of military guards around their prisons, but with guards from the ministry of interior or ministry of justice inside. What are the consequences for life and health of these various arrangements?

Permeability of the system

It is a general experience from cases of violence in the family that such perpetrators attempt to isolate the family. The man, and it is nearly always a man, tries to keep the wife at home, break up her contact with relatives and friends, restrict her to the intimate system where he can establish the standards for acceptable behaviour. Cry quietly, so the neighbours are not disturbed!

Penal systems often attempt to do the same. Penal institutions are closed institutions, closed so insiders cannot come out, physically or by their oral or written messages. But they are also to a large extent closed for outsiders. Visitors are screened, those with records, who will often be those close to the prisoners, might be kept out. So also will journalists, persons from human rights organisations, or dissidents of various sorts. Prisons built in remote areas are also well protected against being confronted with the surprised eye of the ordinary citizen. So are prisons with a reputation for containing exceptionally dangerous inmates – 'sorry, of concern for your own safety you cannot get access to this prison, or to this part of the prison'. Private prisons might create a particular problem – they might claim that what happens inside their walls is a business secret.

In the evaluation of permeability, some questions become essential. Particularly, is it possible for prisoners to complain, and, if so, to whom? Is their mail censored? Does there exist an 'ombudsman' for the prison or for the system as a whole? What sort of contact with the external world exists? Do the prisoners know who the guards are, do the guards wear name-tags?

The more the prison becomes a closed arena, the more dangerous this arena becomes for the inmates. Prisons are by definition a place with extreme differences in power between guards and inmates. The more secluded, the less restrictions on the use of that power. It is therefore of utmost importance to open these systems for inspection; by prison-ombudsmen, by journalists and human rights organisations, by university teachers and their students, and by the most ordinary among ordinary visitors. As in cases of family violence: the more vulnerable the potential perpetrator is, the more protected are the other family members.

Degree of civility

Much of the above reasoning can be captured in the term civility. But that demands a tolerance for the challenges of words with multiple meanings. Of the twenty definitions of civility in the Oxford dictionary (1973), what comes most close to my intentions is number twelve with the simple statement: 'polite or courteous in behaviour to others', and number thirteen: 'Since *civil*: connotes what pertains to the citizen in his *ordinary* capacity, it is distinguished from various words expressing specific departments and thus often opposed to these as a negative term'. Austin, the nineteenth-century legal philosopher, is here quoted in his use of the term as saying 'the word ... is applied to all manner of objects which are perfectly disparate. As opposed to criminal, it means all law not criminal. As opposed to ecclesiastical it means all law not ecclesiastical; as opposed to military it means all law not military, and so on'.

The prison system exemplifies organisations where civil elements are not dominant. Instances of civility can be found, moments of friendship or at least mutual respect between the person in authority and the person under suspicion or the prisoner. But often the persons do not come close enough to establish such sorts of relationships, and if they come close, the meeting is far from civil in basic character. In many countries, military men are literally running the whole penal system. In some, the material conditions are so far below reasonable standards due to hunger, sickness and lack of possibilities for presenting oneself as an ordinary decent person, that any thought of civility is out of the question. Appearing from cages with one square meter per prisoner – that is exactly the minimum established for each fox in Norwegian animal farms[2] – the conditions are not there for presenting oneself as an ordinary human being.

Another measure of civility – closely related to the question of permeability – has to do with the number of rights the prisoner has within the prison. Particularly, is he or she stripped of all civil rights? What about the right to vote? Many countries permit persons in prison to vote. This is the case in countries as diverse as the Czech Republic, Denmark, France, Israel, Poland and Zimbabwe (Donziger 1996: 18). Other countries let categories of prisoners lose their votes for life. The American Sentencing project estimates that 3.9 million US citizens are disenfranchised, including one million who have fully completed their sentences.

Recent trends in modern industrialised countries do not move in the direction of physical atrocities, or in any military direction. Recent trends are a reflection of business-culture, a trend towards managerial dominance of the crime control systems (Feeley and Simon 1992). But again, this is not a civil system. A managerial system is based on rationality and accountability, it is a system of strict planning, one with clear lines of command, and where the small cogs in the system are treated as objects by the big ones at the top. In its managerial character, this system is also one with little room for ordinary human interaction, civil interaction. But at the same time, it is a strong system as exemplified in the Maxi–Maxi prisons. This is, in modern times, the system with the most total control over the individual captive person isolated from all other humans, and at the same time also with the least amount of contact between guards and the captive ever invented. This is the antithesis of civility.

The question of civility is also of relevance within other areas of the institution of penal law. Are the police leaning toward civil standards, or military ones? Indicators here might be how police activities are symbolised; in uniforms and equipment. Do the police people walk, use bicycles or do they use cars, eventually armoured cars? Do they carry arms – always, sometimes, or only on exceptional occasions? How difficult is it for the police-person to get permission to bring a gun, and particularly to use that gun, if that at all is possible? How much reporting – paperwork – is needed after a gun has been used? What sort of evaluation is carried out if a person is killed by the police? In what sort of moral climate do the police operate –

one of war against crime, one of zero-tolerance, or one appreciating the model of an officer of peace? How are the police recruited – from the general population or from military circles? How 'ordinary', that is, representative of the general population, is the police? What is the quota of females recruited each year? How close to the citizens do policemen and women live? How vulnerable are they, in cases of counter-control from the general public?

Similar questions might follow at the court level: from where come the judges, are they close to the population in general, or only to certain segments? If the judges are legally trained, are they recruited from the general universe of law trained people or from selected subgroups; politically, with regard to class, ethnicity or geography? What is their independence *vis-à-vis* state power; are they elected by the voting population, by leading politicians, or by their peers? Is it a job for life, or for election periods? Is the judge equal in power to the prosecution? Has the judge a wide range of alternatives when it comes to punishment, or is it all predetermined by parliament, with highly specified minimum and maximum punishments, seen most clearly in the so-called sentencing tables which convert the judge to a secretary for the law-makers?

Questions can also be raised on the position of the defendant. How much is she or he a participant – how much an object in contrast to a subject? How long did the accused have to wait before the case came before the court, how well prepared is the person, in knowledge of the case, in having had time and space for sleep, for cleaning and dressing as an ordinary being, for presenting her/himself before the judges as an ordinary being deserving an ordinary evaluation? And then to the defence; how strong is the position of the defending side compared to the prosecution, in education, in prestige, in wealth? Is it possible to get to see a defender at any stage of the proceedings, and how free is the prisoner to interact with that person?

On the control of dangerous states

Once more we might look at our experience of dangerous people. Three major problems dominate the criminological/penological debate on these persons.

First, it is the question of the concept of danger. In some penal-law systems, danger is seen as the danger of committing any offence, independent of the character of that offence. In some systems, the concept of danger is limited to recidivism, but then recidivism to all sorts of offences. At the other extreme – and this has gradually come to be the most accepted use – the concept of danger is reserved for more serious acts, often serious violent or sexual acts. A dangerous person is here one dangerous for other people's life, eventually life and body.

A second major question is that of prediction. If we only look at serious acts, is it then possible to identify the perpetrators before they have committed their unwanted serious acts, eventually to predict who will recidivate to such acts? The general view seems to be that rare acts are difficult to predict, and that the number of false positives – those predicted to do the acts, but who would not have done it if they had not been interfered with – will be very high (Von Hirsch 1972; Mathiesen 1998). So, the ethical problem is great if one attempts to sentence people on the basis of prediction.

The third major theme has to do with type of sanction: is the goal of the operation to keep the supposed dangerous person out of circulation for ever or for a pre-determined time, or should the result of treatment or education be used for deciding on release of the supposed dangerous person?

Let us turn to states.

As to the first variable, the definition of the dangerous act, it seems sensible to say that a dangerous state is one that operates with a concept of danger that is all-inclusive. It is a state preoccupied with crime in general, rather than the danger of some individuals selected due to their peculiarly dangerous crimes. Dangerous states are those where mass incarceration is based on triviality, seven bottles of milk, two grams of some sort of drugs, a fist-fight between drunkards, and where extraordinary danger is seen as exhibited through recidivism to such acts. Such a view on dangerous criminals creates an enormous volume of state interference. States become dangerous to their citizens by equalising all they call crimes to danger and all individuals committing them to dangerous criminals.

With this statement, we have an opening for a cure of the situation. A way of reducing the danger in the dangerous state is to force upon the state a serious discussion of the borders of the crime concept. If high incarcerators are seen as a potentially dangerous system, the first step is to slim them, make this tendency a less dominant one. Of course, there are also other reasons than the protection of milk-bottles and the prevention of drug-use behind criminalisation of these acts in the high incarcerating states. But a discussion of the dangers in the expanding system might bring the hidden agenda to the surface. We will – with some good luck – get a discussion of alternative ways of controlling the under-class, rather than undifferentiated opinions in favour of crime-control.

The second variable, prediction, raises a whole set of other questions when we move to the state-level. First, is it possible to predict state-dangers, to predict which states will turn particularly dangerous to their citizens? As we saw from the individual level, problems are great with false positives as well as negatives. And the problems at state-level are even more complex. If Russia makes a break with the present attempts to adapt to the market-economy, what will then happen to its prison population? It is far from certain that the numbers will keep stable. The economic situation might worsen, but pride in being a Russian might get increased value. That pride might make crime less dominant in defining the other person. 'You made an idiotic and deplorable act while you were drunk last Saturday, but you are nonetheless a Russian, one of us. That remains more important than your bad act'. Nationality becomes such an important attribute that the crime-label does not stick. Pride in being a Russian might become so strong a category that it suppresses the distinction between 'Russians' and 'criminals'. Prison figures might shrink to the level of the Tsar-time, which means they would come down to European level with eighty to ninety per 100,000 inhabitants. Maybe. But another scenario is also possible; Russia is filled with minorities. With increased nationalism, prisons would feel a more natural place to contain these outsiders.

Developments in the United States are no more easy to predict. As with Russia, the United States represents today a dangerous state to large segments of its population. But fifteen years back who would have predicted that the United States would develop into a society with such an enormous reliance on imprisonment: it has tripled its prison population during the last fifteen years, and this phenomenal growth just continues. Will this increase continue, or come to a stop – or in the far distance, can we think of a substantial reduction in these figures? The answer is clearly related to the general features of US society. With the monolithic position of concern for trade and money, it is difficult to envisage great changes, particularly the establishment of alternative arenas for those not succeeding in the present system. Without such alternatives, the losers become many, and the winners scared by the prospect of losing what they gained in the monolith. But who knows? Concern for money might create concern for the cost of a bulging prison population. Zero-tolerance in New York City has increased their prison population from 6,000–7,000 inmates in 1980 to between 18,000–21,000 in 1997. The costs have in the same period gone up from $150 million to $800 million. At the same time, because of all the drug arrests being made in the city, 'kids in New York Schools have to attend classes with ninety other kids' (Massing 1998). Another possibility for reduction in the numbers would be more social upheavals among the more suppressed parts of the population. There are already black protests against the drug policy which, rightly, is seen as targeted more against blacks in the ghettos than against whites in the suburbs. More might come, both of incarceration and of protests. But again, unexpected variables might appear. Who would have predicted that Winston Churchill would have been the very person who in the early twentieth century in Britain triggered off a dramatic decrease in the number of British prisoners? It was not right, said this Conservative Secretary for the Home Office, to meet poverty with imprisonment (Downes 1988).

Then to the last variable: can states be influenced, eventually, and how? Particularly, can they be influenced by those of us working with the problems raised in this chapter?

The answer to this question depends on the thrust in cultural activities, the thrust in the intellectual scrutinising of these matters. If we believe in the value of analysis, new concepts, attempts at clarification, attempts to let our societies look at themselves from unexpected angles rather than being too busy looking at their dangerous criminals, then, maybe, we will be able to give the development a little push in a direction more in accordance with our knowledge and values. As for intellectuals, there are no other alternatives.

Notes

1 Jean Wall (1998) is one of the many who write about this. She says:

> In Louisiana an inmate sentenced to life in prison is likely to die there, unless a court intervenes or the sentence is commuted by joint action of the board of pardons and the governor. There are 3014 inmates with life sentences and approximately 1850 more who have 'practical life' – mandatory sentences so long as to effectively preclude release. These inmates represent the future of the already growing population of older inmates, a population that brings with it an increased potential for medical problems and emergencies, circumstances that often develop sooner in prison populations.
>
> (p.136)

2 This minimum is strongly criticised by various organisations supporting the defence of animals.

References

Christie, N. (1981) *Limits to Pain*, Oxford: Martin Robertson and Company.
—— (1994) *Crime Control as Industry*, London: Routledge.
Donziger, S.R. (1996) *The Real War on Crime: The Report of the National Criminal Justice Commission*, New York: Harper.
Downes, D. (1988) *Contrasts in Tolerance. Post-war Penal Policy in the Netherlands and England and Wales*, Oxford: Clarendon Press.
Farmer, P. (1998) 'Cruel and Unusual: Drug-Resistant Tuberculosis as Punishment', *Department of Social Medicine, Harvard Medical School*, 641 Huntington Ave, Boston, MA 02115 USA.
Feeley, M. and Simon, J. (1992) 'The New Penology: Notes on the Emerging Strategy of Corrections and its Implications', *Criminology* 30(4): 419–47.
Massing, M. (1998) 'The Blue Revolution', *New York Review of Books* XLV(18): 32–6.
Mathiesen, T. (1998) 'Selective Incapacitation Revisited', *Law and Human Behavior* 22(4): 455–69.
Moscow Centre for Prison Reform (1998) *Human Beings and Prison*, Moscow: Author.
Schlosser, E. (1998) 'The Prison Industrial Complex', *The Atlantic Monthly* 208(6): 51–77.

Von Hirsch, A. (1972) 'Prediction of Criminal Conduct and Preventive Confinement of Convicted Persons', *Buffalo Law Review* 717–58.
Wall, J. (1998) 'Elder Care', *Corrections Today* 60: 136–8, 195.

Index